791.457
G863

WEST FARGO PUBLIC LIBRARY
109 3rd S̶t̶ s̶t̶
̶ ̶ ̶ ̶ 078

THE COMPLETE IDIOT'S GUIDE® TO

Boomer TV

by Murray Greig

Prentice
Hall
Canada

A Pearson Company
Toronto

alpha
books

Canadian Cataloguing in Publication Data

Grieg, Murray
   The complete idiot's guide to boomer TV

Includes index.
ISBN 0-13-089739-6

1. Television broadcasting—History. 2. Television programs—History. 3. Television programs—Canada—History.
I. Title.

PN1992.2.G73 2000   791.45'09   C00-931446-6

© 2001 Murray Greig

All Rights Reserved. This publication is protected by copyright, and permission should be obtained from the publisher prior to any prohibited reproduction, storage in a retrieval system, or transmission in any form or by any means, electronic, mechanical, photocopying, recording, or likewise. For information regarding permission, write to the Permissions Department.

ISBN 0-13-089739-6

Editorial Director, Trade Division: Andrea Crozier
Acquisitions Editor: Nicole de Montbrun
Copy Editor: Mary Teresa Bitti
Production Editor: Lori McLellan
Art Direction: Mary Opper
Cover Design: Amy Harnden
Cover Image: Courtesy of Adam West
Production Manager: Kathrine Pummell
Page Layout: B.J. Weckerle
Illustrations: Paul McCusker

1 2 3 4 5 WEB 05 04 03 02 01

Printed and bound in Canada.

ALPHA BOOKS and THE COMPLETE IDIOT'S GUIDE TO are trademarks of Pearson Education Inc. All rights reserved. Used under license from Pearson Education Inc.

This publication contains the opinions and ideas of its author and is designed to provide useful advice in regard to the subject matter covered. The author and publisher are not engaged in rendering legal, accounting, or other professional services in this publication. This publication is not intended to provide a basis for action in particular circumstances without consideration by a competent professional. The author, their employees and the publisher expressly disclaim any responsibility for any liability, loss, or risk, personal or otherwise, which is incurred as a consequence, directly or indirectly, of the use and application of any of the contents of this book.

ATTENTION: CORPORATIONS
Books are available at quantity discounts with bulk purchase for educational, business, or sales promotional use. For information, please email or write to: Pearson PTR Canada, Special Sales, PTR Division, 26 Prince Andrew Place, Don Mills, Ontario, M3C 2T8. Email ss.corp@pearsoned.com. Please supply: title of book, ISBN, quantity, how the book will be used, date needed.

Visit the Pearson PTR Web site! Send us your comments, browse our catalogues, and more. **www.pearsonptr.ca**.

A Pearson Company

Contents

Appendices

Dear Reader,

As the world hurtles headlong into the 21st century and all the social, technological, and political impacts of a foreboding future, it's reassuring to know that Boomer TV — classic television from the 1950s, '60s, and '70s — holds all the secrets for coping with what lies ahead. Indeed, I'd go so far as to state that Boomer TV represents one of the most potent medicines of our time. For proof of that, think back to your childhood. When you were sick in bed, what was the first thing your mom plugged in after the vapourizer? The TV, of course. Almost instantly the steady diet of cartoons, sitcoms, westerns, and science fiction went to work unleashing the mystical healing power of the cathode tube, and before you knew it you were back at school. Is it mere coincidence that every major hospital offers TV services to patients during convalescence? Statistics measuring the frequency and duration of hospital television rentals support the theory of "video healing," and the fact that patients are required to pay for the service would seem to indicate the medical profession agrees.

We're older now, but the same irrefutable laws of teleconsciousness still apply. All of us who grew up in the shadow of the Cold War have an "Inner Gilligan" who needs to be nurtured, and the best way to accomplish that is through a steady diet of Boomer reruns. If you can't watch them, the next best thing is to read about them — which is where I think this book might come in handy. If you've ever lost sleep trying to recall the ingredients in Oscar Madison's favourite sandwich or the name of the company Herman Munster worked for, your search is over. If you're curious about which "guest villain" turned Batman and Robin into human postage stamps or you've wondered how Dr. Richard Kimble was finally able to track down the one-armed man, this is where you'll find it.

Think of *The Complete Idiot's Guide® to Boomer TV* as a sort of mental "rewind" through some of the programs, characters, and attitudes that helped to shape pop culture in the mid-20th century. I hope you'll find something here you didn't know — or, at the very least, something that will increase your appreciation of the video gems of yesteryear.

Murray Greig

WEST FARGO PUBLIC LIBRARY
401 - 7th St. East
WEST FARGO, ND 58078

Foreword

Murray Greig has devoted a large hunk of his life to writing a book about a subject that has obviously been an important part of his life. *The Complete Idiot's Guide® to Boomer TV* is staggering in its scope and coverage of television through its turbulent teens and fresh maturity. It was innocent and innovative, endearing and comfortable. Murray covers the television you grew up with, for better or for worse. As you read this book, you become aware of the affection and regard Murray has for his subject and for the folks who brought "Boomer TV" into our lives.

For nearly 40 years I have been one of those folks. Page after page, I read about the shows I have been part of and the fine people with whom I have worked. From *The Outer Limits* to *Maverick*, from *The Big Valley* and *Love, American Style* to *The Detectives*, *Batman* and *The Last Precinct*, I read about things I haven't thought about in years (except *Batman*, of course). You too will find your memories about the shows you grew up with gently stirred.

The Complete Idiot's Guide® to Boomer TV is a book lovingly written. It's a great tribute to the images, the stories and the people that were—and some of us who still are—on your screens. It is an immense and affectionate book of all you ever wanted to know (and some things you didn't) about "Boomer TV." It's also an incredible reference book as well. Now you can dazzle and amaze your friends with what you know about TV.

Thank you, Murray!

Batman *star Adam West*
Ketchum, Idaho
April, 2001

Introduction

Welcome to *The Complete Idiot's Guide® to Boomer TV*.

Before we get into specifics (and at the risk of sounding like Archie Bunker's favourite president), I'd like to make one thing perfectly clear: you don't have to be an idiot to enjoy this book, or to learn something new about some of the most memorable television shows of the 1950s, '60s and '70s. Think of it more as a kind of roadmap through the Vast Wasteland, a user-friendly guide to the good, the bad, and the ugly of Boomer sitcoms, dramas, sci-fi and cop shows. In the appendices, I touch on westerns, cartoons, and variety programs. Most of 'em I liked; some I couldn't stand. Obviously not every series that qualifies as "Boomer TV" is included, and perhaps your all-time favourite show didn't make my final cut. But that's the great thing about TV—we all have our own ideas about what's watchable and what isn't. The shows covered in this book are just my personal picks—nothing more, nothing less.

As you browse through the more than 125 series capsulized on the following pages, I hope you'll occasionally find yourself nodding in agreement with what I have to say. But not always. Some of you will wonder why your favourite series isn't here, or why I've included programs you despised. There's probably even some shows you've never heard of (or at least tried to forget). If nothing else, I hope this book helps trigger both fond memories and hot debates. But don't take it too seriously. Just because I happen to think Ralph Kramden is a fine role model or that Tanya Roberts was the sexiest of *Charlie's Angels* doesn't mean you have to agree. The beauty of Boomer TV is that it will live forever—as will the memories, opinions and arguments it evokes.

The guide is divided into four sections:

Part 1, "Stylish Sitcoms" looks at family-oriented comedy series, beginning with some of the best from the 1950s. There's also chapters on shows that primarily featured married couples, women, and dysfunctional families and an examination of the "country comedy" hits that took primetime by storm in the early '60s.

Part 2, "Enlightened Escapism" spans the sublime to the ridiculous, from a talking horse and a conversational car to the absurd adventures of men and women in uniform. It also includes lengthy chapters on comedies that were pure "magic," and those that featured some of the best ensemble casts in television history.

Part 3, "Distinguished Dramas" covers everything from underwater action heroes to battle-hardened frontline grunts, and from straight-shootin' cops to globe-trotting spies. There are also chapters on favourite family-oriented sagas and TV's most heroic healers.

Part 4, "Superb Sci-fi" runs the gamut from alien invaders and bionic beefcake to lonely vampires and misunderstood superheroes. There's also a special look at some great "terror" TV.

Extras

As with all *Complete Idiot's Guides®*, this one includes elements designed to make for a more enjoyable and informative read. As you flip through, be sure to tune in to:

TeleTrivia

Obscure notes and little-known anecdotes that shed new light on old favourites.

Notable Quotable

Straight-from-the-screen snippets of memorable dialogue.

Fast Forward

Future facts on the stars and shows we've come to love.

Freeze Frame

Facts forever frozen in Boomer consciousness.

Acknowledgments

This project would not have been possible without the patience and encouragement of my wife, Judy, and son, Danny, along with ace editor Nicole de Montbrun and the production and design staff at Prentice Hall Canada. I also want to thank "Brinks" Brennan for coming through in the clutch, and my four cats for putting up with all the cigar smoke. Special thanks to Adam West and Fred Wostbrock.

Permission to reproduce photographs of Topps trading cards was graciously granted by the Topps Co. Inc. of New York. The photos are used for illustrative purposes only and all names, logos, likenesses, etc. remain the property of their respective rights holders. Permission to reproduce photographs of Dart Flipcards trading cards was graciously granted by Dart Flipcards of London, Ontario. All other photos are from the author's personal collection. Their inclusion is for illustrative purposes only and implies no rights, permissions or ownership outside of public domain.

This book is dedicated to Sherrie, Laurie, Debbie and Cathie. Even when we were fighting over the *TV Guide* or arguing about whose turn it was to make the popcorn, deep down I knew they were great sisters. And they still are.

Part 1

Stylish Sitcoms

At the dawn of the television age, the first so-called "situation comedies" were adapted from long-running radio programs like Amos 'n' Andy, The Goldbergs, The Life of Riley *and* Our Miss Brooks. *Initially, the old radio scripts were simply rewritten to incorporate visual gags, and, for the most part, the comedy was even funnier with pictures.*

The Goldbergs, *which debuted on CBS in January 1949, was the first major series to make the move to TV from radio, where it had enjoyed nearly 20 years of enormous popularity. Starring Gertrude Berg as Molly, the matriarch of a middle-class Jewish family in the Bronx, the show became an instant hit—until the spring of 1951 when co-star Philip Loeb (papa Jake Goldberg) was blacklisted by the House Committee On Un-American Activities for alleged communist sympathies. The ensuing controversy caused General Mills to withdraw its sponsorship and CBS subsequently dropped the series.*

When The Goldbergs *moved to NBC in 1952, Harold J. Stone replaced Loeb, and the show remained on the air for another two seasons, ending up on the DuMont network in 1954. Loeb, despite a sworn declaration that he had never been a member of the Communist Party, never worked again. He committed suicide in 1955.*

Amos 'n' Andy was another hit radio series that was dogged by controversy when it graduated to television on CBS in the spring of 1951. Set in Harlem, the show revolved around the comic misadventures of scheming George "Kingfish" Stevens (Tim Moore), the head of the Mystic Knights of the Sea Lodge. His lieutenant was Andy Brown (Spencer Williams Jr.), while Amos Jones (Alvin Childress), who narrated most of the episodes, was the kindly and philosophical cab driver who helped extricate his lodge brothers from their problems.

While Amos 'n' Andy was the first TV series to feature black actors in the lead roles, it immediately came under fire from civil rights groups for racial stereotyping. The fact that the humour was derived from situations that portrayed the principals as gullible, conniving buffoons only reinforced that criticism—particularly since the radio version had been created and performed by two white actors (Freeman Gosden and Charles Correll) who retained creative control when the show moved to television. Due largely to the negative backlash, Amos 'n' Andy was cancelled in 1953. Reruns remained in circulation until the mid-1960s, when the series was finally withdrawn from syndication sale.

In marked contrast to the controversial programming that launched the era of Boomer TV in the early 1950s, by mid-decade a new breed of "sitcom" had transformed a good chunk of prime-time programming into a fairy-tale world that melded perfect families (who never seemed to use the bathroom) and wholesome situations (how will the Beaver pass that math test?) into the kind of harmless humour that still strikes a responsive chord among jaded viewers in the 21st century.

It's a Wonderful Life

Parke Levy, writer-producer of *December Bride* (1954–1961), once defined the situation comedy as "a small hunk of life exaggerated for comic purposes." That's a good start, but Levy might also have added that familiarity is a key ingredient to any good sitcom—a canon that was especially true during the golden age of family comedies. Like old friends we never grow tired of visiting, the Nelsons, Andersons, Cleavers and Bradys are always fresh, always vibrant. No matter how crazy and complicated the real world gets, our favourite TV families are forever frozen in predictability, reacting exactly as we expect them to, every time.

Familiarity also breeds character identity. For the most part, the parents and kids who open each episode of our favourite family sitcoms are doing pretty much the same thing they were the last time we visited them. Jim Anderson has just arrived home from a hard day of selling insurance, while Bud and Kitten are arguing over who has to do the dishes. Ward and June Cleaver are having a cup of coffee in that spotless kitchen while The Beav and Wally are making plans for "messin' around" down at Metzger's Field with Eddie Haskell. Mike and Carol Brady are unpacking the groceries while Alice cooks supper and Marcia worries about auditioning for head cheerleader. Howard and Marion Cunningham are spending a quiet evening at home while Richie and Potsie try to persuade the Fonz to fix Ralph Malph's car.

That combination of comic exaggeration and folksy familiarity became the hallmark of the first family sitcom to become a hit with kids, teens and parents in the 1950s—a show that pioneered the brand of nonsensical, unobtrusive comedy that nearly 40 years later would be a key ingredient in the phenomenal success of *Seinfeld*.

The Adventures of Ozzie and Harriet

Series debut: Oct. 3, 1952 (ABC). Final telecast: Sept. 3, 1966 (ABC). 435 episodes.

With apologies to the *Seinfeld* gang, *The Adventures of Ozzie and Harriet* was truly television's first "show about nothing." On the surface it was a gentle comedy about the trials and tribulations of a middle-class couple raising two sons, but the show's most unique and endearing quality was that it was all, well..."real."

Ozzie and Harriet Nelson were in fact a married couple, and David and Ricky were their real sons. Even the house they lived in on TV was nearly an exact duplicate of their real-life Hollywood home. About the only concession to television fantasy was that Ozzie had no job on the show, other than being the put-upon dad who week in and week out had to cope with a wife, kids and neighbours who always seemed to be at odds with his laid-back character. Two of Ozzie's regular foils were neighbours "Thorny" Thornberry (Don DeFore) and Darby (Parley Baer, who later appeared as Mayor Stoner on *The Andy Griffith Show*).

The Adventures of Ozzie and Harriet began on radio in 1944 with actors voicing the roles of David and Ricky, but by 1949 the real Nelson offspring were playing themselves on the air. When the series moved to television, David was 15 and Ricky was 11, and over the next 14 years viewers watched them grow up and launch their own careers away from the family nest. One of the show's strong points was that both boys were natural actors; there was no forced cuteness or implausible banter—they were simply being themselves.

In 1956 David went off to college and over the next few seasons appeared only sporadically in the series, which gradually became more of a showcase for Ricky's burgeoning talent as a rock 'n' roll singer. An episode late in the 1956 season was devoted to the formation of Ricky's band—which became the focus of many subsequent shows—and after he crooned a version of Fats Domino's "I'm Walkin'" during a telecast the following April, Nelson's real-life release of the single promptly sold over one million copies. All his subsequent hits were likewise included on the show or were featured in short precursors to modern-day music videos, which aired right after the weekly episode.

As the series evolved, *The Adventures of Ozzie and Harriet* often featured musical or "flashback" fantasies to when David and Ricky were younger, with the entire family joining in the singing. It was a winning formula, best showcased in a 1958 episode entitled Tutti Frutti Ice Cream in which all four Nelsons did a musical number during Ozzie's dream sequence about tracking down his favourite frozen dessert.

The final original episode of the series was poignantly nostalgic, with Ozzie purchasing a pool table with the intent of turning his sons' long-vacant bedroom into a den—but Harriet would have none of it! In 1973 Ozzie and Harriet returned to prime time in a short-lived syndicated series (sans sons) called *Ozzie's Girls*, in which the senior Nelsons took in a pair of student boarders, but the magic just wasn't there any more.

TeleTrivia

Unlike his TV character, Ozzie Nelson was a tireless worker. At the age of 13 he became the youngest Eagle Scout in the history of Boy Scouts of America, and in college he was an All-America quarterback at Rutgers. Prior to the Second World War he was a renowned orchestra leader, and he met Harriet when she joined the orchestra as a vocalist.

Fast Forward

After *The Adventures of Ozzie and Harriet* was cancelled, the careers of David and Rick (in his late teens he asked people to quit calling him Ricky) went in opposite directions. David showed up infrequently on television (*The Love Boat, Circus of the Stars*) and in movies (*Cheech and Chong's Up In Smoke*), while Rick became a bonafide rock 'n' roll heavyweight, cranking out 18 top-10 singles between 1957 and 1972. His last big hit was "Garden Party," a whimsical ode to fleeting fame that was eerily autobiographical. Rick continued to perform for years afterwards, but was killed in a plane crash on the way to a concert on New Year's Eve, 1985. His real-life daughter, Tracy Nelson, made her TV debut as ultra-cool Jennifer DeNuccio in the '80s sitcom *Square Pegs*.

Father Knows Best

**Series debut: Oct. 3, 1954 (CBS). Final telecast: April 5, 1963 (ABC).
203 episodes.**

The quintessential TV family of the '50s was the Andersons: Jim and Margaret (Robert
Young and Jane Wyatt) and their three kids, 17-year-old Betty (a.k.a. "Princess," Elinor
Donahue), 14-year-old Bud (Billy Gray) and nine-year-old Kathy (a.k.a. "Kitten," Lauren
Chapin). Like most of the decade's other successful shows, *Father Knows Best* had been
a huge hit on radio, but Young was the only member of the original cast to continue his
role when the series moved to television.

Jim Anderson was a salesman for the General Insurance Company in the generic town
of Springfield, and as head of the household he was the ultimate arbitrator in all family
disputes—of which there were astonishingly few. Inevitably attired in a comfortable
sweater and slippers after a hard day's work, Jim dispensed his sage advice with the same
quiet confidence his real-life alter-ego would bring to the role of Dr. Marcus Welby a
decade later (see Chapter 17). Margaret Anderson was equally kind and sensible,
particularly in helping solve her children's problems—a quality that made her one of

As Jim Anderson on
Father Knows Best,
*Robert Young always had
time for the kids.*

the more realistic TV moms of the era. Margaret was also the first small-screen mom to show an independent streak. On one memorable occasion, fed up with the drudgery of washing dishes, she left the house for a few hours to take a walk on the wild side of town. It wasn't anything earth-shattering, but after the other family members expressed outrage at her strange behaviour, Margaret made it clear she had a mind of her own and would no longer tolerate being taken for granted.

Like the Nelson kids, the Anderson offspring weren't smart-mouthed or overly cute, and their biggest problems revolved around the usual: school life, friends, dating. The entire family was believably intelligent, and despite the show's touchy-feely schmaltziness, *Father Knows Best* routinely featured moments of genuine drama, with writing that was a cut above the usual sitcom fare. Once, after one of Betty's girlfriends taunted a shy orphan boy for "freeloading" all over town, Betty gave the girl a pointed lesson in humility by inviting the boy to stay with the Andersons while Jim and Margaret went through the ups and downs of finding him some parents. On another occasion the family fell in love with a stray dog that in fact belonged to a vagrant who'd been thrown in jail. The man could be released only if a prominent citizen vouched for him—which both Jim and Margaret did, despite never having met the man.

Leave It To Beaver

Series debut: Oct. 4, 1957 (CBS). Final telecast: Sept. 12, 1963 (ABC). 234 episodes.

"Well Beaver, this may be hard for you to believe, but life isn't exactly like television."

So said Ward Cleaver (Hugh Beaumont) at the conclusion of a 1958 episode of one of the true classics of Boomer TV. With wife June (the radiant Barbara Billingsley) at his side, at some point during each show Ward inevitably served up pearls of grown-up

TeleTrivia

Jane Wyatt won three Emmy Awards for best actress in a continuing series role for her portrayal of Margaret Anderson (1957, 1959 and 1960). In 1967 she appeared as Spock's mother in the *Star Trek* episode Journey to Babel, and later reprised the role in the 1986 motion picture *Star Trek IV: The Voyage Home.*

Freeze Frame

Despite ranking sixth among all network programs in the 1959–1960 season, *Father Knows Best* was cancelled when Robert Young decided not to return. Reruns were aired over the next three seasons on CBS and NBC.

wisdom to sons Theodore (a.k.a. "the Beaver," Jerry Mathers) and Wally (Tony Dow), but that's where the similarity to other family sitcoms ended.

Set in the suburban community of Mayfield, the allure of *Leave It To Beaver* was that there wasn't an adult star hogging the spotlight. It was devoted to a kid's perspective on the traumas of everyday life, and in Beaver and Wally millions of youngsters across North America saw a reflection of themselves. The boys were 7 and 12 when the series debuted, and over the next six seasons their experiences parallelled those of real kids in the late '50s and early '60s better than anything else on television.

Notable Quotable

Wally: "Hey Eddie, why are you always givin' Beaver the business?"

Eddie: "I'm not givin' him the business. I'm just tryin' to wise him up. I don't want him goin' out in the world and gettin' slaughtered."

Freeze Frame

Jerry Mathers enlisted in the U.S. Air National Guard during the Vietnam War and was mistakenly reported as "killed in action" when a wire-service editor misread a similar name on one of the weekly casualty lists. After actress Shelly Winters mentioned The Beaver's "death" during an appearance on *The Tonight Show*, Mathers had to go public to assure distraught fans that he was, indeed, still alive.

Besides good writing and strong acting, what gave *Leave It To Beaver* its timeless charm was the interaction between the two brothers, their friends and their parents. Beaver's buddies—most notably Larry Mondello (Rusty Stevens), Whitey Whitney (Stanley Fafara) and Gilbert Bates (Stephen Talbot)—were just like him: unremarkable, naive and decidedly middle class. Wally's best friends—Clarence "Lumpy" Rutherford (Frank Bank) and the weasely Eddie Haskell (Ken Osmond)—were exact opposites who played off Wally's straight-arrow persona. Lumpy was shy and somewhat dimwitted, while Eddie was a hip, smart-mouthed opportunist who could instantly transform himself into a slimy suck-up in the presence of adults.

Leave It To Beaver never went for the big laughs; its humour was derived from viewer identity with the simple, common foibles we could all easily imagine happening in our own lives. Beaver personified every kid who ever tried to understand the adult world without causing too much trouble. It was a formula that was both human and wholesome, and as long as there are kids who grow up to be parents, that combination will never go out of style.

In March 1983 a made-for-TV movie entitled *Still The Beaver* brought back most of the original cast in a bittersweet reunion that saw Beaver as the divorced father of two young sons, Wally as a successful lawyer and Eddie Haskell as a crooked building contractor. Barbara Billingsley reprised her role as June, and spent much of the movie reminiscing beside Ward's grave in the Mayfield Cemetery (Hugh Beaumont passed away in 1982). The movie attracted a huge audience and led to a cable series called *The New Leave It To Beaver* on the TBS superstation in the spring of 1986.

Family Affair

Series debut: Sept. 12, 1966 (CBS). Final telecast: Sept. 9, 1971 (CBS). 138 episodes.

Bill Davis (Brian Keith) was a suave, successful bachelor engineer with a swanky apartment in the heart of Manhattan when his life was suddenly turned upside down by the arrival of 15-year-old Cissy (Kathy Garver) and 6-year-old twins Buffy and Jody (Anissa Jones and Johnnie Whitaker), the children of his brother and sister-in-law, who had been killed in an accident.

Not knowing anything about kids, "Uncle Bill" hired Giles French (the rotund and perfectly proper Sebastian Cabot) as a combination butler/babysitter, and the chemistry (or lack thereof) between the rambunctious kids and the stuffy English neat-freak became the foundation for most of the story lines. In many episodes Uncle Bill appeared only for a few minutes (he was often out of town on business), leaving the exasperated Mr. French to cope with Cissy's dating, Jodie's horseplay and Buffy's cutie-pie curiosity. The other "regular" in the cast was Buffy's faithful rag doll, Mrs. Beasley.

Family Affair was primarily a show about compromise, and as the series evolved both Uncle Bill and Mr. French dramatically adjusted their lifestyles to cope with the unexpected twists of living with kids who were, at least initially, total strangers. Still, there was a genuine warmth between the adults and their young charges, and both men could always be counted upon to bring a satisfactory resolution to any problems by the end of each episode.

On a personal note, a few years after *Family Affair* was cancelled, Sebastian Cabot was on vacation in Victoria, B.C., and happened to visit the department store where I was working at my first "real" job during high school: selling shoes. The store was in the midst of a big promotion on English leather Oxfords, and although I'd only been working for a couple of weeks, I figured this was my chance to show the boss that I could really sell. It didn't turn out that way. Early in my shift, laden down with a dozen or so boxes of shoes from the storeroom, I turned down an aisle and was startled to see Mr. Cabot, not five feet away, examining some Oxfords. Stunned, I simply dropped the load of shoes all over the floor and blurted out "Mr. French! Mr. French!" so loudly that the other customers stopped to gape. I recovered my composure long enough to stammer an apology, and then, amazingly, Mr. Cabot actually helped me pick up the mess and put the

Fast Forward

Anissa Jones was an adorable eight-year-old when she landed the role of Buffy on *Family Affair,* and over the five-year run of the series she and her doll, Mrs. Beasley, became its most popular stars. Sadly, Jones got heavily involved in the dark side of child stardom after the series ended and died from a drug overdose in 1976 at the age of 18.

shoes on a display rack, all the while making cheerful small talk. He even autographed a box lid for me! Not surprisingly, the boss was horrified by such unprofessional behaviour, and an hour later I was summoned to his office and fired.

The Brady Bunch

Series debut: Sept. 26, 1969 (ABC). Final telecast: Aug. 30, 1974 (ABC). 116 episodes.

Introduced by one of the most hummable theme songs in television history ("Here's the story, of a lovely lady, who was bringing up three very lovely girls..."), *The Brady Bunch* transformed the simple premise of a widow with three daughters marrying a widower with three sons into an entertainment franchise that spawned four spinoff series, a couple of made-for-TV movies, a live theatrical production and two hit motion pictures. All from a show that barely made it onto the fall schedule in 1969 and never cracked the top 25 network programs during its five-year run!

The Brady Bunch tried hard to become the *Leave It To Beaver* of the '70s, but with a war raging in Vietnam, chaos on college campuses and riots in the streets, America had simply changed too much. Ironically, that's exactly why the series struck a chord with its loyal viewers. Like slipping into a favourite pair of bell-bottoms and a tie-dyed T-shirt, the comforting sameness of the sanitized Bradys tapped into our deep-rooted yearning for simplicity. Three decades later, it still works.

Freeze Frame

Big-screen veteran Gene Hackman was series creator Sherwood Schwartz's first choice to play Mike Brady before the role was offered to Robert Reed. From 1969 to 1974 Reed also appeared as Lieut. Adam Tobias on the CBS detective drama *Mannix*, thereby becoming one of the very few actors in TV history to appear concurrently on rival networks.

Face it, we all wanted parents like Mike (Robert Reed) and Carol (Florence Henderson). And who wouldn't want brothers and sisters like Greg (Barry Williams), Peter (Christopher Knight), Bobby (Mike Lookinland), Marcia (Maureen McCormick), Jan (Eve Plumb) and Cindy (Susan Olsen)? Add a wacky heart-of-gold housekeeper like Alice Nelson (Ann B. Davis) to the mix, and the recipe for suburban bliss was complete. *The Brady Bunch* was a refreshing oasis of polyester non-reality that quenched our thirst for answers to such memorable kid problems as getting braces, going steady, that first cigarette or flunking a driving test. Maybe that last one is why the Brady kids spent so much time fixing their bicycles.

There were other reasons for tuning in, especially for boys. Marcia was, in a word, babe-o-licious—the ultimate '70s pop tart. Long blonde hair, short skirts, high heels...you get the picture. Eye candy aside, all six kids were accomplished actors, as were Reed and Henderson—the last TV couple to have a linear connection to their '50s counterparts. Mike Brady was an architect who travelled a

Notable Quotable

The pilot episode includes the following telephone exchange between drug-dependent Mike Brady and his bride-to-be:

Mike: "I'm so nervous, it feels like I've got flying saucers in my stomach."

Carol: "Why don't you take a tranquilizer?"

Mike: "I already did."

Carol: "Maybe you should take another one."

Mike: "Nothing doing. I want to be calm for the ceremony, but there's the honeymoon to consider!"

Carol: "That's an architect for you—always planning ahead!"

lot (in a classic three-episode adventure in 1972 the whole gang accompanied him to Hawaii) while Carol was a stay-at-home mom who worked tirelessly for volunteer groups.

When the series debuted, the Brady kids ranged in age from 7 to 14, and most of the early story lines revolved around their adjustments to the blended family and their efforts to assert independence. The pilot episode (The Honeymoon) features Mike and Carol's outdoor wedding, which was ruined when the boys' dog Tiger started chasing the girls' cat, Fluffy. The ensuing chaos culminated with Mike doing a face plant into the wedding cake, but by the end of the half hour everything worked out and the kids, Alice, Tiger and Fluffy all accompanied the newlyweds on their honeymoon.

Right from the start Reed was at odds with series creator/producer Sherwood Schwartz on the show's direction. As a highly respected "serious" actor, he wanted to avoid turning *The Brady Bunch* into a slapstick spoof, but it was a losing battle. Over the course of the series, as the kids got older and Mike and Carol became little more than window dressing, the hostility between Reed and Schwartz festered to the point where they barely spoke to each other, culminating in Schwartz's decision not to include Reed in the final original episode. But time has a way of healing old wounds, and Reed reprised his role as one of TV's best-loved dads in *The Brady Bunch Hour*, an eight-episode comedy/variety series in 1977; *The Brady Brides*, a 10-episode effort in 1981 (Marcia and Jan both got married in the opener); and *The Bradys*, a "serious" limited series for CBS in 1990. He also appeared in 1988's *A Very Brady Christmas*, one of the highest-rated TV movies of the year.

Freeze Frame

Maureen McCormick was a show business veteran long before she was cast as Marcia Brady. A veteran of more than 50 TV commercials and guest roles on everything from *Bewitched* to *My Three Sons*, McCormick also recorded the words for all the Mattel Toy Company's talking dolls in the 1960s (remember Chatty Cathy?) and was the voice of Peppermint Patty in the Peanuts cartoon specials. From 1972 to 1974 all six Brady siblings provided the voices for their animated counterparts on *The Brady Kids*, a Saturday morning cartoon on ABC.

TeleTrivia

A lot of famous faces guest-starred on *The Brady Bunch*, among them pro athletes (Joe Namath, Don Drysdale, Deacon Jones), musicians (Davy Jones, Desi Arnaz Jr., Don Ho) and actors (Jim Backus, Jay Silverheels, Jackie Coogan). Davy Jones, lead singer for The Monkees, was Marcia's date for the prom in a 1971 episode and reprised his role in *The Brady Bunch Movie* 25 years later when he crooned the same song: "Girl."

Reed passed away at age 59 on May 12, 1992, but you can't help thinking he would have appreciated the irony of *The Brady Bunch* being turned into two hugely successful motion pictures a few years later—both of which perfectly skewered the loveable non-reality of the original series that he fought so hard to change.

The Partridge Family

Series debut: Sept. 25, 1970 (ABC). Final telecast: Aug. 31, 1974 (ABC). 96 episodes.

Loosely based on The Cowsills, a real-life family band in the '60s, *The Partridge Family* was living proof that the public will buy anything that comes in a pretty package.

Fronted by vocalist/mom Shirley Partridge (Shirley Jones, who won an Academy Award for her stunning portrayal of Lulu Baines in *Elmer Gantry*) and singer/guitarist/teen idol Keith (Jones' real-life stepson David Cassidy), the musical Partridges lived in the California beach community of San Pueblo and toured the country in a colourfully painted school bus. According to the show's original theme song (which changed after the first season), the kids—Keith, Laurie (Susan Dey), Danny (Danny Bonaduce), Chris (Brian Forster) and Tracy (Suzanne Crough)—formed an impromptu garage band with the idea of playing locally, "and it all came together when mom sang along." Their first single was "I Think I Love You," (Jones and Cassidy sang, backed by studio musicians), which in real life sold nearly five million copies.

DOING HIS THING

The Partridges were an "all-for-one, one-for-all" family, but Keith (David Cassidy) quickly became the show's biggest draw.

THE PARTRIDGE FAMILY

Fast Forward

Susan Dey was an accomplished model who had very little acting experience when she was cast in the role of Laurie, but her willowy good looks and girl-next-door sweetness quickly made her one of the most popular Partridges with viewers. More than a decade after the series was cancelled, Dey brought the same understated excellence to her role as deputy district attorney Grace Van Owen on *L.A. Law.*

As the first family sitcom with a musical theme, *The Partridge Family* was heavily promoted in the real-world recording industry. At 16, the talented Cassidy instantly became a teen idol and one of the biggest concert draws on the planet. As a comic actor he was passable, and his interaction with 9-year-old Danny became the crux of many of the show's best episodes. Danny's other main foil was Reuben Kincaid (Canadian-born Dave Madden), the band's exasperated manager.

Like *The Brady Bunch, The Partridge Family* was pure fluff—innocent story lines leading up to the bubble gum musical performance that capped each episode. Whether

TeleTrivia

The Partridge Family was one of the most heavily marketed programs in television history. In addition to the nine albums and seven singles released by the group, dozens of toys, books, paper collectibles and a line of clothing featured the Partridge logo. The items ranged from the usual lunch boxes, board games and bubble gum cards to such bizarre offerings as the The David Cassidy Love Kit (which contained 40 wallet-sized photos and a "secret love message") and David Cassidy Choker Luv Beads. The original series was also spun off into one of the more improbable animated efforts of the 1974–1975 season—*The Partridge Family, 2200 A.D.*—with Dey, Bonaduce, Madden, Forster and Crough all voicing their cartoon counterparts.

involving Laurie dating an irascible biker named "Snake" (Rob Reiner), Danny's latest money-making scheme (he once set up a kissing booth to sell Keith's smooches for 10 cents each, explaining: "When you've got a shoddy product, you gotta go for bulk,") or Keith's romantic pursuit of a foreign princess (he dressed up as a bellboy to whisk her away from her hotel room), the plots were always wacky, but inevitably contained enough nuggets of warmth and wisdom to keep viewers satisfied until the next show. In the final season (1973–1974), a precocious four-year-old neighbour named Ricky Stevens (Ricky Segall) joined the cast and performed with the band.

Happy Days

Series debut: Jan. 15, 1974 (ABC). Final telecast: July 12, 1984 (ABC). 255 episodes.

Happy Days was a spinoff from a 1972 segment of the ABC comedy anthology series *Love, American Style*, and quickly cashed in on the nostalgia for the 1950s that followed the release of the motion picture *American Graffiti* a year later.

Henry Winkler's performance as "Da Fonz" propelled Happy Days *to the top of the ratings in 1974.*

Set in Milwaukee, *Happy Days* was originally conceived as a showcase for Jefferson High School pals Richie Cunningham (Ron Howard) and Warren "Potsie" Weber (Anson Williams). By the end of the first season, the show's most popular star was Arthur "Da Fonz" Fonzarelli (Henry Winkler), the ultra-cool motorcycle rebel whose "thumb's up" and signature greeting of "Aaaay!" became personal trademarks. Richie's parents, Howard and Marion Cunningham (Tom Bosley and Marion Ross), and kid sister Joanie (Erin Moran) rounded out the primary cast, while an assortment of friends and hangers-on—most notably Ralph Malph (Donnie Most) and the owners of the gang's hangout, Arnold's Drive-In (Pat Morita, 1974–1976, and Al Molinaro, 1976–1982)— anchored the supporting cast.

Freeze Frame

During the first season of *Happy Days*, Richie had an older brother named Chuck (played by Gavin O'Herlihy and Randolph Roberts) who attended college and was forever bouncing a basketball around the house. He was soon written out of the show, and the Cunningham family never mentioned him again.

For the first couple of seasons *Happy Days* was content to focus on the relationship between Richie, Potsie, Fonzie and Ralph (with occasional forays into the lives of Howard and Marion), but by 1976 the plots were getting stale and the comedy looked forced. The network then started introducing a string of "occasional regulars," including Fonzie's sexy sweetheart Pinky Tuscadero (Roz Kelly) and her sister Leather (real-life rock star Suzi Quatro). Fonzie's young cousin Chachi Arcola (Scott Baio) joined the cast in 1977 and served as a romantic interest for Joanie.

At the end of the 1977 season, Richie, Potsie and Ralph graduated from Jefferson High and enrolled at the University of Wisconsin, but after a couple of years as college men they left the series (their absence was explained by their having joined the army), and by 1980 Winkler was clearly carrying the show on his own. Richie eventually married long-time girlfriend Lori Beth Allen (Lynda Goodfriend) in a long-distance telephone ceremony from his army base in Greenland (Fonz served as his stand-in), and in the final episode, Richie and the rest of the gang returned to their old stomping grounds for Joanie and Chachi's wedding, while Fonzie bought a house and adopted a son.

Fast Forward

Squeaky-clean Richie Cunningham was Ron Howard's second major TV role. From 1960 to 1968 he portrayed freckle-faced Opie Taylor on *The Andy Griffith Show* (see Chapter 4), and he'd guested on several other prime-time programs, including *The Twilight Zone* and *Dennis The Menace*. As an adult he became one of the most powerful and respected directors in Hollywood, with a string of big-screen hits including *Splash!*, *Cocoon*, *Backdraft*, *Apollo 13*, and *The Grinch*.

TeleTrivia

Happy Days became such a huge hit that in 1980 Fonzie's black leather jacket was enshrined in a permanent display of pop culture memorabilia at the Smithsonian Institution in Washington. And in keeping with the retro feel of the series, the original theme song—Bill Haley's 1955 hit "Rock Around The Clock"—again made the top 10 in 1974. In 1976 Haley's opening track was replaced by an original composition entitled "Happy Days," which likewise became a top-selling single.

The Least You Need to Know

➤ *The Adventures of Ozzie and Harriet* was the first prime-time series to incorporate music videos, featuring a young Rick Nelson and his rock 'n' roll band.

➤ Two decades after *Leave It To Beaver* was cancelled most of the original cast returned for a TV reunion movie entitled *Still The Beaver*, which spawned a cable remake of the classic series.

➤ *The Brady Bunch* was spun off into three other television series, an animated cartoon show and two successful feature-length movies.

➤ *The Partridge Family* was loosely based on the real-life rock group The Cowsills.

➤ During the first season of *Happy Days*, the Cunningham family included three children: Richie, Joanie and college-aged Chuck. But after he was written out of the series, Chuck was never mentioned again!

Not Quite Normal

On the cusp of the 21st century, television has truly become the Boomer generation's mythology for the new millennium; the folklore of our time. Theme songs like *The Brady Bunch* and *Happy Days* are the soundtracks of our youth, indelibly indexed as common reference points in our collective experience.

You want proof? Next time you're out with friends or attending a social function, make a mental note of how many Boomer TV references find their way into casual conversation. Somebody might refer to their portly boss as "The Skipper" or the new guy in marketing as "a real Eddie Haskell." The doofus down the hall might have a heart of gold "but he's a bit of a Gomer," while that jerk on the subway this morning sounded "just like Archie Bunker."

The subliminal absorption of sitcom slang into our everyday vocabulary can be traced to the first wave of family comedies that flooded prime time through the late 1950s and early '60s. After all, these were the only shows a lot of kids were allowed to watch on school nights, so we drifted off to sleep with happy visions of the Nelsons, Cleavers, Bradys and Partridges still fresh in our impressionable minds. Even though many of the

WEST FARGO PUBLIC LIBRARY

family-oriented programs of that era flirted with themes destined to become television staples in the '80s and '90s—single parents, working women, home-alone kids—for the most part they stuck pretty close to what had worked so well in the 1950s: well-grounded WASP couples living in the burbs with polite, obedient kids.

The traditional family sitcom was still very much alive and well by the mid-1960s, but when the networks started subtly tweaking their tried-and-true recipe for ratings success, the decade produced some of the most memorable "non-traditional" family shows of all time—and paved the way for the ground-breaking debut of the single most important situation comedy in the history of the medium.

My Three Sons

Series debut: Sept. 29, 1960 (ABC). Final telecast: Aug. 24, 1972 (CBS). 369 episodes.

Stage and screen veteran Fred MacMurray, who starred as aviation engineer Steve Douglas, a widowed father of three boys, was once described by a critic as "bland as white bread"—but that didn't prevent *My Three Sons* from becoming one of the very few sitcoms to bracket the entire decade of the '60s.

MacMurray was well known to viewers as the soft-spoken and sensible father in a string of Walt Disney movies (*The Shaggy Dog, Son of Flubber*, etc.), which only reinforced the believability of his performance as Steve Douglas. When the series debuted, his "sons"— Mike (Tim Considine), Robbie (Don Grady) and Chip (Stanley Livingston)—were 18, 14 and 7, and when Steve was away on one of his frequent business trips the brood was chaperoned by his father-in-law and housekeeper, Michael Francis "Bub" O'Casey (William Frawley). Frawley, who had previously starred as the cantankerous Fred Mertz on *I Love Lucy* (see Chapter 3), died in 1965 and was replaced on the show by Uncle Charley (William Demarest), a retired sailor who did his best to keep the fragmented Douglas household shipshape.

My Three Sons was a perfect vehicle for MacMurray, whose laid-back style was as comfortable as an old pair of slippers. He had an especially good rapport with Considine (another Disney alumnus), but by the start of the 1965–1966 season the 24-year-old had outgrown the role of Mike and wanted out of the series. In a memorable episode he married long-time girlfriend Sally Ann Morrison (Meredith MacRae), and the couple moved east so that Mike could become a college professor. To maintain the "three sons" scenario, Steve adopted Chip's orphaned pal Ernie Thompson (Stanley Livingston's real-life younger brother Barry), and other than a stronger focus on the two younger boys, the gentle comedy never skipped a beat.

In 1967 Steve's company transferred him from the Midwest to California, and much of that season's episodes revolved around adjusting to the move. One of the benefits was that Robbie met and fell in love with Katie Miller (Tina Cole) and they were married before the season ended. The first episode the next fall revealed that Katie was pregnant, and when she gave birth to triplets (Steve Jr., Robbie Douglas II and Charley) a whole new set of story lines opened up—aided by the fact Robbie, Katie and the babies continued to live in the Douglas home. In 1969 Steve finally found love and married vivacious schoolteacher Barbara Harper (Beverly Garland), and when she moved in with her nine-year-old daughter Dodie (Dawn Lyn), the ranks of the Douglas family swelled to 11.

That house must have been a lot bigger than it looked on TV.

The Patty Duke Show

Series debut: Sept. 18, 1963 (ABC). Final telecast: Aug. 31, 1966 (ABC). 104 episodes.

It's only fitting that one of the most versatile actresses of all time starred in this quirky series about a "typical" New York City teenager and her refined, sophisticated Scottish cousin. The hook was that the girls were exact lookalikes, which led to all kinds of comedic twists at home and school. As Patty Lane, the 17-year-old Duke was a mischievous and uninhibited tomboy with a taste for blue jeans, hot dogs, rock 'n' roll and men in uniform (her boyfriend Richard Harrison [Eddie Applegate] was a part-time delivery boy for Western Union). As cousin Cathy Lane, Duke transformed herself into a beautiful and demure young lady, well versed in the nuances of classical literature and Renaissance art. Patty's father Martin was a stuffy newspaper editor (played by the wonderfully banal William Schallert) while mom Natalie (Jean Byron) and annoying little brother Ross (Paul O'Keefe) rounded out the family.

While *The Patty Duke Show* was essentially a one-joke gimmick, it managed to last three full seasons thanks to strong writing and excellent acting—particularly by the star. Though still a teenager, Duke was a seasoned veteran, having made her screen debut at the age of 8 in the motion picture *I'll Cry Tomorrow* and the Paul Newman classic *Somebody Up There Likes Me*. By 1957 she was appearing regularly on TV anthology programs and in commercials, and at age 12 she became an international sensation with her stunning portrayal of Helen Keller in the Broadway hit *The Miracle Worker*. In 1960 she transferred that role to the big screen and won an Academy Award for her performance. *The Patty Duke Show* was her first extended venture into comedy, but she tackled the dual role with characteristic gusto and earned an Emmy Award nomination in 1962.

Freeze Frame

William Schallert and Jean Byron, the parents on *The Patty Duke Show*, had been regulars on *The Many Loves of Dobie Gillis* (1959–1963), which starred Dwayne Hickman. Another member of the *Gillis* cast was a young Warren Beatty (yes, THAT Warren Beatty), in the role of spoiled rich kid Milton Armitage.

Notable Quotable

"Whoever thought up boys must've made a million dollars!"

—Patty Lane

TeleTrivia

In scenes on *The Patty Duke Show* that included both Patty and identical cousin Cathy in the shot, actress Rita McLaughlin served as the double—always with her back to the camera.

After the series was cancelled, Duke was rarely seen on television for the rest of the decade. She later married John Astin (Gomez on *The Addams Family*), then returned to the small screen with an Emmy-winning performance in the made-for-TV movie *My Sweet Charlie* in 1970. Duke was also nominated for Emmys for her work in two terrific mini-series—*Captains and Kings* (1976) and *The Miracle Worker* (1979), in the latter playing Helen Keller's teacher. A string of "relevant" TV movies followed, including the ground-breaking *Don't Hit Me, Mom* (about child abuse), prior to a couple of short-lived returns to series comedy in the early '80s: *It Takes Two* (with Richard Crenna) and *Hail to the Chief*, in which Duke starred as Julia Mansfield, the first female president of the United States.

The Addams Family

Series debut: Sept. 18, 1964 (ABC). Final telecast: Sept. 2, 1966 (ABC). 64 episodes.

Just as the theme song promised, *The Addams Family* was "creepy and kooky, mysterious and spooky." It was also one of the most clever ensemble comedies of the decade— a faithful live-action adaptation of the genius of cartoonist Charles Addams, whose comic strip in the *New Yorker* magazine inspired the series.

Starring bug-eyed John Astin as Gomez Addams and the beautiful Carolyn Jones as his ghoulishly gorgeous wife Morticia, the show was kind of a Marx Brothers-meets-Frankenstein spoof of the idealized families we were accustomed to seeing on TV. Everything about these folks was strange. In the foyer of their house—which looked like a combination dungeon-mausoleum—there was a hangman's noose that when pulled sounded a gong to summon a seven-foot butler named Lurch (Ted Cassidy). There was also a disembodied hand named "Thing" that lived in a black box and routinely answered the phone or provided Gomez with a lit match. Then there were the kids: 10-year-old Pugsley (Ken Weatherwax), who liked to play with sharp objects, and 7-year-old Wednesday Thursday Addams (Lisa Loring), who carried around a doll with no head and liked nothing better than spending time with the family pets—a full-grown lion, an octopus named Aristotle and a six-foot Venus flytrap. Bald-headed Uncle Fester (the inimitable Jackie Coogan), Cousin Itt (a three-foot androgynous creature made entirely of hair) and Grandmama (Blossom Rock) completed the macabre mix.

Despite their bizarre trappings, the Addams were a close-knit clan. There was genuine love and affection between Gomez and Morticia (whenever his wife spoke French, Gomez would react by taking her hand and planting passionate kisses all the way up her arm), and as parents they never passed negative judgments on their kids or on outsiders. In their own oddball way, the Addams were both stylish and graceful. Even as a youngster I was struck by the way Gomez wielded his ever-present cigar as a sort of personal exclamation mark. Whether dissertating on "the good old days of the Spanish

Notable Quotable

Like all good TV moms, Morticia Addams took an active interest in her children's education. Horrified by the "extremism" depicted in the storybooks they brought home from school, Morticia decided to write one of her own. "Imagine those juvenile delinquents Hansel and Gretel pushing a sweet little old lady into an oven!" she told Gomez. "And what was the name of that mean little brat who was so beastly to those three lovely bears? Ah yes, Goldilocks! Trust a blonde to bring on trouble!"

Former child star Jackie Coogan portrayed Uncle Fester on The Addams Family.

Notable Quotable

Cosmetics clerk: "What kind of powder does your mommy use?"

Wednesday Addams: "Baking powder."

Cosmetics clerk: "No dear, I mean on her face."

Wednesday Addams: "Baking powder."

Inquisition" or plotting another scheme with Uncle Fester, he waved and rolled his Havana with roguish panache. Very cool.

Speaking of Fester, it's doubtful anyone other than Coogan could have pulled off the character with such aplomb. He was at once both pathetic and patronly; a man-child perpetually on the periphery of something great. His harebrained schemes always backfired, but to this day Uncle Fester remains the show's most memorable character for kids who grew up in the '60s.

Coogan was Hollywood's original child prodigy, having co-starred (at the age of four) with the legendary Charlie Chaplin in *The Kid* (1921). The movie was a world-wide smash and led to a five-year merchandising blitz during which Coogan's face and name were plastered on everything from toys and candy bars to clothing and shoes. By 1925, perched as the No. 1 box-office attraction in the world, he was worth millions and owned a film company headed by his father, Jackie Sr. Tragically, Jackie Sr. was killed in a car accident just weeks before his son's 21st birthday and when the boy reached legal age and tried to collect the millions he'd

TeleTrivia

Except for a truly awful 1977 made-for-TV reunion movie (*Halloween With The Addams Family*), the main cast members went their separate ways after the series was cancelled. Astin briefly replaced Frank Gorshin as Riddler on *Batman* and married actress Patty Duke in 1972. He later starred as Lt.-Cmdr. Matthew Sherman on the ABC naval sitcom *Operation Petticoat*, and in the mid-'80s he had a recurring role as Harry Anderson's eccentric father on *Night Court*. Jones guest-starred as the evil Marsha, Queen of Diamonds, on *Batman* and was a regular on the CBS daytime soap opera *Capitol* until her death from cancer in 1983. Coogan passed away in 1984 at age 69, while Cassidy died of complications following open heart surgery in 1979. He was only 46. Lisa Loring, who portrayed little Wednesday Thursday Addams starred for four years as teen sexpot Cricket Montgomery on the CBS soap opera *As The World Turns*.

earned, his mother and the family's business manager refused to release the funds. At the time, under California law, a minor's earnings were the legal property of the parents and they could spend it however they saw fit. Jackie launched a widely publicized lawsuit against his mother and business manager for what was rightfully his, but when a settlement was finally reached more than a decade later, all he received was $126,000 from a fortune that at one time was estimated at nearly $10 million.

Bitterness over the way he'd been treated haunted Coogan for the rest of his life, but as a direct result of his legal battle the California State Legislature instituted what is officially titled the Child Actor's Bill (a.k.a. the Coogan Act) to prevent such abuses of young performers from ever being repeated. The bill stipulates that at least 50 percent of a child actor's earnings be deposited in a trust fund or some other form of secured savings account that the child can access when he or she reaches legal age.

The Munsters

Series debut: Sept. 24, 1964 (CBS). Final telecast: Sept. 1, 1966 (CBS). 70 episodes.

Debuting just a week after *The Addams Family*, *The Munsters* took the same premise of a family of ghoulish misfits adapting to everyday life and added an extra twist. The family was headed by Frankenstein-clone Herman (Fred Gwynne) and his pasty-faced wife Lily (Yvonne DeCarlo). It also included a Count Dracula–like grandpa (Al Lewis) who wasn't above transforming himself into a bat, and a "wolf boy" son named Eddie (Butch Patrick). The only normal member of the family was Herman's niece, a pretty blonde named Marilyn (Beverly Owen, later Pat Priest). The ongoing joke about Marilyn's "plainness" became a plot staple, along with the predictable results when her boyfriends met the rest of the family.

The Munsters lived at 1313 Mockingbird Lane, and Herman worked for the funeral home of Gateman, Goodbury and Graves. Unlike *The Addams Family*, a lot of the humour of *The Munsters* stemmed from their adventures outside the home. Herman's co-workers, Eddie's schoolmates and Grandpa's business ventures were often used to set up the situation, and even though the series was more formulaic and predictable than *The Addams Family*, it was almost as funny.

One of the highlights of *The Munsters* was the comedic chemistry between Herman and Grandpa. Gwynne and Lewis had earlier teamed up as Officer Francis Muldoon and Officer Leo Schnauser on *Car 54, Where Are You?* (see Chapter 9), and their styles were seamlessly complementary. Herman was big, dumb and loveable while Grandpa was small,

Freeze Frame

Herman and Lily Munster were the first prime-time television couple to regularly be shown occupying the same bed.

TeleTrivia

Yvonne DeCarlo was born in Vancouver, B.C., in 1922 and had once been named "The Most Beautiful Woman In The World." In the 1940s she was one of Hollywood's most recognizable glamour queens, specializing in exotically sensual characters. Other than guest roles and the dreadful Munsters TV reunion movie in 1981, she never again appeared on network television after the series was cancelled.

conniving and a bit maniacal—especially when he was working in his dungeon laboratory. In addition to being a vampire, Grandpa fancied himself one of history's great wizards and he had a trunk containing items like a Mother's Day card from Lizzie Borden, a compass from the Titanic and a rabbit's foot once owned by General George Custer.

The Courtship of Eddie's Father

Series debut: Sept. 17, 1969 (ABC). Final telecast: June 14, 1972 (ABC). 73 episodes.

Warm and fuzzy almost to a fault, this gentle comedy about the relationship between widowed magazine publisher Tom Corbett (Billy Bixby) and his precocious seven-year-old son Eddie (Brandon Cruz) was based on the 1962 hit movie of the same name, which starred Glenn Ford and little Ronny Howard.

Freeze Frame

Future Academy Award winner Jodie Foster made several guest appearances on *The Courtship of Eddie's Father* as Eddie's tomboy pal, Joey Kelly. The show's catchy theme song ("Best Friend") was written by pop star Harry Nilsson.

Bixby was familiar to viewers as harried newspaper reporter Tim O'Hara on *My Favorite Martian* (see Chapter 6), and while the role of a kind, understanding, "mod" father was a bit of stretch, he pulled it off nicely. The real star, however, was the freckle-faced Cruz, who had never acted before. He landed the part after his mother submitted a homemade audition tape to the studio, and there was an instant chemistry between the inquisitive little guy and his TV dad. Each episode opened with a distance shot of the two of them walking or playing together, and a voice-over by Eddie that inevitably started with "Hey, dad ...?" followed by a thoughtful query. The comedy centred around Eddie's tireless efforts to find a new mom, aided and abetted by the Corbett's Japanese housekeeper Mrs. Livingstone (Miyoshi Umeki), who always referred to Tom as "Mr. Eddie's Father." The other principal cast members were Tom's ditzy secretary Tina (Kristina Holland) and swinging photographer Norman Tinker (James Komack).

All In The Family

Series debut: Jan. 12, 1971 (CBS). Final telecast: Sept. 21, 1983 (CBS). 202 episodes.

To describe *All In The Family* merely as a show about a bigot is like equating The Rolling Stones with a garage band or calling Evel Knievel just another motorcycle enthusiast. *All In The Family* was (and still is) the Super Bowl of sitcoms, a tour de force that single-handedly reshaped the way all television is written, edited, performed and watched. Without Archie Bunker (Carroll O'Connor), his "dingbat" wife Edith (Jean Stapleton), their daughter Gloria (Sally Struthers) and son-in-law Mike "Meathead" Stivic (Rob Reiner) paving the way, none of the so-called "relevant" shows of the past 30 years— everything from *M*A*S*H* to *Seinfeld* and *Sex And The City* to *The Sopranos*—could have got on the air. *All In The Family* broke the mould for all time by shattering every TV taboo and setting a standard so high above the rest that today, almost 20 years after the final episode, the series is still responsible for producing 6 of the top 50 highest rated programs in the history of television.

Inspired by a British series called *Till Death Do Us Part*, which revolved around a slovenly Cockney father and his rebellious son-in-law in the ethnic melting pot of London's East End, *All In The Family* was originally pitched by creator Norman Lear to ABC in 1968 under the working title Justice For All. For the lead character—a blue-collar New Yorker named Archie Justice—Lear tried to recruit Mickey Rooney, who graciously declined. Lear next contacted O'Connor, a veteran character actor who had distinguished himself in several films (most notably as a general in *What Did You Do In The War, Daddy?*) and more than 100 television roles. He agreed to shoot the first pilot, titled Those Were The Days, with Stapleton as Edith, Kelly Jean Peters

Freeze Frame

Sally Struthers, who portrayed Gloria Stivic on *All In The Family*, provided the voice of Pebbles on the long-running animated series *The Flintstones*.

as Gloria and Tim McIntire as the Irish-American son-in-law Richard, but after ABC executives screened the finished product they turned it down. In 1969 a second pilot was shot with O'Connor and Stapleton as Archie and Edith and Chip Oliver and Candy Azzara as the kids, but once again ABC declined to purchase the series, leaving Lear and his writing partner Bud Yorkin free to offer it to another network.

Freeze Frame

Before he accepted the role of Archie Bunker, Carroll O'Connor unsuccessfully auditioned for the part of the Skipper on *Gilligan's Island.* "It was the luckiest thing in the world for him that he didn't get it," *Gilligan's Island* creator Sherwood Schwartz later said. "If Carroll had become identified with the Skipper, no way would he have been chosen for Archie Bunker."

Freeze Frame

All In The Family creator Norman Lear is on record as saying he patterned Archie Bunker after his real-life father, Herman. "My father had a habit of silencing my mother with 'stifle yourself' and he used to call me 'the laziest white man' he ever saw," said Lear.

Over at CBS, where sweeping changes were taking place, Lear and Yorkin found a home for their show. Network president Robert B. Wood was in the process of cancelling such long-time staples as *The Ed Sullivan Show, Red Skelton* and *The Beverly Hillbillies* and was looking for something fresh and cutting-edge. In late 1970 Lear shot a third pilot under the title All In The Family with Struthers and Reiner in the supporting roles. Another change saw the son-in-law renamed "Mike Stivic." The plot centred on Archie and Edith coming home early from church to find Mike playfully trying to tempt Gloria upstairs to the bedroom. In the key scene Archie roars that "it's still daylight of a Sunday morning," then launches into a hilarious verbal assault on "you longhairs and hippies," welfare cheats, college bums, blacks, Jews—and his "pinko Polack atheist" son-in-law. It was exactly the kind of show CBS was looking for, and the network promptly ordered 13 episodes.

All In The Family debuted on Jan. 12, 1971 (right after *Hee Haw*)—but before the screen lit up with the opening bars of Archie and Edith singing "Those Were The Days," CBS took the unusual precaution of airing a voiced-over announcement that warned: "The program you are about to see is called *All In The Family*. It seeks to throw a humourous spotlight on our frailties, prejudices and concerns. By making them a source of laughter, we hope to show, in a mature fashion, just how absurd they are."

The network really needn't have bothered, as ratings for the debut were dismal, to say the least. In fact, *All In The Family* registered minimal viewer interest in the Nielsen ratings throughout its initial 13-episode run and was on the verge of being cancelled when, in a last-ditch effort to save the show, the cast performed a live sketch on the high-profile Emmy Awards telecast and then won three of the coveted statuettes, for Outstanding New Series, Outstanding Comedy Series and Outstanding Continued Comedy Performance by an Actress in a Leading Role (Stapleton). Summer reruns of the original 13 episodes subsequently attracted a massive following, and by fall *All In The Family* was the most talked about show on television, with one-third of all TV sets in America tuned in to the weekly dose of explosive satire emanating from 704 Hauser St. in Queens.

Seemingly overnight, Archie Bunker, the lowly loading-dock foreman for the Prendergast Tool and Die Company (and occasional cab driver), became a symbol of the little guy struggling against forces he can't control to maintain his precarious place in the food chain. No television character before or since spat such inflammatory opinions on race, politics, sex and religion. He routinely referred to blacks as "coons" and "spades." Jews were "Hebes." Orientals were "chinks" and Puerto Ricans were "spics." England was "a fag country." Archie worshipped President "Richard E. Nixon," hated gun control, rabidly supported the war in Vietnam and frequently (mis)quoted the Bible, usually prefacing it with "you can look it up in your Good Book there...." His malapropisms became the stuff of legend, as he constantly "misconscrewed" words and facts. Female doctors were "groinocologists." The sexual act "was never constipated." In Archie's interpretation of the Bible, Abel's brother beat him to death with a cane.

You get the drift.

In the pivotal eighth episode, which saw the black Jeffersons move in next door, Archie calls a family meeting to express his concern: "Jim Bowman's done it—sold his home to a family of spades!" When Mike, Gloria and Edith don't think it's a big deal, he gets hysterical, shrieking: "I'm all alone here! Don't you get it? Our world is crumblin' down...the coons are comin'!" When Gloria replies that she thinks it's "wonderful," Archie bellows: "Yeah? Well let's see how wonderful it is when the watermelon rinds come flyin' out the windows!" Later, when he confronts Bowman about "double-crossing the whole block," the ex-neighbour suggests Archie get everyone else on the street to chip in to buy back the house by offering the Jeffersons a $2,000 profit. "Do ya think they'll go for it?" Archie asks. Bowman replies: "They'll be so happy, they'll be tap dancing all the way back to Harlem!"

In another memorable first-season episode, Archie was involved in a minor car accident. Though unhurt, he sees it as an opportunity to land an insurance settlement if he can get "a real sharp Jew lawyer." Flipping through the phone book, he comes across a firm

Notable Quotable

Mike: "Arch, if there's no personal contact, there's no danger of further infection."

Archie: "That's with regular American germs. But them Polack bugs you got are probably too dumb to know the rules and regulations. And if those germs of yours got any sense at all, they're poppin' out of you right now, lookin' for a better home."

called Rabinowitz, Rabinowitz and Rabinowitz (in a later episode he describes the firm as "seven savage Jews who will pick your bones clean.") He launches a lawsuit, but his case falls apart when the opposing lawyer produces some surprise witnesses: a station wagon full of nuns.

While prejudice and bigotry often served to set up the situation on *All In The Family*, the story of Archie, Edith, Gloria and Mike was really about the average person's everyday struggle for survival. When Archie couldn't sleep because the Prendergast Tool and Die Company was on strike, he mirrored the anxieties of millions of viewers facing the same situation in real life. When an affirmative action program prevented Mike from getting a high-paying job in Minnesota, millions of viewers on both sides of that controversial issue identified with his predicament. When Edith couldn't serve a favourite Sunday supper because the price of beef had gone through the roof, the audience could immediately empathize with her.

TeleTrivia

In the spring of 1972 an impromptu "Archie Bunker For President" campaign spawned tens of thousands of T-shirts, posters, bumper stickers and political buttons. Five months later, at the Democratic National Convention, one delegate gave Archie a write-in vote for vice-president on George McGovern's ticket.

Perhaps surprisingly, some of the very best episodes revolved around Edith, whom Stapleton infused with a sympathy and believability rarely matched before or since in any sitcom character. In the episode Edith's Christmas Story (Dec. 22, 1973), she puts up a brave front and goes about her cheery holiday preparations despite having found a tiny lump in her breast. In a poignant conversation between Edith and neighbour Irene Lorenzo (Betty Garrett), Irene reveals that she had a mastectomy years ago and urges Edith to undergo tests. In the examination room, when the doctor informs Edith that it's only a cyst, she jumps for joy...and breaks her ankle. In the stunning hour-long episode Edith's 50th Birthday (Oct. 16, 1977), while everyone else is next door preparing for a surprise party, Edith opens the door at 704 Hauser to a young man posing as an undercover police officer investigating a string of rapes. She lets him in, and within seconds it's revealed he's the rapist. There are some genuinely chilling scenes as Edith realizes what her fate will be, but as the man begins undressing her, the cake she's baking starts to burn. She runs into the kitchen with the rapist in hot pursuit, removes the burning cake from the oven and shoves it in his face before escaping out the back door.

Another brilliant hour-long offering was Edith's Crisis Of Faith, which aired on Christmas Day, 1977. Mike and transvestite Beverly LaSalle, who had befriended the Bunker family after Archie (not knowing she was a he) saved her life in his cab, are mugged on the street on Christmas Eve. Mike escapes unharmed, but Beverly is beaten to death. Edith, who was very fond of Beverly, is shaken to the point of renouncing her Christianity. Again, the powerful sympathy Stapleton manages to evoke in the character is overwhelming. The episode concludes with a heart-felt conversation between Edith and Mike, the life-long atheist, who tells her that the only kind of Christianity he ever understood or appreciated was the kind she's always demonstrated.

Freeze Frame

The controversial rape episode on *All In The Family* was originally written for Ann Romano (Bonnie Franklin), the young divorced mom on another Lear creation, *One Day At A Time*. Edith Bunker wound up as the target when the writers and producers decided the story would have more impact by showing that rape victims come in all ages.

Over its 12-year run *All In The Family* underwent myriad changes. The Jeffersons and Lorenzos came and went as the Bunkers' neighbours before Mike and Gloria moved into the house next door. In a three-part story to open the 1977–1978 season, Archie finally quit his job on the loading dock and bought Kelsey's Bar, which he renamed Archie's Place. A year later Mike and Gloria moved to California with their infant son Joey, and Archie and Edith were joined by Edith's young niece Stephanie Mills (Danielle Brisebois), who had been abandoned by her father. Shortly afterwards they found out Stephanie had been raised in the Jewish faith, which irked Archie no end. During the 1979–1980 season the series focused almost exclusively on Archie's bar and its "regulars," and in the opening episode of the 1980–1981 season, it was revealed Edith had died of a stroke, leaving Archie and Stephanie to soldier on.

Through all the changes, including its final incarnation as *Archie Bunker's Place* (1979–1983), the series remained a ratings winner and a timeless showcase for how TV's best comedy could often also be its best drama. Archie Bunker became an American icon, and 30 years after first telling Edith to "stifle it," he was deservedly voted television's all-time greatest character in a *TV Guide* poll.

The Least You Need to Know

➤ Michael Francis "Bub" O'Casey, the original housekeeper on *My Three Sons*, was played by the irascible William Frawley, who also portrayed Fred Mertz on *I Love Lucy*.

➤ Teenager Patty Duke had already won an Academy Award when she took on the dual role of identical cousins on *The Patty Duke Show*.

➤ Jackie Coogan, who portrayed Uncle Fester on *The Addams Family*, had been the world's No. 1 box-office draw as a child star.

➤ Herman and Lily Munster (Fred Gwynne and Yvonne DeCarlo) were the first prime-time sitcom couple to be shown in bed together.

➤ *All In The Family* was originally pitched to ABC under the working title *Justice For All*, and Carroll O'Connor got the starring role after flunking an audition for the part of the Skipper on *Gilligan's Island*.

Chaotic Couples

The astonishing success of *All In The Family* forever shattered the long-standing network credo that viewers would welcome only wholesome, inoffensive TV families into their living rooms. Certainly there would always be a place in the pantheon of sitcom immortals for the Nelsons, Andersons, Cleavers and Bradys, but the sledge-hammer effect the Bunker clan had on redefining domestic comedy heralded a new era of in-your-face sitcoms that reflected the real lives of viewers more accurately than anything that had come before.

The post–Archie Bunker broadening of prime-time parameters encompassed much more than just comedy programming. Soap operas, game shows and dramas also became bolder and more cutting-edge, as did current affairs programs like *60 Minutes* and *NBC Reports*. The fact that such a full-scale facelift of network norms could be traced to a single situation comedy was incredible—but not without precedent.

Albeit in a kinder, gentler way, a full two decades before *All In The Family* hit the airwaves the standard for television's first golden age was established by a zany redhead and her Cuban husband, who together put an indelible stamp on the sitcom "look" by pioneering the use of three-camera photography and proving that tight writing and brilliant characterizations were far more effective than precocious kids, dopey parents or cheap sexual innuendo in getting laughs.

That simple formula, based almost entirely on physical comedy and interaction between two adult lead characters, became the foundation for some of the greatest programs in television history.

I Love Lucy

Series debut: Oct. 15, 1951 (CBS). Final telecast: May 6, 1957 (CBS). 179 episodes.

"Larry and Lucy Lopez? A Latin bandleader and his kooky wife? C'mon, where's the laugh appeal in that?"

According to Melanie Anscomb, author of *Why We Loved Lucy*, that was the reaction of one high-ranking CBS executive after he screened the original pilot episode of *I Love Lucy*, which was kinescoped on March 2, 1951, but didn't air on American television until 1990. And that nameless network suit was right. The "audition show," as pilots were then called, bears little resemblance to the series that went on to become arguably the best loved in television history. For one thing, Lucille Ball and her real-life husband, Desi Arnaz, weren't all that funny. The plot was a simple rewrite of a sketch from their touring vaudeville act, patched together with a script from Lucy's *My Favorite Husband* radio show, and the end result was...well...boring. Neighbours Ethel and Fred Mertz (Vivian Vance and William Frawley) hadn't yet been cast, so there was no sustainable counterpoint to the antics of the two principals.

TeleTrivia

Lucy Ricardo's maiden name was MacGillicuddy. On *Here's Lucy* (1962–1965) Lucille Ball's character was "Lucy Carter," and on *The Lucy Show* (1965–1974) she was "Lucy Carmichael."

Lame as it was, the audition show was good enough to convince CBS to order 13 episodes, and by the time *I Love Lucy* debuted as a full-fledged network production seven months later, series creators Jess Oppenheimer, Madelyn Pugh and Bob Carroll Jr. had done an extensive rewrite. The lead characters were now Lucy and Ricky Ricardo, who resided in apartment 4A at 623 East 68 St. in Manhattan. Ricky was a $150-a-week bandleader at the Tropicana Club, while Fred and Ethel Mertz were the Ricardo's landlords and best friends. The most important tweak, however, was that the show's creators unanimously agreed to allow Lucy to exploit her over-the-top physical comedy to the fullest.

It was an instant smash. Most of the first-season episodes revolved around Lucy's screwball attempts to break free of her humdrum housewife routine in order to land a show business job at Ricky's club. Ethel served as her partner in crime, while Fred, always the fuddy-duddy cynic, did his best not to get involved. As the series evolved, so did the sophistication of the comedy. Ricky's show business career blossomed, he got his own television show and bought a night club—providing even more fodder for Lucy's magnificent misbehaviour. The plots, while sometimes convoluted, were incredibly inventive and always showcased Lucy's peerless talent for physical comedy. Her overblown crying jags quickly became an audience favourite, as did her penchant for charging headfirst into hilarious situations. By the spring of 1952, when there were barely 15 million television sets in America, *I Love Lucy* commanded a weekly audience of 11.5 million viewers. The following season's episode featuring the birth of "Little Ricky" attracted the kind of media attention usually reserved for royalty, and drew more viewers than the inauguration of President Dwight Eisenhower.

Freeze Frame

The birth of "Little Ricky" on *I Love Lucy* occurred on the exact same day that Lucille Ball gave birth to Desi Arnaz Jr.—Jan. 19, 1953. Lucy's pregnancy had been the focal point of the series for months beforehand, and that night's episode—Lucy Goes to the Hospital—became the most-watched show in television history to that point. When Little Ricky joined the cast in 1956, the part was played by Richard Keith.

Today, more than 40 years after they first aired, the classic episodes are still legendary: Lucy finagling her way onto Ricky's TV show to do a commercial for a health tonic called Vitameatavegamin, then getting drunk on its high alcohol content; Lucy and Ethel working on an assembly line in a chocolate factory, only to have the candy-laden conveyor belt speed up as they attempt to wrap the sweets; the pair using two cartons of yeast to bake bread, then having the dough explode from the oven in an eight-foot loaf that pinned them to the kitchen wall. For my money, the funniest sustained stunt in the entire run of the series came when the Ricardos and Mertzes visited Italy in 1956. Lucy is spotted on the street by a famous Italian director named Vittorio Fellipi, who offers her a role in his new movie, entitled Bitter Grapes. Assuming the film is about the wine industry, Lucy immediately sets out to immerse herself in researching the role. Dressed in peasant garb and unable to speak a word of Italian, she journeys to a wine-making centre on the outskirts of Rome, where the supervisor takes one look at the size of her feet and quickly assigns her to a huge grape-filled vat with orders to stomp. After a disagreement acted out in sign language, the hapless redhead and her frumpy Italian co-stomper engage in a full-blown wrestling match inside the vat, rolling and sloshing through the mush with uninhibited gusto. The scene lasts nearly five full minutes, after

Notable Quotable

"So what if I'm not sitting in the lap of luxury? I'm happy where I am, on the bony knees of nothing."

—Lucy Ricardo

which Lucy finally drags herself out of the vat, soaking wet and covered in grape pulp. She returns to Rome only to learn that the movie has nothing to do with wine-making; Vittorio was merely looking for a woman to portray "a typical American tourist." Adding insult to injury, he offers the part to Ethel.

What keeps *I Love Lucy* fresh and funny after all these years is the sheer exuberance of its star. By rejecting the expected and defiantly refusing to act her age, Lucy became a timeless personification of the little kid in all of us who just can't help testing the limits of disobedience. Forever in the midst of money problems and always with the heavy hand of a dominant male dictating her every move (first Ricky, then on *The Lucy Show* and *Here's Lucy*, Mr. Mooney and Uncle Harry respectively, both played by Gale Gordon), Lucy let us all in on a big secret between the laughs: not every woman dreams of a spotless home and a perfect marriage. Desi's insistence on filming the series like a movie, with three cameras in front of a live audience rather than on the traditional kinescope gave the show a crisp, natural flow—and perfect high-quality prints for the reruns, which provided the network such a lucrative income in the decades to follow.

I Love Lucy was still the No. 1 show on television when it ceased production as a weekly series at the end of the 1956–1957 season, but the kooky redhead and the exasperated

TeleTrivia

Lucille Ball's immortal status as the first lady of television came precariously close to being harpooned before it was ever established. In 1952 she was summoned before the House Committee On Un-American Activities, a de facto vigilante board headed by Senator Joe McCarthy to "expose" Communist sympathizers in all facets of American society—with a particular emphasis on the entertainment industry. *The Los Angeles Herald-Tribune* ran a four-inch front page headline proclaiming "LUCILLE BALL NAMED RED!" along with a photograph of a 1936 voter registration card on which Lucy allegedly had indicated her intention to vote for a Communist candidate. After a thorough investigation she was cleared, and weeks later the Arnazes, Vivian Vance and William Frawley were invited to the White House for dinner with President Dwight Eisenhower.

Cuban bandleader made regular appearances over the next two years on the *Lucille Ball & Desi Arnaz Hour*—still with the Mertzes in tow. In later years the prestige of appearing with Lucy became a badge of honour, even for Hollywood heavyweights who normally shunned television. William Holden, Tallulah Bankhead, Jack Benny, Richard Burton, Elizabeth Taylor and John Wayne were among the big names who appeared on the hour-long specials or Lucy's subsequent solo efforts, *Here's Lucy* (1962–1965) and *The Lucy Show* (1965–1974).

In 1986, at a spry 75, Lucy attempted a TV comeback in *Life With Lucy*, playing a free-spirited grandmother who inherited half of a run-down hardware store in California. The other half was owned by Curtis McGibbon, played by long-time foil Gale Gordon, who was 80. The old chemistry between the two was still evident, but sight gags and slapstick by a couple of senior citizens just didn't catch on with viewers and the series was cancelled after just eight episodes.

I Married Joan

Series debut: Oct. 15, 1952 (NBC). Final telecast: April 6, 1955 (NBC). 98 episodes.

While *I Love Lucy* is acknowledged as television's pioneering domestic sitcom, many Boomers remember *I Married Joan* as the medium's first copycat comedy. In fact, so closely did the antics of ditzy housewife Joan Stevens (Joan Davis) and her straight-laced

TeleTrivia

The first appearance of National Hockey League film footage on a U.S. sitcom was in the second episode of *I Married Joan*, entitled The Birthday. In order to get Joan out of the house so her friends can arrange a surprise party, Judge Stevens takes her to a hockey game between California and Florida. Of course, the episode was filmed a full 15 years before there was an NHL team in California and nearly 40 years before Florida joined the league, so the producers inserted footage from two different games from the old six-team NHL. The first sequence, which follows a shot of Judge Stevens in the crowd, rabidly cheering for "California," is a clip from a game between the New York Rangers and Boston Bruins. Seconds later, after another crowd shot showing fans cheering for both "California" and "Florida," the on-ice action is from a game between the Montreal Canadiens and Detroit Red Wings.

Notable Quotable

Judge Stevens: "How can you write cheques with no money in the bank?"

Joan: "I figured they'd trust us. After all, when they've got our money we don't go nagging them about it, do we?"

husband, Judge Bradley Stevens (Jim Backus), parallel the Ricardos that one critic suggested the series be retitled "I Married a Clone."

Davis, who was 45 years old when the series debuted, was never Lucy's match when it came to physical comedy, but she gave it the old college try. Like Lucy, she did all her own stunts on the show, but they were never quite as complex or athletic as the redhead's. Davis' best attribute was her gift for making goofy faces during banter with the droll Backus, who portrayed the stuffy judge as sort of a hybrid of two future roles that would establish him as a TV icon: Mr. Magoo and Thurston Howell III.

Like *I Love Lucy*, most of the plots on *I Married Joan* revolved around the star's efforts to break free of her household routine—at any cost. She never had money, rarely thought things through, and in the end inevitably had to rely on her husband to get her out of a jam. During the first season, Joan's next-door neighbour Minerva Parker (Hope Emerson) served as her co-conspirator (she was even frumpier than Ethel Mertz), but in 1953 Parker was replaced as the only other regular in the cast by Davis' real-life daughter, Beverly Wills, in the role of Joan's college-aged sister.

The Honeymooners

Series debut: Oct. 1, 1955 (CBS). Final (original) telecast: Sept. 10, 1956 (CBS). 39 episodes.

I Love Lucy and *I Married Joan* were both splendid examples of the affection between principal characters being palpable enough to transcend even the most outrageous situations. Whether it was the Ricardos and Mertzes bracing for a Martian invasion on the roof of their Manhattan apartment building or Judge Stevens and his scatter-brained wife trapped in a kitchen filled with popcorn, there was an undercurrent of warmth and fondness that flowed through each episode. The same was true with *The Honeymooners*, but with a twist. In bus driver Ralph Kramden (Jackie Gleason), his wife Alice (Audrey Meadows) and their best friends Ed and Trixie Norton (Art Carney and Joyce Randolph), viewers were treated to the same uncommon chemistry—with a heaping helping of genuine pathos on the side.

More than any situation comedy that had appeared on television to that point, *The Honeymooners* managed to wring belly laughs from situations that were almost exclusively negative. Ralph, a blustering, pig-headed driver for the Gotham Bus Company was a loveable loser—a '50s prototype for Archie Bunker. Perpetually broke and with a bowling ball-sized chip on his shoulder, he treated Alice like a hired hand and punctuated their screaming matches with wild histrionics and threats of physical

Jackie Gleason, Audrey Meadows, Art Carney and Joyce Randolph turned The Honeymooners *into a timeless classic of Boomer TV.*

violence: "One of these days, Alice, ONE OF THESE DAYS...Pow! Right in the kisser!" or the classic, "Bang, zoom, to the moon!" The Nortons lived upstairs in the same shabby Brooklyn apartment building at 328 Chauncey St. and were the Kramdens only real friends. Ed was a cheerful, wisecracking sewer worker whose puppy-like devotion to Ralph made up for his lack of smarts, while Trixie was a sensible and sympathetic confidant for the long-suffering Alice. Even the setting was radically different from the TV norm; there was no comfortable suburban home or white picket fence here. The Kramdens' two-room apartment, which Gleason based on his childhood home, was shabby and decrepit, with just a few pathetic sticks of furniture and an old-fashioned ice box that rarely contained anything more than a leftover chicken leg.

In the same way the trappings of middle-class familiarity became the cornerstone for virtually every other sitcom of the day, the lack of creature comforts in the dismal lives of the Kramdens and Nortons was the foundation for most of the comedy on *The Honeymooners*—and it worked magnificently. The superb chemistry between Gleason and Carney and Gleason and Meadows made Ralph, Norton and Alice three of the most believable characters in television history, and explains why their predicaments continue to be as poignant and amusing today as they were when the episodes first aired. Half a century later, it's still easy to forget they were merely actors playing roles and not real people who might have lived down the street. As long as Ralph and Norton could find

Notable Quotable

"A man's home is his castle, and in that castle you're the king! Tomorrow afternoon when Agnes says 'I do,' that's the last decision you allow her to make."

—Ralph Kramden's advice to a friend getting married

TeleTrivia

Jackie Gleason's first series role was as Chester A. Riley on the NBC sitcom *The Life of Riley* (1949). Although the character bore a striking resemblance to the "loveable loser" that became Ralph Kramden, the series was a ratings flop and lasted only one season. When a revamped version of *The Life of Riley* returned in 1953 with William Bendix in the lead it did much better, staying on the air for five seasons.

refuge in the Raccoon Lodge or the corner pool room to plot their hopeless money-making schemes (glow-in-the dark wallpaper, no-cal pizza, making a commercial to sell 2,000 Happy Housewife Helper apple corers), they were just like us...and that was oddly comforting.

The Honeymooners was TV's first spinoff series, having begun as a semi-regular sketch on Gleason's first series on the DuMont network, *Cavalcade of Stars* (1949–1952). The idea was hardly original: a blue-collar worker comes home at night, demands dinner, then fights with his wife about lack of money, household drudgery, etc. Actress Pert Kelton was the original Alice in the five-minute segments, and Carney was added to the mix simply to bring in another face. By the time the renamed *Jackie Gleason Show* moved over to CBS in 1952, expanded Honeymooners sketches (with Meadows replacing Kelton) were part of each hour-long program. Like *I Love Lucy*, the shows were filmed in front of a live audience, but unlike Desi Arnaz, Gleason didn't believe in stopping to reshoot corrections for the little glitches that sometimes arose—and the resulting ad libs were often better than the original lines. In the very first episode with Meadows, for example, Ralph burst into the kitchen screaming, "You're not going to serve me frozen steak again, are you?" He then picked up the "steak," which was really a piece of wood painted to look like meat, and slammed it down on the table...at which point it broke in two pieces, with one part flying into the audience. Without missing a beat, Meadows saved the scene by calmly picking up the piece that was still on the table and dead-panning, "No, Ralph. I'm not serving you frozen steak again. I'm serving you HALF a frozen steak!"

In early 1955, when Gleason accepted an offer to develop a half-hour program with Buick as the main sponsor, the misadventures of bus driver Ralph Kramden and his dimwitted sidekick became a full-blown sitcom. Meadows and Randolph came on board full time, and a genuine TV legend was born.

Gleason's deal with Buick called for 78 episodes to be filmed (two seasons of 39 shows each), with an option for a third season. His company would be paid $65,000 per show, and half of that for summer reruns. Unfortunately, dropped into a tough Saturday night time-slot opposite the phenomenally popular *Perry Como Show* on NBC, *The Honeymooners* never gained an audience toehold the first time around, and after one season Gleason cancelled the contract. The "Classic 39," as the original episodes came to be called, were locked away in a network vault and didn't resurface for more than a decade. *The Honeymooners* was revived as an occasional hour-long feature on Gleason's variety show in 1966, with Sheila MacRae as Alice and Jane Kean as Trixie, and those episodes were rerun sporadically until 1971, but by then the original 39 had been released into syndication and a whole new generation of viewers was introduced to the "real" Kramdens and Nortons.

Notable Quotable

Ralph: "I'm a hero, Alice. Do you know what a hero is?"

Alice: "Yeah. It's a fat sandwich that's full of baloney."

Since the mid-1970s *The Honeymooners* has never been off the air in North America, and the Classic 39 will no doubt continue to be popular as long as television exists. The show's timeless appeal is a testament not only to the comedic genius of Gleason and Carney and the uncommon chemistry between the cast but to the universality of its premise. Every single situation on *The Honeymooners* was based on something that could happen to any one of us. The characters were legitimate, real people who worried and bickered and made up like real people. In the end, *The Honeymooners* was all about truth. You knew Ralph really was sorry and that Alice really did forgive him when he hugged her and said, "Baby, you're the greatest!"—just as you knew that the next time he roared, "You're goin' to the moon, Alice!" he really meant that, too. And that's why the honeymoon will never be over.

The Dick Van Dyke Show

Series debut: Oct. 3, 1961 (CBS). Final telecast: Sept. 7, 1966 (CBS). 158 episodes.

The Dick Van Dyke Show was the first TV sitcom about a TV sitcom—and the show that made a star out of Mary Tyler Moore.

Conceived by Carl Reiner in the fall of 1959, the original name of this series was Head Of The Family. Reiner himself portrayed Rob Petrie in the first pilot, which was flatly rejected when shopped to the networks in 1960. It was only after veteran actor/director Sheldon Leonard got hold of Reiner's 13 scripts later that year that the true potential of the concept was realized. Leonard convinced Reiner that he was a better writer and producer than he was an actor, and suggested they find somebody new to play Rob Petrie, the shy-but-talented head writer for the fictitious Alan Brady Show. Before they

TeleTrivia

➤ The Petries lived at 448 Bonnie Meadow Rd. in New Rochelle, New York.

➤ Rob's favourite breakfast was cold spaghetti.

➤ Buddy Sorrell's pet name for his wife (played by Barbara Perry and Joan Shawlee) was "Pickles," but her real name was Fiona.

➤ Jamie Farr, who went on to portray Cpl. Max Klinger in *M*A*S*H*, appeared in a semi-regular role as the guy who delivered snacks to the Brady Show writing staff.

settled on the rubber-faced Van Dyke for the lead, Reiner and Leonard gave serious consideration to Johnny Carson, but they opted for the gangly Van Dyke because, as Reiner later put it: "We wanted a guy who was shy, like a writer, but who was also a naturally funny performer. Dick had both those qualities."

In supporting roles as Rob Petrie's writing partners Buddy Sorrell and Sally Rogers, Reiner and Leonard scored a major coup by signing show business veterans Morey Amsterdam and Rose Marie. Amsterdam, the acid-tongued king of one-liners, was an old vaudeville performer (he once cracked that TV stood for "tired vaudeville"), while Rose Marie had been a national sensation as radio songstress "Baby Rose Marie" at the age of three before going on to a long and distinguished career on radio and the stage. Richard Deacon was cast as Mel Cooley, the bald no-nonsense producer of The Alan Brady Show. He also happened to be the brother-in-law of Brady (Reiner), whose favourite expression was "Shut up, Mel." Jerry and Millie Helper, the Petries' next-door neighbours, were played by Jerry Paris and Ann Morgan Guilbert.

By the time the troupe was ready to shoot a second pilot, the only key role left to fill was that of Rob's wife Laura—and Leonard and Reiner were running out of time. It was then that Leonard's business partner, Danny Thomas, suggested a relatively unknown actress who had unsuccessfully auditioned for the part of his oldest daughter on *The Danny Thomas Show*. It was Moore. Her only other TV work had been one season as David Janssen's sultry-voiced secretary, Sam, on *Richard Diamond, Private Detective*. What was unusual about that role was that Moore's face was never seen—only her legs! "I had Mary come in and read three lines," Reiner recalled years later. "One of the lines was simply 'Hello, Rob'...but that's all it took. I took her over to Sheldon's office and said, 'This is our Laura Petrie. She said hello like a real person!'"

Dick Van Dyke and Mary Tyler Moore became one of TV's all-time favourite couples as Rob and Laura Petrie on The Dick Van Dyke Show.

The second pilot for the renamed *Dick Van Dyke Show* was shot in January 1961 and was good enough for Procter and Gamble to make an offer to sponsor the show as a weekly series on CBS. It premiered nine months later but, like a lot of other great shows, it had difficulty finding an audience in a competitive time-slot (Tuesday night at 8). Leonard felt the slot was too early to attract sophisticated urban viewers, and the dismal ratings reflected his concern. At the end of the season the ratings were so bad that Procter and Gamble withdrew sponsorship and the network actually issued a cancellation notice, but after Leonard's 11th-hour plea it was given a stay of execution.

Beginning in 1962, *The Dick Van Dyke Show* was moved to Wednesday night at 9:30, and over the next few months it rocketed from 80th to 9th place in the Nielsen ratings. As the audience swelled, so did America's love affair with pert, sexy Mary Tyler Moore, whose understated comedy was the perfect complement for Van Dyke's over-the-top physical style. As Laura Petrie, Moore's prolonged crying jags (usually prefaced with "Oh, Rob!...") rivalled Lucy Ricardo's for comic effect, and since the series regularly employed dream sequences and flashbacks, Moore was often called upon to act out the same kind of broad slapstick that had become Lucy's trademark.

Freeze Frame

Like a lot of other '60s sitcoms, *The Dick Van Dyke Show* occasionally featured rock 'n' roll performers as guests. In the 1964 episode The Redcoats Are Coming, real-life British rock duo Chad and Jeremy portrayed "Ernie and Freddie," on The Alan Brady Show.

One of the more memorable examples of Moore's versatility was a raucous 1962 episode entitled It May Look Like A Walnut. After chiding Laura about being too scared to join him, Rob watches a late-night horror movie about aliens who take over human bodies by an "absorbatron" hidden in walnuts. The next morning, when Laura gives him walnuts for breakfast, Rob laughs it off as mere coincidence. Later, at the office, he learns that the guest star on the upcoming Alan Brady Show is Danny Thomas (playing himself), who bears a startling resemblance to Colak, the evil leader of the alien invaders. As the "coincidences" mount, Rob starts to panic. He returns home, but can't unlock the door because he's lost his thumbs—a sure sign of alien takeover. When he finally gets inside, he opens the hall closet and Laura comes cascading out on top of a mountain of walnuts, evilly exhorting her fellow aliens to join in the fun. Colak then emerges from the kitchen, followed by Buddy, Sally and Mel, who have likewise been "transformed." It's all been a nightmare, of course, and when Rob wakes up in a cold sweat, his adoring wife is there to comfort him.

Even more than the acting, which was always terrific, the consistent high quality of the writing is what made *The Dick Van Dyke Show* one of the best loved series of the '60s. A favourite gimmick used to set up the situation was a Petrie house party, which always attracted a strange mix of folks. In one of the best party episodes, a two-parter that aired on March 14 and March 21, 1962, Rob's brother Stacy drops by for a visit, hoping to launch a stand-up comedy career in the Big Apple. The trouble is, Stacy (played by Van Dyke's real-life brother Jerry) is funny only when he's sleep-walking! Rob and Laura arrange a party and invite Alan Brady to hear Stacy's schtick (at one point he does a hilarious imitation of General Custer, saying, "I don't know what's the matter with them Indians, they was all right at the dance last night..."), with predictable chaotic results. In the end, however, Stacy is able to perform wide awake, everybody loves him and he gets a guest spot on the Brady Show.

TeleTrivia

The famous opening sequence to *The Dick Van Dyke Show* in which Rob trips over the ottoman, does a full flip on the floor and then bounces up to shake hands with everyone is actually the second of four openings that were used over the course of the series. The first simply features photos over a drum mix of the theme song, while in the third sequence Rob is heading for the ottoman and looks like he's going to trip, but at the last second he does a nifty shuffle around it. In the fourth opening sequence, he again is headed for the ottoman, but sidesteps it—only to trip on the rug before shaking hands with Buddy.

The Dick Van Dyke Show won 15 Emmy Awards during its five-year stint (including two each for Van Dyke and Moore as outstanding lead performers in a comedy) and was still ranked in the top 20 programs when it was cancelled in the fall of 1966. Van Dyke appeared sporadically on the small screen right through the 1990s, highlighted by yet another Emmy Award for best comedy variety for *Van Dyke & Company* (1977). As for Mary Tyler Moore, her star would shine even brighter a few years later (see Chapter 10).

The Odd Couple

Series debut: Sept. 24, 1970 (ABC). Final telecast: July 4, 1975 (ABC). 114 episodes.

The hook for this underrated masterpiece was neatly explained in the voiced-over opening: "On November 13th, Felix Unger was asked to remove himself from his place of residence. That request came from his wife. Deep down he knew she was right—but he also knew that some day he would return to her. With nowhere else to go, he appeared at the home of his friend, Oscar Madison. Sometime earlier, Madison's wife had thrown him out, asking that he never return. Can two divorced men share an apartment without driving each other crazy?"

Felix (Tony Randall) was a freelance commercial photographer ("Portraits a specialty!") and a compulsive neat freak. Oscar (Jack Klugman) was a slovenly sportswriter for The New York Herald who smoked cigars, had a penchant for putting food in his pockets and loved nothing more than watching TV, drinking beer, playing poker with his friends and talking sports. On a personal note, Oscar was also the role model for my life's work.

TeleTrivia

Fans of *The Odd Couple* will be familiar with Oscar's favourite sandwich: ham, corned beef, salami, cream cheese and tomato on rye, with lots of mustard. His other "first string" snacks included sardines on raisin–bread toast with ketchup, and creamed chipped beef with raisins on a glazed donut. In one episode he said that the "ideal meal for romance" is red wine and fish sticks, and in another he demonstrated the best way to make a tasty hot meal: cook one Chinese and one Italian TV dinner, then press the trays together and shake. Another Madison culinary tip: always serve beer in cans, never glasses or bottles, "in order to preserve that good can taste."

Developed for television by Garry Marshall and Jerry Belson, the series was a small-screen spinoff of the hit Broadway play by Neil Simon, who also wrote the screenplay for a 1967 movie version starring Jack Lemmon as Felix and Walter Matthau as Oscar. Of the many *Odd Couple* incarnations, however, the TV effort by Randall and Klugman ranks as the absolute best. With impeccable craftsmanship, each actor imbued his character with so many layers of physical and emotional comic stylings that it's virtually impossible to view any of the 114 episodes without laughing out loud at least once. The core of the supporting cast was equally outstanding: Murray the cop (Al Molinaro), Oscar's ex-wife Blanche (played by Klugman's real-life ex-wife, Brett Somers), Oscar's whiny secretary Myrna (Penny Marshall), Felix's girlfriend Miriam Welby (Elinor Donahue) and his ex-wife Gloria (Janis Hansen).

Although most episodes revolved around the interaction between the two principals, the jokes never got predictable or stale, thanks to the subtle nuances Randall and Klugman brought to their roles. Part of what made them so funny was that each actor appeared to be born to play the part. Felix was hilarious every time he flitted around the living room spraying air freshener or went into one of his prolonged "honking" fits (it was his way of clearing stuffed sinuses), and Oscar was equally brilliant as the unrepentant slob. The scenes in his bedroom, with dirty laundry, pizza boxes and newspapers all over the place, are especially memorable. And you just knew that every time Felix prefaced a statement with "Oscar, Oscar, Oscar...," something special was about to happen.

The conflict on which *The Odd Couple* was based was resolved when Felix and Gloria remarried in the series finale, entitled "I Do Two." When Felix discovers Gloria has been dating another man, he goes ballistic, screaming, "You're making a mockery of our entire divorce!" He begs her to take him back, but she's still too leery of the finicky Felix who drove her crazy with his neatness. To prove he's changed, he lets Oscar do the cooking for a week (Oscar gets his recipes out of *Racing Digest*) and he even sleeps in Oscar's room. Oscar tells Gloria how Felix is a changed man, and she's moved to the point where she agrees to take him back. At the wedding, which is held in Oscar's apartment, Felix goes back to his old ways. He doesn't like Gloria's dress, he doesn't like the flowers...and when a water pipe in the ceiling starts leaking he wants to cancel the ceremony and call a plumber. Oscar brings him back to his senses with a terse warning: "If you blow this now, I'll break both your legs." The ceremony goes off without a hitch, and the happiest person in the room is Oscar, who starts dancing under the leaky pipe while belting out a very bad rendition of "Singin' In The Rain."

Notable Quotable

"It's like living with a crop duster."

—Oscar, describing Felix's love affair with aerosol air fresheners

In the final scene of the series, Felix is about to leave the apartment for the last time. As a gesture of how much he's "grown," he says, "Oscar Madison, I salute you!"—then overturns a wastepaper basket. Visibly moved, Oscar replies with: "You know how I'm gonna salute you? I'm gonna clean that up!" Felix nods triumphantly: "Then it hasn't been in vain!" After Felix leaves, Oscar looks down at the mess and says, "I'm not gonna clean that up," then saunters down the hallway to his bedroom. Seconds later, Felix creeps back into the apartment and scoops up the papers, muttering "I *knew* he wouldn't clean it up...."

For his portrayal of Oscar, Klugman won the Emmy Award for outstanding continued performance by an actor in a comedy series in both the 1970–1971 and 1972–1973 seasons. Randall won the same award for his role as Felix in 1974–1975.

The Least You Need to Know

- ➤ *I Love Lucy* was the first sitcom to be filmed with three cameras.
- ➤ The first film footage of the National Hockey League used in a U.S. sitcom appeared in the second episode of *I Married Joan* in 1952.
- ➤ Jackie Gleason's real-life childhood home in Brooklyn was the model for the Kramdens' shabby apartment on TV's first spinoff series, *The Honeymooners*.
- ➤ Ratings for *The Dick Van Dyke Show* were so low after the first season that the series was officially cancelled.
- ➤ In the final episode of *The Odd Couple*, finicky Felix Unger remarried Gloria, the wife who had thrown him out at the start of the series five years earlier.

Chapter 4

Rural Roots

In This Chapter

➤ California dreamin': *The Real McCoys*

➤ Homespun humour: *The Andy Griffith Show*

➤ Strangers in a strange land: *The Beverly Hillbillies*

➤ Sweet 'n' sexy: *Petticoat Junction*

➤ Twisted transplant: *Green Acres*

Domestic sitcoms and so-called "character" shows were the first wave of television comedy, but by the end of the 1950s the familiar format was beginning to look a tad tired. After all, how many successful shows can be milked from different takes on the same married-couple-with-kids-in-suburbia gimmick? The classics—*I Love Lucy, I Married Joan, The Honeymooners*—had ceased first-run production years earlier, and old staples like *Father Knows Best, Leave It To Beaver* and *The Danny Thomas Show* were starting to show their age.

In early 1957, writer Irving Pincus pitched a sitcom idea to NBC that initially seemed just too hokey, even for TV: pluck a happy-go-lucky family out of the sticks of West Virginia and put 'em on a farm in California's San Fernando Valley. NBC wasn't convinced there was enough laugh potential in transcontinental culture shock to sustain a weekly series and quickly passed, but ABC gave the idea a lukewarm reception and grudgingly agreed to finance the pilot.

As it turned out, Pincus was a visionary. His creation was the first in the wave of rural-based comedies that virtually took over prime time in the early-to-mid '60s and paved the way for writer/producer Paul Henning to earn a well-deserved reputation as television's all-time king of cornpone comedy.

The Real McCoys

Series debut: Oct. 3, 1957 (ABC). Final telecast: Sept. 22, 1963 (CBS). 224 episodes.

Notable Quotable

"It's just plain foolishness, squattin' all day in front of a little black box, starin' bleary-eyed at people who ain't no more than two inches high. It's a passin' fancy, I tell ya, like buggy whips and high-button shoes."

—Amos McCoy, describing television

The main objection Irving Pincus encountered when he first pitched the idea for this series was that it didn't appear strong enough to attract urban viewers. But by the time the script was reworked and presented to ABC, big-screen veteran Walter Brennan had joined the cast as crotchety grandpa Amos McCoy, head of a clan of naive West Virginians who moved lock, stock and barrel to "Californy" to start a new life on a farm in the San Fernando Valley.

The 63-year-old Brennan, who was the first actor to win three Academy Awards (1936, 1938 and 1940) was a perfect choice to play the illiterate, cantankerous head of the household, and his presence virtually guaranteed that big-city viewers would tune in—if only to see how a well-respected movie star fared on TV. The family also included Amos' grown-up grandson Luke (Richard Crenna), Luke's

Fast Forward

Richard Crenna, who portrayed Luke McCoy, made his TV debut as gawky, dimwitted student Walter Denton on the Eve Arden sitcom *Our Miss Brooks* (1952–1955). After *The Real McCoys* he starred in a pair of dramas (*Slattery's People* and *Centennial*) and a couple more sitcoms (*All's Fair* and *It Takes Two*) before winning an Emmy Award as best actor in a TV special for the ground-breaking *The Rape of Richard Beck* (1986). He also won acclaim for his steely portrayal of Col. Sam Trautman, Sylvester Stallone's commanding officer in the Rambo movie trilogy.

wife Kate (Kathy Nolan), along with his 12-year-old brother "Little Luke" (Michael Winkleman—apparently their parents weren't very imaginative), and sister Hassie (Lydia Reed). Farmhand Pepino Garcia (Tony Martinez) and elderly neighbour George MacMichael (Andy Clyde) rounded out the regular cast, but over the course of the six-year run several minor characters came and went, including Joe the mailman (Howard McNear, who went on to TV immortality as barber Floyd Lawson on *The Andy Griffith Show*) and MacMichael's spinster sister Flora (Madge Blake).

When the series moved to CBS in the fall of 1962 Luke became a widower (Kathy Nolan left the show to pursue other projects), and over the final season, as the action moved increasingly off the farm and into town, most of the plots revolved around grandpa's efforts to find Luke a new wife.

The Andy Griffith Show

Series debut: Oct. 3, 1960 (CBS). Final telecast: Sept. 16, 1968 (CBS). 249 episodes.

The Real McCoys started the trend, but *The Andy Griffith Show* was the series that steered rural humour into the mainstream of television comedy. Set in the town of Mayberry, North Carolina, the show about widowed sheriff Andy Taylor (Griffith), his inept deputy Barney Fife (Don Knotts), son Opie (Ronny Howard) and housekeeper Aunt Bea (Frances Bavier) has become a metaphor for the idyllic small-town American Dream. The humour was always gentle and philosophic, and mostly revolved around the relationships between the principal characters. Andy was the strong, silent type (he never wore a gun), while Barney, the stereotypical 98-pound weakling, did his best to project a tough image. Barney packed heat, but Andy let him carry just one bullet—which the twitchy deputy meticulously polished and kept in his shirt pocket. Other memorable Mayberrians included town drunk Otis Campbell (Hal Smith), barber Floyd Lawson

Freeze Frame

Andy Griffith Show cast members Howard McNear (Floyd Lawson) and Parley Baer (Mayor Stoner) had both been regulars on the original *Gunsmoke* radio series, portraying Doc Adams and deputy Chester Goode respectively. McNear was also a close friend of Elvis Presley and appeared in several movies with the king of rock 'n' roll, including *Blue Hawaii, Follow That Train* and *Viva Las Vegas.*

As sheriff of Mayberry, Andy Taylor (Andy Griffith) dished out a lot of laughs between apprehending chicken thieves and writing out parking tickets.

(Howard McNear), gas pump jockeys Gomer and Goober Pyle (Jim Nabors and George Lindsey) and Andy and Barney's girlfriends, schoolteacher Helen Crump (Aneta Corsaut) and the surname-less Thelma-Lou (Betty Lynn). Town clerk Howard Sprague (Jack Dodson), Mayor Stoner (Parley Baer) and rock-throwing hillbilly Ernest T. Bass (Howard Morris) were semi-regulars.

The Andy Griffith Show was a spinoff from an episode of *The Danny Thomas Show* in which New Yorker Danny Williams (Thomas) and his vacationing family were pulled over for speeding by a small-town sheriff (Griffith), who was singularly unimpressed with Williams' show biz status. The character of Barney Fife was introduced as Andy's cousin after the series debuted, when Knotts called his long-time pal Griffith and suggested that the star needed a bumbling sidekick. Barney instantly became a favourite with viewers, and the role earned Knotts five Emmy Awards for Best Supporting Actor in a Comedy.

Viewed today, most episodes of *The Andy Griffith Show* still work as pure comedy, but the ingredient that made the series so special in its time and what continues to shine through after endless reruns is the homey familiarity. The extraordinary comic timing between Griffith and Knotts could turn a meal at the Mayberry Diner or a car ride to Mt. Pilot (a whole 12 miles away) into a memorable event, with no more than conversation or the simplest props to sustain the laughs.

Notable Quotable

"When a man carries a gun all the time, the respect he thinks he's getting might really be fear. So I don't carry a gun because I don't want the people of Mayberry to fear a gun; I'd rather they would respect me."

—Sheriff Andy Taylor

The series was still highly rated when Griffith decided to pull the plug in 1968, and in the final episode Andy married Helen and took a job as a postal inspector in Cleveland. The supporting cast (without Knotts, who had left in 1965) appeared in a follow-up series called *Mayberry R.F.D.* (starring Ken Berry), which lasted three seasons, but most of the originals reunited for a feature-length production called *Return To Mayberry*, which aired in April 1986 and was the highest rated TV movie of the year.

Fast Forward

Andy Griffith went on to star as chili-dog lovin' lawyer Ben Matlock in the long-running crime series *Matlock* (1986–1993), but he never forgot his Mayberry roots. Don Knotts had a recurring role as Matlock's obnoxious neighbour Les Calhoun, while Aneta Corsaut was cast as a feisty no-nonsense judge who regularly showed Ben who was boss in the courtroom.

The Beverly Hillbillies

Series debut: Sept. 26, 1962 (CBS). Final telecast: Sept. 7, 1971 (CBS). 274 episodes.

With the possible exceptions of *The Odd Couple* (see Chapter 3) and *Gilligan's Island* (see Chapter 6), no sitcom in history was more succinctly explained in its musical opening than this creation of writer/director Paul Henning, who wrote both the music and lyrics to the wonderfully catchy "Ballad of Jed Clampett" (c. 1962 by Carolintone Music Co. Inc.):

> Come 'n listen to my story 'bout a man named Jed,
> Poor mountaineer, barely kept his fam'ly fed.
> An' then one day, he was shootin' at some food,
> An' up through the ground came a bubblin' crude.
> Oil, that is. Black gold. Texas tea.
> Well, the first thing you know, Jed's a millionaire.
> Kin folk said, 'Jed, move away from there.'
> Said, 'Californy is th' place ya oughta be,'
> So they loaded up the truck and they moved to Beverly.
> Hills, that is. Swimmin' pools, movie stars....

And the verse that closed each episode:

> Well now it's time to say goodbye to Jed and all his kin.
> An' they would like t' thank you folks fer kindly droppin' in.
> Yer all invited back again to this locality,
> To have a heapin' helpin' of their hospitality.
> Hillbilly, that is. Set a spell. Take yer shoes off.
> Y'all come back now, hear?

Yup, for Jed (Buddy Ebsen), his daughter Elly May (Donna Douglas), nephew Jethro Bodine (Max Baer Jr.) and mother-in-law Granny Daisy Moses (Irene Ryan), that swanky 35-room California mansion was about as far removed from their shack on the outskirts of Bug Tussle, Tennessee, as Hawaii is from Siberia.

Freeze Frame

Buddy Ebsen was the original choice to play the Scarecrow in *The Wizard of Oz* before being recast as the Tin Man, but early in the filming he became seriously ill after ingesting the powdery aluminium makeup used to paint his face. His lungs were coated with aluminium dust and permanently damaged, so the role was passed on to Jack Haley.

During nine years and 274 shows, as the original $25 million paid to Jed by the OK Oil Company swelled to $95 million, the family never quite got used to their luxurious digs. From the opulent "cee-ment pond" (swimming pool) to the wood-burning still that Granny built to brew her "rheumatiz medicine," the Clampett's abode—like almost everything else in their new lives—was a study in contrasts. This led to endless problems, especially for Commerce Bank president Milburn Drysdale (Raymond Bailey) and his prissy secretary Jane Hathaway (Nancy Kulp), who did everything in their power to "citify" the family. Adding to the chaos was Elly May's penchant for adopting stray critters (everything from a kangaroo named Sidney to a swimming cat named Rusty) and Jethro's never-ending search for a career befitting a guy "who done gradjeeated sixth grade."

Even though the series was panned by critics as a one-joke aberration, *The Beverly Hillbillies* was a huge hit with viewers, beginning with the very first episode, which attracted an audience of nearly 50 million. The lack of critical acclaim didn't faze

Freeze Frame

In addition to distilling the most potent moonshine this side of Bug Tussle, Granny was famous for preparing first-rate "vittles." High on her list of culinary masterpieces was possum shanks with pickled hog jowls, Southern-fried muskrat with sow belly and hand-slung chitlins, and devilled hawk eggs with stewed squirrel and turnip greens. As Jethro would say, "Boy, them's eats!"

Henning, who said: "I created the show for the viewers, not the critics. My purpose is to give the public pure escapist entertainment and comedy, not phony 'heart' and synthetic 'warmth' dreamed up by a bunch of sophisticated writers sitting around in a smoke-filled room. I believe that true warmth and heart can come only from the characters themselves, and I believe these characters have it."

He was right, of course. As Jed and Granny, old pros Ebsen and Ryan were the show's anchors, but goofy Jethro and Elly May quickly became viewer favourites. Donna Douglas imbued Elly May with a sexy naivete that male viewers found irresistible. By the end of the first season she was receiving thousands of fan letters per week. Baer, the son and namesake of a former world heavyweight boxing champion, likewise became somewhat of a sex symbol—even if his alter-ego rarely had much luck with the ladies. Like the rest of the family, Jethro never fully fathomed that his uncle was obscenely rich, and some of the most memorable episodes revolved around his ongoing quest to find gainful employment. Among his career aspirations were: double-naught spy; five-star general; fry cook (he briefly opened an eatery called The Happy Gizzard); movie producer; atomic scientist; bullfighter; and brain surgeon. During the first season, when some episodes featured flashbacks to the Clampetts' previous life in the Ozarks, Max Baer Jr. appeared in drag as Jethro's twin sister, Jethrine. Their mother, Cousin Pearl Bodine, was portrayed by Bea Benaderet.

After seven straight seasons as one of television's top 12 ratings leaders (including being No. 1 in 1962–1963 and 1963–1964), *The Beverly Hillbillies* slipped to No. 18 in 1969–1970 and dropped out

Notable Quotable

"As Elly May Clampett, Donna Douglas has done more for blue jeans in seven months than cowboys did in 110 years."

—*TV Guide*, 1962

Freeze Frame

Actress Sharon Tate, whose 1969 murder by members of the infamous Manson Family triggered one of the largest manhunts in U.S. history, had a semi-regular role during the second and third seasons of *The Beverly Hillbillies* as Janet Trego, a trainee in the Commerce Bank's secretarial pool.

of the top 25 the following year. The show was cancelled in the fall of 1971, and to this day remains the highest rated series to be completely shut out of the Emmy Awards.

Petticoat Junction

Series debut: Sept. 24, 1963 (CBS). Final telecast: Sept. 12, 1970 (CBS). 222 episodes.

The unexpected success of *The Beverly Hillbillies* made series creator Paul Henning the hottest name in Hollywood in the early '60s, and CBS rewarded him by offering to purchase another series without even looking at a pilot episode. Since Henning had been looking for a showcase for versatile actress Bea Benaderet (Cousin Pearl on *The Beverly Hillbillies*), he accepted the offer and created "Petticoat Junction," a character comedy set in the whistle-stop hamlet of Hooterville, where widow Kate Bradley (Benaderet) and her three lovely daughters Billie Jo, Bobbie Jo and Betty Jo ran the Shady Rest Hotel along with Kate's uncle, Joe Carson (Edgar Buchanan). Over the course of the series three different actresses portrayed Billie Jo (Jeannine Riley, Gunilla Hutton and Meredith MacRae) and two were Bobbie Jo (Pat Woodell and Lori Saunders), while the only Betty Jo was Linda Kaye Henning—daughter of the show's creator. Other regulars were Charlie Pratt (Smiley Burnette) and Floyd Smoot (Rufe Davis), the hayseed engineers who ran the Cannonball steam engine between Hooterville and neighbouring Pixley; general store proprietor Sam Drucker (Frank Cady); and Homer Bedloe (Charles Lane), vice-president of the C.F. & W. Railroad, who was always threatening to shut down the line to

Notable Quotable

Floyd Smoot, the philosophic Cannonball engineer, had a talent for malapropisms. He was fond of saying: "Remember, it's always darkest before you lead a horse to water," and when things went wrong he placated his partner, Charlie Pratt, with: "Don't forget, Charlie, every cloud has a stiff upper lip!"

Hooterville and put the Shady Rest out of business. The name of the series was explained in the opening credits, which showed the three Bradley daughters bathing in a water tower "at the junction" with their petticoats slung over the side.

The delectable daughters were certainly a good enough reason for men to watch *Petticoat Junction*, but the series was also well written and the characterizations were bang on—particularly Kate and Uncle Joe. There was a chemistry between Benaderet and Buchanan that lit up every exchange between the two. Despite Kate's stern admonitions, you knew that every time Uncle Joe hatched another of his harebrained schemes to bring more business to the Shady Rest, she'd be there to bail him out. Sadly, Benaderet died soon after production began for the 1968–1969 season, and the show

Freeze Frame

Bea Benaderet's first television role was as Blanche Morton, next-door neighbour to George and Gracie on *The George Burns and Gracie Allen Show* (1950–1958). She also provided the voice of Betty Rubble on *The Flintstones* from 1960 to 1964.

was never the same afterwards. Janet Craig (June Lockhart) was introduced as Hooterville's matronly doctor to fill the void, but her character never really fit and the series limped through one more season before being cancelled.

Two years after *Petticoat Junction* hit the airwaves, CBS added *Green Acres* to its prime-time lineup (see next listing), and for the remainder of both series' runs there were regular crossovers of characters. For a 1969 Thanksgiving special, the lead characters from *The Beverly Hillbillies*, *Green Acres* and *Petticoat Junction* all gathered at the Shady Rest Hotel for a memorable holiday feast.

Green Acres

Series debut: Sept. 15, 1965 (CBS). Final telecast: Sept. 7, 1971 (CBS). 167 episodes.

Created by Jay Sommer with an assist from Paul Henning and writer Dick Chevillat, *Green Acres* was one of the strangest sitcoms of the decade. On the surface the show was merely the flip side of *The Beverly Hillbillies*, revolving around a stuffy former Manhattan lawyer named Oliver Wendell Douglas (Eddie Albert) and his spoiled, society-conscious wife Lisa (Eva Gabor), who bought "a pile of dirt and a run-down shack" on the outskirts of Hooterville (Lisa called it "Hootersville") and spent the duration of the series trying to farm it. "I want to get more out of life...get back to the land, get my hands dirty, the way it must have been for our forefathers," said Oliver. Whenever he talked like that, patriotic music would start playing in the background and somebody in the scene would look up and mutter, "There goes that patriotic music again...."

Yes, this was a strange show indeed. Where *The Beverly Hillbillies* and *Petticoat Junction* were homey and sentimental, *Green Acres* was edgy and cynical. Where the Clampetts and Bradleys were over-the-top, knee-slappin' funny, the odd assortment of geeks and weirdoes on *Green Acres* was sometimes downright disturbing. Indeed, perhaps the best way to describe the show, which lasted a healthy 167 episodes, is that it was the Twilight Zone of cornpone comedy.

While the relationship between Oliver and Lisa was the show's main catalyst, most of the laughs were milked from the array of social outcasts who lived and worked in Hooterville. There was handyman Alf Monroe (Sid Melton) and his sister Ralph (Mary Grace Canfield); Fred and Doris Ziffel (Hank Patterson and Barbara Pepper) and their affable "son" Arnold—who was a corpulent pink pig. Arnold wore hats, was drafted into the army, squealed contentedly while watching television (*The Dick Van Dyke Show* was his favourite program), and "talked" to Lisa. Then there was county agricultural agent Hank Kimball (Alvy Moore), who often talked in gibberish, weasely snake-oil salesman Mr. Haney (Pat Buttram); storekeeper-postmaster-newspaper editor Sam Drucker (Frank Cady, who played the same role on *Petticoat Junction*) and, last but certainly not least, hired hand Eb Dawson (Tom Lester), a dorky lout who referred to Oliver and Lisa as "dad" and "mom." A first-season episode shed some light on Eb's inner demons after Lisa discovered an abandoned puppy on the porch. Unsure of what to feed the pooch, she asked Eb, who replied: "When we was kids, mom fed the pups the same thing she fed us."

"What was that?"

"Dog food."

That little exchange pretty much sums up the whole attitude on *Green Acres*. Even the show's opening credits, which were painted on everything from the roof of a barn to the side of a real cow, were different. For Oliver Wendell Douglas it was a six-year sentence to an alien planet populated by some of the nuttiest misfits in sitcom history. For the rest of us, it was pure fun.

The Least You Need to Know

➤ Walter Brennan, star of *The Real McCoys*, was the first actor to win three Academy Awards.

➤ *The Andy Griffith Show* was a spinoff from an episode of *The Danny Thomas Show*. Howard McNear, who portrayed Mayberry barber Floyd Lawson, was a close friend of Elvis Presley and appeared in several of The King's movies.

➤ *The Beverly Hillbillies* remains the highest rated program in television history to be completely shut out of Emmy Awards.

➤ *Petticoat Junction* and *Green Acres* were both based in the fictitious Hooterville, and characters regularly crossed over between the two series.

Distaff Laughs

With a few notable exceptions (*Green Acres* being at the top of the list), most of the best sitcoms in the first 20 years of television were based on relationships, whether between couples (*I Love Lucy, The Honeymooners*), family members (*Father Knows Best, Leave It To Beaver*) or work-based (*The Andy Griffith Show, The Dick Van Dyke Show*). Exploring the ways in which the main characters complemented or contrasted each other was the foundation for most of the comedy, and it proved to be an eminently sustainable recipe for ratings success.

Starting in the mid-'60s, however, a new wind was blowing across the prime-time landscape. Couples like Gomez and Morticia Addams, Lily and Herman Munster and Tom and Eddie Corbett were redefining the traditional relationship sitcom, and waiting in the wings was the next wave of fantasy comedies that would herald a rebirth of slapstick silliness (see Part 2).

At the same time that relationship sitcoms started yielding to the more fertile fantasy format, all three networks unveiled so-called "girl shows" that struck a chord with the burgeoning feminist movement. These first tentative experiments in building a comedy series around a single, independent female star became the blueprint for a formula that would continue to pay ratings dividends well into the 21st century.

Fast Forward

Before she blossomed into one of the biggest movie stars of the 1980s, Sally Field starred in two other TV sitcoms: *The Flying Nun* (see Chapter 7) and *The Girl With Something Extra* (1973). She also had a recurring role on *Alias Smith and Jones* (see Appendix 2).

Gidget

Series debut: Sept. 15, 1965 (ABC). Final telecast: Sept. 1, 1966 (ABC). 32 episodes.

Based on the series of Gidget movies that kicked off in 1959 with Sandra Dee in the title role, this cheery exercise in beach blanket etiquette was largely forgettable except for the performance of future Academy Award winner Sally Field, who starred as Francine "Gidget" Lawrence, 15-year-old daughter of widowed college professor Russ Lawrence (Don Porter). Field was 18 years old and had never acted professionally when she was picked for the lead, and though the series lasted just one season the bubbly personality and wide-eyed enthusiasm she brought to the role no doubt helped put her on the path to Hollywood superstardom.

Teenager Sally Field made her TV debut as the star of Gidget. *Don Porter portrayed her father.*

The series was shot on location at beaches in the Malibu district of Los Angeles and featured lots of sun-drenched teenage bodies and endless surfing scenes. The plots revolved around Gidget's efforts to assert her independence from her father and overprotective older sister Anne Cooper (Betty Conner), and she often recruited her best friend Larue (Lynette Winter) to help carry out her schemes. Peter Deuel, who later co-starred in *Alias Smith and Jones* (see Appendix 2), portrayed Anne's analytical husband John, a psychology student. The show's theme song, sung by Johnny Tillotson, became a minor hit in 1966.

That Girl

Series debut: Sept. 8, 1966 (ABC). Final telecast: Sept. 10, 1971 (ABC). 136 episodes.

This series, starring Danny Thomas' gorgeous daughter Marlo as aspiring actress Ann Marie, holds special significance for me because I was absolutely head over heels in love with her. The fact that a young woman in my Grade 9 social studies class bore an uncanny resemblance to the dark-eyed beauty only made it worse.

That Girl was the harbinger of all the "independent woman" sitcoms that flooded the prime-time schedule over the next decade. Cleverly written and with a strong supporting cast headed by Ann's journalist boyfriend Donald Hollinger (Ted Bessell), her parents Lou (Lew Parker) and Helen (Rosemary DeCamp) and best friends Jerry and Ruth Bauman (Bernie Kopell and Carolyn Daniels, who was later replaced by Alice Borden), the series chronicled Ann's misadventures in Manhattan after leaving the family nest in staid Brewster, New York. Forever searching for that elusive big break, Ann supported herself with a variety of odd jobs between bit parts in TV commercials and off-off-off-Broadway plays. Donald, a writer for Newsview magazine, provided the emotional support when her dreams of stardom crumbled with depressing regularity, while Harvey Peck and George Lester (Ronnie Schell and George Carlin) were the pie-in-the-sky agents who kept lining up auditions for her.

After *That Girl* was cancelled, Thomas stopped acting for a few years and put her talents to work behind the camera. She produced and starred in the Emmy Award–winning children's special *Free To Be...You and Me* in 1974, and won Emmys for Best Performer in a Children's Program for *The Body Human: Facts For Girls* (1981) and for Best Actress in the TV special *Nobody's Child* (1986). She later married obnoxious talk show host Phil Donahue, and in the late 1990s made several guest appearances as Rachel's mom on *Friends*.

TeleTrivia

That Girl was the second TV series in which Marlo Thomas portrayed a struggling young actress. In 1961–1962 she was cast as Joey's kid sister, Stella Barnes, on *The Joey Bishop Show*.

Julia

Series debut: Sept. 17, 1968 (NBC). Final telecast: May 25, 1971 (NBC). 86 episodes.

Starring Diahann Carroll as single mom Julia Baker, this show was notable for two things: It was the first comedy series to feature a black female lead who wasn't a maid (that dubious honour goes to *Beulah*, which starred Ethel Waters and ran from 1950 to 1953 on ABC), and it was the first sitcom to acknowledge the terrible cost of the Vietnam War. In a touching scene in the debut episode, Julia explained to her young son Corey (Marc Copage) that his father, a helicopter pilot, had been killed in combat in Southeast Asia. Mother and son then moved to Los Angeles, where Julia, a nurse, was hired by gruff-but-good-hearted Dr. Morton Chegley (Lloyd Nolan) in the medical office at Astrospace Industries. The scene in which she applied for the job over the phone was another TV first of sorts, considering America's racial climate at the time:

Julia: "Did they tell you I'm coloured?"

Dr. Chegley: "Hmmm. What colour are you?"

Julia: "Why, I'm a Negro!"

Dr. Chegley: "Oh I see. Have you always been a Negro, or are you just trying to be fashionable?"

The series was completely integrated, which was also something of a novelty in 1968, and over the course of its run *Julia* had just as many white friends as black ones. The head nurse at Astrospace Industries was feisty Hannah Yarby (Lurene Tuttle), who took Julia under her wing and adored little Corey. Corey's best friend and rambunctious partner in mischief was next-door neighbour Earl J. Waggedorn (Michael Link).

Fast Forward

Even though *Julia* was a ratings winner, Diahann Carroll wasn't convinced she would continue to make a living as an actress. She earned a university degree in child psychology for a "backup career" in case performing didn't work out, and in later years put that training to good use as a youth counsellor in Los Angeles. After hosting *The Diahann Carroll Show* (variety) for one season in 1976, she went into semi-retirement, but in 1984 Carroll was lured back to the small screen to play scheming businesswoman Dominique Deveraux on the prime-time soap opera *Dynasty*.

Maude

Series debut: Sept. 12, 1972 (CBS). Final telecast: April 29, 1978 (CBS). 140 episodes.

Maude was the first spinoff from *All In The Family* and the second jewel in Norman Lear's prime-time crown, which eventually included, among other gems, *The Jeffersons; Sanford and Son; One Day At A Time; Good Times; Mary Hartman, Mary Hartman* and *Fernwood 2-Night*. Like all those shows, *Maude* took dead aim at topical social and political issues and didn't flinch in espousing a decidedly pro-feminist point of view.

Maude Findlay (Beatrice Arthur) was Edith Bunker's large, loud cousin, and made two guest appearances on *All In The Family* before getting her own show. In her first visit to the Bunker household (1971), Maude fussed over Edith, Mike and Gloria, who were all suffering from the flu, but flat-out refused to lift a finger to help Archie, whom she regarded as a bigoted lout. To make matters worse, Maude insisted on sitting in Archie's favourite chair while expounding on the merits of Franklin Roosevelt, whom Archie despised. The episode featured some classic verbal sparring, and when Maude returned the next year to invite the Bunkers to her daughter Carol's wedding (unbeknownst to Archie, Carol was marrying a Jew), the jabs continued, with predictably hilarious results.

On her own show, Maude lived in Tuckahoe, New York, with her fourth husband, Walter (Bill Macy), who owned Findlay's Friendly Appliances. Carol (Adrienne Barbeau) was now divorced and lived with them, along with her young son Phillip (Brian Morrison). The Findlays' best friends were acid-tongued conservative Dr. Arthur Harmon (Conrad Bain) and his wife Vivian (Rue McClanahan), while Florida Evans (Esther Rolle) was the Findlays' maid. When Rolle left the series in 1974 to star in *Good Times*, Hermione Baddeley stepped in as gin-swilling English housekeeper Nell Naugatuck.

Like *All In The Family*, Maude took a sledgehammer approach in dealing with controversial issues, and viewers responded by making it one of the most popular shows of the decade. The Lear trademark of using comedy to explore serious topics shone through in episodes that featured Maude getting an abortion (a prime-time first) and Walter dealing with alcoholism, but in between there were enough laughs to keep things lively and upbeat. In 1976

Notable Quotable

"God will get you for that, Walter."

—Maude's pet response to anything disagreeable her husband said or did

Notable Quotable

"It's only common sense, Maudie. If God wanted people to be gay He wouldn't have created Adam and Eve, He would have created Adam and Steve."

—Dr. Arthur Harmon

TeleTrivia

A year after *Maude* was cancelled, Bill Macy, who portrayed Walter Findlay, resurfaced as the star of *Hangin' In*, yet another Norman Lear creation that saw Macy in the unlikely role of Louis Harper, a former pro football hero turned humanitarian who becomes president of a university in Washington, D.C. If casting the paunchy, diminutive Macy as an ex-gridiron great didn't stretch the imagination of viewers, the show's disjointed premise certainly did, and *Hangin' In* was cancelled after just four forgettable episodes.

Maude launched a one-woman crusade to get Henry Fonda elected president via a write-in vote, and the ongoing story line culminated with the venerated movie star appearing as himself to graciously discourage her from continuing the campaign. The next season saw Maude take her own plunge into politics when she was appointed to finish out the term of a New York congressman who died in office, but after the Findlays moved to Washington, Bea Arthur decided she didn't want to continue in the role and the series was cancelled.

Rhoda

Series debut: Sept. 9, 1974 (CBS). Final telecast: Dec. 9, 1978 (CBS). 106 episodes.

I don't know about you, but I always thought Mary's pal Rhoda Morgenstern (Valerie Harper) was the funniest, most vibrant character on *The Mary Tyler Moore Show* (see Chapter 10). Ergo, when Rhoda got her own series, it seemed a pretty safe bet that Harper's comedic brilliance would continue to grow and shine. But a funny thing happened when she moved from Minneapolis to New York. Instead of being the hip, wisecracking character we'd come to know and love, Rhoda became...well...tamer. Much, much tamer. The Big Apple was the perfect place for her to really take a bite out of life, but in just the seventh episode (an hour-long special) she married Joe Gerard (David Groh), owner of the New York Wrecking Company, who had 10-year-old son Danny (Tood Turquand). After their honeymoon the newlyweds moved into the same building as Rhoda's sister Brenda (Julie Kavner), and settled into a formulaic routine that was only occasionally funny.

Freeze Frame

The telecast of Rhoda's wedding on Oct. 28, 1974, attracted 51 million viewers—by far the largest single audience in the four-year run of the series. Mary, Lou, Murray and the rest of the cast from *The Mary Tyler Moore Show* travelled to New York for the nuptials—as did Phyllis Lindstrom (Cloris Leachman), who forgot to pick up Rhoda to drive her to the church in Brooklyn. In what ranks as the funniest prolonged scene in the series, Rhoda, dressed in her wedding gown and flowing veil, ran into the street to try to hail a cab (the show was shot on location). When she couldn't get a taxi to pull over, she did what any determined Gothamite would do: hopped the subway to her mom's house!

Inevitably, as Rhoda's life as a married, working-from-home freelance window dresser became increasingly dull, the focus of the series shifted to Brenda, who worked as a bank teller and was always hunting for Mr. Right. The girls' parents, Ida and Martin (Nancy Walker and Harold Gould) were also regulars, as was the drunken voice of unseen "Carlton, your doorman" (Lorenzo Music), who was constantly slurring messages over the apartment intercom.

Shortly after the start of the 1976–1977 season, the Gerards separated, which left the writers free to introduce some goofy potential suitors for Rhoda—the most memorable being Las Vegas lounge lizard Johnny Venture (Mike Delano). Brenda, meanwhile, was wooed by a succession of losers, including clothing store owner Gary Levy (Ron Silver),

Fast Forward

Years after *Rhoda* was cancelled, Julie Kavner, who portrayed chubby, neurotic Brenda Morgenstern, scored her greatest television success by providing the grating voice of big-haired Marge Simpson on the animated classic *The Simpsons.*

musician Nick Lobo (Richard Masur) and geeky Benny Goodwin (Ray Buktencia). By the third season Joe was completely written out of the series and Rhoda found a new job working for costume designer Jack Doyle (Ken McMillan), a gimmick that temporarily boosted the show's ratings. But alas, after four years of Rhoda's quest for emotional stability, Brenda's whiny dependence on her sister and Ida's caustic cynicism, the series simply ran out of ideas and the solo career of one of TV comedy's all-time great supporting characters was cancelled with nary a whimper.

Laverne & Shirley

Series debut: Jan. 27, 1976 (ABC). Final telecast: May 10, 1983 (ABC). 178 episodes.

Laverne De Fazio (Penny Marshall) and Shirley Feeney (Cindy Williams) were best friends and roommates who worked as bottle-cappers at the Shotz Brewing Company in Milwaukee in the late 1950s. The series was a spinoff from an episode of *Happy Days* (see Chapter 1), in which the girls were dates for Richie and Potsie. The time frame and setting were the same on both shows, so there were occasional crossovers.

Laverne was plain, quick-tempered and fiercely loyal, while Shirley was cute, perky and childishly naive. They bickered a lot (usually about men) but always looked out for each other's best interests. Other main characters included idiotic Shotz truck drivers Lenny Kosnowski (Michael McKean) and Andrew "Squiggy" Squiggman (David L. Lander), who lived upstairs from the girls and constantly tried to romance them; Carmine "The Big Ragoo" Ragusa (Eddie Mekka), a talented dancer who was in love with Shirley; and Laverne's crusty father Frank De Fazio (Phil Foster), who owned the Pizza Bowl restaurant. Most of the comedy was derived from the girls' efforts to forge better lives for themselves, even though they were always broke, worked at dead-end jobs and had little education. The series was created by Garry Marshall (Penny's real-life brother), who also created *Happy Days*.

Laverne & Shirley was crucified by the critics right from the start (one reviewer referred to the series as "indigestible TV junk food"), but the show was a huge hit with viewers and ended up being the No. 1 prime-time program in 1977–1978. The following season Frank De Fazio married sardonic Edna Babish (Betty Garrett), and their relationship provided grist for a humorous secondary story line. In 1980, Frank and Edna moved to California and opened a restaurant called Cowboy Bill's, and soon afterwards Laverne, Shirley and Carmine joined them, with the idea of breaking into the movies. The change in locales didn't do much for the show's slumping ratings, and in 1982 Cindy Williams quit. On the show, Shirley married an army doctor named Walter Meany (thus becoming Shirley Feeney Meany) and they moved overseas, leaving Laverne and the rest of the gang to limp through the last dozen or so episodes.

Freeze Frame

Laverne's favourite beverage (other than Shotz beer, of course) was a "half 'n' half" of milk and Pepsi.

TeleTrivia

The theme song for *Laverne & Shirley*, "Makin' Our Dreams Come True," was written by Norman Gimbel and Charles Fox, and sung by Cyndi Grecco. It made the Billboard Top 50 in the summer of 1976.

The Least You Need to Know

➤ Future Academy Award winner Sally Field had never acted professionally when she was cast in the starring role of *Gidget* in 1966.

➤ After starring in *That Girl*, Marlo Thomas became an Emmy Award–Winning producer.

➤ *Julia* was the first sitcom to star a black female in a nondomestic role.

➤ *Maude* was the first sitcom in which the lead character had an abortion.

➤ Rhoda Morgenstern's wedding to Joe Gerard on Oct. 28, 1974, attracted more than 50 million viewers.

➤ *Laverne & Shirley* was a spinoff from *Happy Days* (see Chapter 1), and there were occasional crossovers between the two series.

Part 2
Enlightened Escapism

Relationship-based sitcoms have remained at the forefront of the medium's most basic entertainment genre simply because they're the farthest removed from the "real world" problems viewers might encounter on cop shows, medical dramas and soap operas. Still, the timeless excellence of I Love Lucy, The Honeymooners, All In The Family *and* The Odd Couple *notwithstanding, relationship comedies have always, in the final analysis, been formula for formula's sake; a simplified problem/solution equation designed to be solved within the confines of one or two episodes in order to reinforce the viewer's faith in the cultural status quo.*

The so-called fantasy sitcoms of the 1960s advanced that tried-and-true format to the next level by further widening the buffer zone between TV comedy and the real world. The end result was that some of the most outrageous and implausible "situations" ever loosed upon the network landscape became unforgettable classics of escapist entertainment.

Like the Twinkies and Kool-Aid that to this day continue to fuel my marathon sessions in front of the tube, these shows still have an extraordinarily high CQ (comfort quotient) despite their near-universal lack of esthetic merit. But hey, isn't that what TV comedy is all about?

Chapter 6

Flights of Fantasy

In This Chapter

➤ Unbridled laughs: *Mr. Ed*

➤ Out of this world: *My Favorite Martian*

➤ Tale of a fateful trip: *Gilligan's Island*

➤ A honkin' good time: *My Mother The Car*

➤ Holy funny bone!: *Batman*

➤ Na-nu, na-nu: *Mork and Mindy*

There's no rule that states nostalgia has to necessarily be intelligent, and nowhere is this more evident than on the television comedies that evoke the fuzziest flashbacks among members of the Boomer generation. Oh sure, *The Adventures of Ozzie and Harriet, The Dick Van Dyke Show* and *The Courtship of Eddie's Father* were all superbly written, but in terms of rekindling nostalgic memories of school nights spent huddled in front of the family Philco with a bag of Fritos and a frosty can of grape Shasta, could they hold a candle to a talking horse, a friendly Martian or seven stranded castaways? Not hardly.

In their time, most of television's campiest classics were dismissed as either childishly numbing or just plain dumb by the critics (most of whom wouldn't have known Mr. Ed from Mr. Freeze anyway), but, as *Beverly Hillbillies* creator Paul Henning was fond of pointing out, television is created for viewers, not critics. And if viewers "get it," what difference does it make if Uncle Martin's cheesy antennae look like they came out of a box of Cracker Jacks, or that there's no rational explanation for Thurston and Lovey Howell packing so many clothes for a three-hour cruise?

Boomer TV is about memories, not metaphysics; what ya sees is what ya gets. Unlike the 1950s, when most prime-time fare was written for an adult audience, the "gimmick" and fantasy programs of the '60s were aimed squarely at kids—which is why today it's easier for most of us to explain *F Troop* or *Get Smart* than the Cuban missile crisis or thalidomide.

And when you think about it, that's not so terrible.

Mr. Ed

Series debut: Oct. 1, 1961 (CBS). Final telecast: Sept. 8, 1965 (CBS). 143 episodes.

Taking a cue from the phenomenal success of the seven *Francis The Talking Mule* movies that lit up the big screen between 1949 and 1956, show biz legend George Burns put up $75,000 in 1958 to finance the pilot for a TV series about a talking horse. After a series of rewrites and recasting, *Mr. Ed* was introduced in the fall of 1961—along with a curiously hummable theme song that became something of an anthem on the nation's playgrounds over the next four years.

Ed was owned by Wilbur Post (Alan Young), a self-employed architect who lived with his wife Carol (Connie Hines) in a rambling country home on the outskirts of Hollywood. The horse was part of the deal when they bought the house, but it wasn't until after they'd moved in that Wilbur discovered Ed could talk—but only to him. For

Notable Quotable

Wilbur: "What's new, Ed?"

Mr. Ed: "What can be new with a horse? Just standin' around, eatin', sleepin' and swattin' flies."

Wilbur: "Don't you sometimes wish you were a human being?"

Mr. Ed: "Never. How can you beat eatin', sleepin' and swattin' flies?"

Wilbur: "Sure beats working, worrying and paying taxes."

Mr. Ed.: "Naturally."

the first couple of seasons, the Posts' neighbours were Roger and Kay Addison (Larry Keating and Edna Skinner), followed by Gordon and Winnie Kirkwood (Leon Ames and Florence MacMichael). The voice of Ed was former big-screen cowboy star Allan "Rocky" Lane.

What made *Mr. Ed* a funny show was that the horse was the more rational of the two lead characters. Wilbur was always worried someone would discover his secret, and he became more jittery and paranoid as the series wore on. Ed, on the other hand, was thoughtful and pragmatic. He wore giant glasses when he read the newspaper, he loved comic books and TV, and whenever Wilbur came out to the barn to watch the late, late show, it was always Ed who ordered pizza. Ed also had an eye for the ladies—and a jealous streak. In a classic 1962 episode entitled Clint Eastwood Meets Mr. Ed, the laconic star of the hit western *Rawhide* (see Appendix 2) moved next door to the Posts and his "tall, dark and handsome" stallion Midnight stole all of Ed's fillies. To get even, Ed tapped into the telephone party line and wreaked havoc with Clint's business and romantic life. It all worked out in the end, however, when Eastwood agreed to take part in a benefit play the Posts were organizing to raise money for a youth centre.

In order to make Ed appear to be "talking," a thin layer of peanut butter was applied to the inside of the horse's mouth. When he licked the peanut butter, his lips moved. Some of Ed's best comments were reserved for when he was alone. He'd turn directly toward the camera and say things like: "You can fool all of the horses part of the time and part of the horses all the time, but you can't fool THIS horse anytime!" or "Wilbur is a simple man; sometimes you just gotta frighten him into things." As for why he would only talk to Wilbur, Ed offered his master a simple explanation: "Because you're the only one I like well enough to talk to."

Notable Quotable

"Wilbur, beat me, take away my food, my water, my TV...but don't ever take away my comic books."

—Mr. Ed

My Favorite Martian

Series debut: Sept. 29, 1963 (CBS). Final telecast: Sept. 4, 1966 (CBS). 107 episodes.

Tim O'Hara (Bill Bixby), an earnest cub reporter for the *Los Angeles Sun*, was on his way to yet another mundane assignment when he was the lone witness to the crash of a small, one-man space craft. Though dazed, the silver-suited pilot of the ship survived and Tim took him back to his rooming house with the intention of writing a story that would earn him star billing on the newspaper's reporting staff. Once the human-looking visitor (Ray Walston) recuperated, however, Tim discovered he was a friendly, lonely Martian who spoke impeccable English and possessed amazing powers, including the

Notable Quotable

"The only way you could ever have a high IQ is to go up in a blimp."

—Martin O'Hara to Det. Brennan

ability to make himself disappear. He could move faraway objects with the flick of a finger and hear conversations taking place in another room. The Martian also had a vast knowledge of technology, and by activating the six-inch antennae that sprung from the back of his head, his brain worked faster than the world's most advanced computer. Realizing he couldn't reveal the visitor's true identity, Tim adopted him, introducing him as "Uncle Martin" to friends and acquaintances, including his landlady, Lorelei Brown (Pamela Britton), and his boss, editor Harry Burns (J. Pat O'Malley).

Most of the plots revolved around Tim's efforts to protect the true identity of Uncle Martin, while the Martian worked tirelessly to repair his damaged ship in order to return home. During the first season, Mrs. Brown's teenage daughter Angela (Ann Marshall) also lived in the rooming house, and later on the landlady became romantically involved with police detective Bill Brennan (Alan Hewitt), who was always suspicious of Uncle Martin.

Gilligan's Island

Series debut: Sept. 26, 1964 (CBS). Final telecast: Sept. 4, 1967 (CBS). 98 episodes.

"Inept, moronic and humourless."

"Vapid and trite."

"Preposterous...professional actors should know better."

Those were some of the *kinder* reviews after this series about seven castaways marooned in the South Pacific premiered in 1964. What none of the critics grasped was that creator Sherwood Schwartz intentionally—and very cleverly—clichéd the characters in order to present a social microcosm. Their story was told in Schwartz's brilliant opening theme song:

> Just sit right back and you'll hear a tale,
> A tale of a fateful trip,
> That started from this tropic port,
> Aboard this tiny ship.
> The mate was a mighty sailing man,
> The Skipper, brave and sure;
> Five passengers set sail that day,
> For a three-hour tour (a three-hour tour).
> The weather started getting rough,

The tiny ship was tossed;
If not for the courage of the fearless crew,
The Minnow would be lost (the Minnow would be lost!)
The ship set ground on a shore of this uncharted desert isle,
With Gilligan, the Skipper too
The Millionaire and his wife;
The movie star, the Professor and Mary Ann—
Here on Gilligan's Isle.

...and the equally snappy closing tune:

So this is our tale of the castaways,
They're here for a long, long time;
They'll have to make the best of things,
It's an uphill climb.
The first mate and the Skipper too
Will do their very best
To make the others comfortable
In this tropic island nest.
No phone, no lights, no motor cars—
Not a single luxury;
Like Robinson Crusoe,
It's primitive as can be.
So join us here each week my friends,
You're sure to get a smile,
From seven stranded castaways,
Here on Gilligan's Isle!

The castaways were led by the Skipper, Jonas Grumby (Alan Hale Jr.), a large, likeable seafaring man whose greatest misfortune was to have the bumbling, accident-prone Gilligan (Bob Denver) as his first mate. Together they made up the entire crew of the S.S. Minnow, a charter cruiser aboard which tourists took a three-hour tour around the Hawaiian islands. Along with five passengers—millionaire Thurston Howell III (Jim Backus) and his wife "Lovey" (Natalie Schafer); voluptuous movie star Ginger Grant (Tina Louise); high school science teacher Roy Hinkley (Russell Johnson), known as "the Professor", and naive Kansas farm girl Mary Ann Summers (Dawn Wells)—they became stranded on an uncharted island when the Minnow was shipwrecked during a storm.

Despite the heroic efforts of the Skipper and the Professor, week after week, through three years and 98 episodes, the stranded group's efforts to be rescued were always

The Skipper (Alan Hale) and his "little buddy" Gilligan (Bob Denver) were the entire crew of the ill-fated S.S. Minnow.

unintentionally sabotaged by the hapless Gilligan. The show featured a lot of slapstick and plenty of pratfalls, and quickly won a huge following, particularly among younger viewers. Some armchair psychologists have even advanced the theory that *Gilligan's Island* was a Biblically inspired morality play of sorts, with the seven characters representing the seven deadly sins of Pride (the Professor), Envy (Mary Ann), Lust (Ginger), Avarice (Mr. Howell), Sloth (Mrs. Howell), Gluttony and Anger (both personified in the Skipper), leaving poor little Gilligan as a kind of lunkhead Lucifer—but that's a whole 'nother book!

According to the Professor's calculations, the "uncharted desert isle" was located 250 nautical miles southeast of Hawaii. Its lush vegetation provided the castaways with coconuts, mangos, bananas and papaya, and was home to monkeys, gorillas, tigers and other wild beasts. Fresh water came from an underground cavern, while the lagoon provided a steady supply of tuna, mackerel and swordfish. Hostile headhunters lived on a neighbouring island, and over the run of the series numerous visitors "dropped in," only to depart without helping the castaways do likewise. Among the more memorable guests was a Japanese soldier still fighting the Second World War (Vitto Scotti), socialite Erika Tiffany Smith (Zsa Zsa Gabor), Russian cosmonauts Igor and Ivan (Vincent Beck and Danny Klega) and a jungle boy (14-year-old Kurt Russell).

The castaways' only contact with the outside world was through a battery-operated transistor radio, for which the Professor invented a primitive recharger by utilizing salt

TeleTrivia

There was a lot of speculation during the original run of *Gilligan's Island* as to the first names of Gilligan and "Lovey" Howell. While Gilligan's first name was never mentioned in the series, years later Bob Denver revealed that in the pilot script his character's full name was Willy Gilligan. Creator Sherwood Schwartz subsequently disclosed that he came up with the name "Gilligan" by thumbing through the white pages of the Los Angeles telephone directory. As for Mrs. Howell, in episode 67, entitled Mr. and Mrs.?, the radio broadcaster mentions "Lovey's" full maiden name: Miss Eunice Wentworth.

Freeze Frame

The famous opening scene of *Gilligan's Island*, which shows the S.S. Minnow leaving Honolulu Harbour for its fateful voyage, was actually the last scene shot for the original pilot episode and was scheduled to be filmed Nov. 22, 1963—the day president John F. Kennedy was assassinated in Dallas. Like all U.S. naval and military installations, the harbour was closed for a two-day mourning period, and the filming was delayed until Nov. 25.

water and copper tubing from the Minnow's motor. In fact, the Professor was so resourceful when it came to fashioning things out of bits of scrap metal and the native flora and fauna that you half expected him to build a nuclear reactor out of coconuts and papaya leaves. In the original pilot episode the role of the Professor was played by John Gabriel, while Kit Smythe was Ginger and Nancy McCarthy was "Bunny"—the character that became Mary Ann Summers. Before the second pilot was filmed the network insisted all three be replaced, and Schwartz subsequently recruited Johnson, Louise and Wells.

Freeze Frame

Some "name" actors unsuccessfully auditioned for roles in *Gilligan's Island*, including Carroll O'Connor, who tested for the part of the Skipper, and Raquel Welch, who didn't make it when she tried out for the role of Mary Ann. Even Bob Denver was Schwartz's second choice to play Gilligan; he first offered the role to Jerry Van Dyke, who turned it down in order to star in *My Mother The Car* (see next listing).

While *Gilligan's Island* was a marginal hit during its three-year life in original production, in reruns it has become a genuine phenomenon, ranking right up there with *The Honeymooners* and *Star Trek* as one of the longest-running programs in the history of television. In 2000, the series was airing seven days per week in more than 50 major U.S. and Canadian markets, as well as in dozens of foreign countries. *Entertainment Weekly* succinctly summed up the show's appeal by commenting: "Sophocles' *Antigone*. Da Vinci's *Mona Lisa*. Mozart's *Jupiter Symphony*. Sherwood Schwartz's *Gilligan's Island*. All great works of art have one thing in common: they endure."

More than a decade after the series was cancelled, the castaways finally made it back to civilization in *Rescue From Gilligan's Island*, a two-part TV movie that attracted huge ratings when it aired on Oct. 14 and Oct. 21, 1978. All the original cast returned with the exception of Tina Louise (Ginger), who was replaced by Judy Baldwin. As fate would have it, at the end of the movie another storm developed during a reunion cruise aboard the Minnow II, and the group found themselves marooned on the exact same island! On March 3, 1979, a second made-for-TV movie entitled *The Castaways On Gilligan's Island* again scored huge ratings. This time, Gilligan found two semi-demolished Second World War airplanes in the jungle, and the Professor figured out a way to use parts from both to make one of them serviceable. The gang took off to fly to Hawaii, but in order to keep the overloaded plane airborne they had to throw out their luggage. Naturally, Gilligan got in the way and fell out with the bags, but (surprise!) he was wearing a parachute and made it safely back to the island. Meanwhile, U.S. Air Force radar located the plane and dispatched a rescue party. The Howells were so grateful that they decided to remain on the island and build a resort hotel, which became the catalyst for the third (and final) reunion movie, 1981's *The Harlem Globetrotters On Gilligan's Island*.

My Mother The Car

Series debut: Sept. 14, 1965 (NBC). Final telecast: Sept. 6, 1966 (NBC). 29 episodes.

Not to be confused with *My Son Jeep*, an equally short-lived 1953 sitcom starring Jeffrey Lynn and Betty Lou Keim, this hopelessly contrived series revolved around the misadventures of a small-town lawyer named Dave Crabtree whose dead mother was reincarnated as a 1928 Porter automobile. Jerry Van Dyke had the starring role, along with Ann Sothern, who provided the voice of the talking car. Crabtree's wife Barbara (Maggie Pierce), their kids Cindy (Cindy Eilbacher) and Randy (Randy Whipple) and antique car dealer Capt. Mancini (Avery Schreiber) rounded out the principal cast.

My Mother The Car was similar to *Mr. Ed* in many ways, but not nearly as funny. In the pilot episode Dave discovered the vehicle on a used car lot while searching for an inexpensive beater. When he climbed behind the wheel for a test drive, a voice came from the dashboard, informing him that the spirit of his dear departed mom had come back in the form of the car. Of course, the car would talk only to Dave, and he was the only person who could hear it. When others were around, Mother would simply honk her horn to indicate delight or displeasure. As the series chugged along and it became apparent to everyone the car was indeed something special, the nefarious Capt. Mancini concocted all kinds of crazy schemes to try to get it away from Dave.

While *My Mother The Car* is at or near the top of most critics' lists of the worst sitcoms of all time, the series was not without its moments. Van Dyke brought a certain resigned exasperation to his role, which was genuinely funny (as he did years later as Luther Van Damme on *Coach*), but the supporting cast was uniformly dull and one-dimensional. Sothern, who'd had a long and distinguished movie career before breaking into television on the sitcom *Private Secretary* in the mid-1950s, did her best to make Mother believable (she sounded a lot like a stereotypical Jewish mother), but somehow a talking car is just never as entertaining as a conversational horse, and the series was permanently parked after just one season.

Freeze Frame

The year and make of the "star" in *My Mother The Car*—a 1928 Porter—is revealed in the show's theme song. In real life there was never an automobile by that name.

Batman

Series debut: Jan. 12, 1966 (ABC). Final telecast: March 14, 1968 (ABC). 120 episodes.

It was clever. It was goofy. It was delightfully deranged.

TeleTrivia

Batman was one of the first series in the 1960s to be shot entirely in colour, and in syndication it has joined *I Love Lucy, The Honeymooners, Gilligan's Island* and *Star Trek* as one of Boomer TV's ultrarare "evergreens"—an industry tag for perennial sales and ratings success.

In many ways, Batman was the defining series of the second half of the 1960s, when the so-called Love Generation captured the hearts and minds of television programmers and pop-culture marketing gurus all over North America. It appealed to the audience on two different levels. To young viewers, it was a colourful, swashbuckling live-action comic book. To adults, it was pure camp, liberally punctuated with witty dialogue and high-profile "guest villains." At a time when the generation gap was growing wider by the minute, it was one of those rare programs that children and parents could watch and enjoy together.

The character of Batman was created by Bob Kane in Detective Comics No. 27, way back in 1939. Four years later, the cowled crimefighter made his first appearance on celluloid in a serial starring Lewis Wilson as Batman and Douglas Croft as his young ward, Robin the Boy Wonder; apart from their costumes the tandem bore little resemblance to Kane's creations and soon disappeared. A second Batman serial in the early 1950s featured Robert

Adam West was sensational as Batman (below), but the real stars of the series were villains like The Joker (Cesar Romero) and The Riddler (Frank Gorshin).

Lowery and John Duncan in the lead roles, but once again the characters were wooden and static—not at all like Kane's dashing heroes.

In 1965, ABC approached writer/producer William Dozier about the possibility of resurrecting Batman in a weekly TV series. A year earlier, Dozier, the former vice-president of Columbia Pictures' television division, had formed his own company, Greenway Productions. He was intrigued with the concept but knew nothing about the characters. After immersing himself in a study of Batman comic books, Dozier decided the only way to make the idea work on the small screen would be to make it full-blown camp. As he later recalled: "I just came up with the simple idea of overdoing it ... of making it so square and so serious that adults would find it amusing. I knew kids would go for the derring-do stuff, the adventure, but the trick would be to find adults who would either watch it with their kids or say to hell with the kids and watch it on their own." The result was TV's first over-the-top live action cartoon—complete with words like "Pow!" "Zap!" and "Biff!" exploding across the screen during the carefully-choreographed fight scenes. Everything about the show was new and exciting, from its twice-a-week airings to the clever use of crooked camera angles in the credits to identify the crooks.

In a stroke of casting genius, Dozier awarded the lead role to Adam West who had originally been introduced to the Batman character by reading Kane's comic books as a boy in Walla Walla, Washington. West was an established big-screen actor familiar to television viewers for his guest spots on top-rated shows like *Bewitched, Maverick, The*

TeleTrivia

Adam West was picked to play Batman without having to do the traditional screen test. In 1964 he co-starred with William Shatner in the pilot film for an unsold series entitled Alexander The Great (set in 333 BC!), and the following year he lit up the screen as the droll Captain Quik, pitching chocolate drink mix in a high-profile television commercial. He was on his way to Europe to star in a spaghetti western when his agent persuaded him to read the Batman pilot script in Dozier's office. Having seen the Captain Quik spot and knowing West's uncanny talent for quickly grasping the essence of a role, the producer offered him the job on the spot! As for Aunt Harriet, Dozier is on record as saying the role was created "to keep Bruce Wayne and Dick Grayson from looking like homosexuals. We put a woman in the house to balance the act."

Outer Limits and *Gunsmoke*, and he'd also portrayed Sgt. Steve Nelson, Robert Taylor's subordinate on *The Detectives* during the 1961–62 season. As Batman's sidekick, Robin the Boy Wonder, Dozier selected a 19-year-old real estate agent named Bert "Sparky" Gervis, a former ice-skating star who changed his name to Burt Ward after being picked for the part.

In their alter-egos as millionaire philanthropist Bruce Wayne and his young ward Dick Grayson, Batman and Robin lived in "stately Wayne Manor" on the outskirts of Gotham City. The household also included butler Alfred Pennyworth (Alan Napier), who was the only one who knew their secret identities, and Bruce's aunt, Harriet Cooper (Madge Blake.) Ensconced beneath the palatial mansion was the Bat Cave, a cavernous hideaway that housed multiple laboratories, banks of giant computers, an exotic array of crimefighting equipment, and vehicles such as the atomic-powered Batmobile and the Batcopter. Bruce and Dick accessed the Bat Cave from the main house by sliding down a pair of Bat-poles hidden behind a false bookcase. When trouble broke out, Police Commissioner Gordon (Neil Hamilton) activated the Bat Signal, a beam of high-intensity light flashed into the night sky to summon the caped crusaders to police headquarters.

Other recurring characters included Gotham City Police Chief O'Hara (Stafford Repp), Batgirl/Barbara Gordon (Yvonne Craig, third season only), Gotham Prison warden Crichton (David Lewis) and Mayor Linseed (Byron Keith). Dozier himself served as the off-camera narrator for the series, opening and closing each episode with a suitably melodramatic flourish.

Freeze Frame

➤ The Batmobile, equipped with everything from surface-to-air missiles to an on-board computer, was in fact a 1955 Ford Futura, modified by renowned car designer George Barris. The Futura was a test model that was manufactured but never marketed.

➤ Lee Meriwether (*Time Tunnel, Barnaby Jones*) portrayed Catwoman in the hugely successful 1966 movie version of *Batman*, which also starred West, Ward, Gorshin, Meredith and Romero.

➤ The 1966 national edition of *TV Guide* with Adam West on the cover remains one of the most valuable and sought-after issues among collectors. West also appeared in costume on the cover of *Life* magazine that year.

Besides the kitschy gadgets and colourful fight scenes, the attraction of Batman was the all-star cast of "guest villains," ranging from regulars like Riddler (Frank Gorshin, later John Astin), Penguin (Burgess Meredith), Joker (Cesar Romero) and Catwoman (Julie Newmar, Eartha Kitt) to The Siren (Joan Collins), Egghead (Vincent Price) and Fingers Chandell (Liberace). Frank Sinatra was originally pencilled in to play Riddler, but a movie commitment prevented him from taking on the role. Since the series initially aired two nights per week (Wednesday and Thrusday), the episodes were written as two-part cliffhangers, giving each week's villain plenty of time to set elaborate traps for Batman and Robin—like when they were dipped in wax to make human candles (Riddler), or chained to a giant perforating machine to create human-sized postage stamps (Col. Gumm). Another draw for adult viewers was the hokey dialogue, overloaded with bad puns and Robin's trademark expression of "Holy (fill in the blank) Batman!" Indeed, some of the Boy Wonder's observations were truly inspired, such as when he exclaimed "Holy uncanny photographic mental processes!" and "Holy priceless collection of Etruscan snoods!".

In 1966 producer William Dozier expected to score another hit when he unveiled *The Green Hornet* in a weekly series on ABC (see Chapter 16), but this time he played it straight rather than going for camp, and the result was a decidedly dull and humourless show. Not surprisingly, many Boomers recall that the Hornet's finest moment came in a guest appearance on *Batman* (March 1–2, 1967), highlighted by a classic scene in which Bruce Wayne meets the Hornet's alter-ego, newspaper publisher Britt Reid, at a Gotham society ball. Of course, neither knows of the other's secret identity, so when Bruce strikes up the following conversation, it's in his trademark deadpan whisper.

Bruce: "May I join you?"

Britt: "Of course."

Bruce: "I'm very disturbed by certain rumours. It seems people think I'm The Green Hornet."

Britt: "That's funny. People think I'm Batman."

Bruce (squinting): "You're not really Batman ... are you?"

Britt: "Are you kidding? Me get dressed up in that crazy cowl?"

The attraction of this series was that it never took itself too seriously. Gloriously goofy and always absurd, yes, but never boring. In the fall of 1967, Batgirl (Yvonne Craig) became a permanent cast member, but shortly thereafter production was cut back to one show per week. Batman was still notching respectable ratings when the last episode aired on March 14, 1968, and in syndication it has attained the cult-like status reserved for the very cream of the Boomer TV crop.

"I loved playing Batman ... giving him a grandiose verve," West says today. "Making the series and the (1966) feature film was a wonderfully satisfying experience. We had such talented people on the show—both in front of the camera and behind the scenes. Frank

Fast Forward

Twenty years after Batman was cancelled, Adam West shot another pilot for a sitcom called Lookwell, in which he starred as an aging former TV crime fighter who puts his "experience" to use solving real crimes. It was one of the funniest half-hour presentations of the unenlightened '80s, but inexplicably never got picked up by the networks.

Gorshin's Riddler was my favourite villain, and I think his appearance in the very first episode was crucial in helping establish the characters of Batman and Robin and the direction of the series. Frank was absolutely magical ... his body movements, facial expressions, the laugh. And all with no make-up! He was terrific ... they all were. I adored Julie Newmar, and I thought it was great fun that Cesar Romero refused to shave off his moustache to play Joker. Burgess Meredith, Roddy McDowall, Vincent Price, Victor Buono, Liberace ... the list goes on and on. They were all tremendously talented performers, and they certainly helped make my job easier."

In order of appearance, here's a complete list of the major guest villains who appeared in the 120 episodes of Batman (several made multiple appearances): Riddler (Frank Gorshin and John Astin); Penguin (Burgess Meredith); Joker (Cesar Romero); Catwoman (Julie Newmar and Eartha Kitt); Mr. Freeze (George Sanders, Otto Preminger, Eli Wallach); Zelda (Anne Baxter); Mad Hatter (David Wayne); False Face (Malachi Throne); King Tut (Victor Buono); Bookworm (Roddy McDowall); The Archer (Art Carney); The Minstrel (Van Johnson); Ma Parker (Shelley Winters); Clock King (Walter Slezak); Egghead (Vincent Price); Chandell (Liberace); Marsha, Queen of Diamonds (Carolyn Jones); Shame (Cliff Robertson); Puzzler (Maurice Evans); Sandman (Michael Rennie); Col. Gumm (Roger C. Carmel); Black Widow (Tallulah Bankhead); The Siren (Joan Collins); Lord Marmaduke Ffogg (Rudy Vallee); Lola Lasagne (Ethel Merman); Louie the Lilac (Milton Berle); Nora Clavicle (Barbara Rush); Dr. Cassandra Spellcraft (Ida Lupino); Minerva (Zsa Zsa Gabor).

Mork and Mindy

Series debut: Sept. 14, 1978 (ABC). Final telecast: June 10, 1982. 95 episodes.

If comedian John Byner hadn't been such a busy guy the world might never have heard of Mork from Ork. Byner was picked by producer Garry Marshall to play the guest role of a wacky extra-terrestrial who meets Richie and Fonzie on an episode of *Happy Days* in February 1978, but when the standup comic's schedule prevented him from accepting the part, Marshall offered it to a young comedian named Robin Williams. Although he was virtually unknown and had very little acting experience, Williams infused Mork with such inspired nuttiness that Marshall quickly decided to create a spinoff series around the character.

At first glance, *Mork and Mindy* was just a hipper, slicker update of *My Favorite Martian*, but after the first few shows it was obvious Williams brought an unusual talent to the starring role. In the debut episode Mork's egg-shaped ship landed on the outskirts of Boulder, Colorado, where he met Mindy McConnell (Pam Dawber), a music-store clerk who had gotten lost on her way back to the city. Mindy befriended the polite, inquisitive stranger and invited him to her apartment for a glass of iced tea—which Mork proceeded to "drink" through his fingers. When she asked him to sit down, he did—on his head. When Mindy demanded to know what was going on, Mork told her truthfully: He was an alien from the planet Ork—30 million light years

Notable Quotable

"I was a test-tube baby. My father ran away with a bottle of nose drops."

—Mork, explaining to Mindy how he'd grown up on Ork as an orphan

from Earth—sent to our planet by the Orkan ruler, Orson, to study Earth customs. Much to the chagrin of Mindy's straight-laced father Frederick (Conrad Janis), Mork moved into the attic above Mindy's apartment and the ensuing combination of broad slapstick and burgeoning romance between the two lead characters quickly translated into mammoth ratings.

After that first season, during which *Mork and Mindy* was TV's No. 1–rated prime-time series, the producers inexplicably tampered with the winning format by trying to inject "relevancy" into the story lines. It was a huge mistake. The new "meaningful" plots

As the alien Mork from Ork, Robin Williams honed the comedic stylings that later made him one of Hollywood's biggest movie stars.

resulted in wholesale changes to the supporting cast and robbed the show of its best asset—Williams' manic, off-the-wall comedic stylings. The ratings plummeted, only to recover the next season when yet another overhaul returned the show to its original course...with a few notable tweaks. One was the addition of Mork's friend Exidor (Robert Donner), the crazed leader of an invisible cult called The Friends of Venus. Another was the subsequent marriage of Mork and Mindy and their prolonged honeymoon on Ork, which was populated by a wild assortment of bizarre creatures. At the beginning of the fourth and final season, Mork gave birth by ejecting a small egg from his navel. The egg grew and grew until it finally cracked open to reveal a 250-pound baby (Jonathan Winters) that looked like a full-grown middle-aged man. The proud parents named the baby Mirth, and since biological maturation was reversed in Orkans, he would presumably grow younger with each passing year.

Despite the magical comedic chemistry between Williams and Winters over the last dozen or so episodes, Mork uttered his final "na-nu, na-nu" (goodbye in Orkan) in the summer of 1982. He went on to become one of the busiest motion picture stars of the 1980s and '90s, while Dawber, after a short-lived TV comeback in *My Sister Sam* (1986), has made only occasional appearances on the small screen in the years since.

The Least You Need to Know

➤ George Burns "ponied up" $75,000 in seed money to finance the original *Mr. Ed* pilot.

➤ After the first pilot for *Gilligan's Island* was shown to network executives, new actors were cast in the roles of the Professor, Ginger and Mary Ann.

➤ Jerry Van Dyke took on the starring role in *My Mother The Car* after rejecting the part of Gilligan.

➤ Renowned concert pianist and showman Liberace portrayed villain Fingers Chandell on *Batman*.

➤ Robin Williams' role as the extra-terrestrial on *Mork and Mindy* was originally offered to comedian John Byner.

Sugar and Spice

Fantasy shows like *Mr. Ed, My Favorite Martian* and *Gilligan's Island* were clearly aimed at younger viewers, but it wasn't until *Batman* came along that the enormous dollar potential for cross-merchandising so-called "kiddie-coms" was fully realized. Certainly there had been TV-inspired toys, cereal premiums and lunch boxes since the medium's infancy, but those pre-*Batman* merchandizing efforts were on a relatively penny-ante scale compared to what started in the late 1960s and continues to this day.

"Bat-mania," as it was called, swept across North America like a tidal wave within weeks of the series debut. Overnight, Adam West and Burt Ward became two of the most photographed men on the planet, and marketing gurus were quick to cash in. Everything from Bat-toothpaste and Bat-telephones to bubble gum cards and bed sheets was adorned with the faces and/or logo of Gotham City's fabled dynamic duo, and like the show itself, the trinkets and collectibles were targeted at both kids and adults. While 10 year olds pestered their parents to purchase the Batman Magic Slate or the Batman & Robin Repeating Tin Rifle, mom and dad might also pick up a set of shot glasses inscribed "Property of Gotham City Jail" for their bar or a roll of Batman vs. Catwoman Authentic Bat-Wallpaper for the rec room.

A couple of years before the *Batman*-inspired maturation of kiddie-coms into major merchandizing franchises, all three networks unveiled fantasy shows aimed primarily at adult male viewers. None of them triggered the marketing bonanza ignited by the Caped Crusader (nor were they expected to) but each succeeded in rocketing its female star to the forefront of media attention—ignited by a not-so-subtle spark of sexuality.

Bewitched

Series debut: Sept. 17, 1964 (ABC). Final telecast: July 1, 1972 (ABC). 252 episodes.

One of the most beloved and imaginative series of the decade was this story about a modern suburban witch named Samantha Stephens (Elizabeth Montgomery) and her dull-as-dishwater mortal husband Darrin (Dick York, later Dick Sargent), an advertising executive at the agency of McMann & Tate in New York City. Larry Tate (David White) was Darrin's boss, and Larry's wife Louise (Irene Vernon, later Kasey Rogers) was Samantha's best friend. Other regulars included members of Samantha's extended family, all of whom were either witches or warlocks: mother Endora (Agnes Moorehead), father Maurice (Maurice Evans), Uncle Arthur (Paul Lynde), Aunt Clara (Marion Lorne) and trouble-making cousin Serena (played by Montgomery in a black wig). Samantha's physician, the grandiloquent warlock Dr. Bombay (Bernard Fox) appeared semi-regularly, as did the Stephens' next-door neighbours, Abner and Gladys Kravitz (George Tobias and Alice Pearce, later Sandra Gould). In 1966 Samantha gave birth to a daughter, Tabitha (portrayed as a two year old by twins Erin and Diane Murphy), and three years later the Stephens had a son, Adam (David and Greg Lawrence). Naturally, both kids inherited their mom's magical powers.

Freeze Frame

Dick York, the first Darrin Stephens, was one of TV's busiest actors through the late 1950s and early '60s, with multiple appearances on such hits as *The Twilight Zone*, *Wagon Trail* and *Alfred Hitchcock Presents*, as well as a co-starring role opposite Gene Kelly and Leo G. Carroll in *Going My Way*, a 1962–1963 comedy based on the 1944 film. A serious illness forced York to permanently retire from acting in 1969, and he was replaced on *Bewitched* by Dick Sargent.

While *Bewitched* was essentially a one-joke show, it was extremely well written and cleverly acted. Darrin and Samantha were married in the series premiere, and upon learning his wife could disappear into thin air, move objects, time-travel to the past or perform a thousand other tricks simply by twitching her nose or invoking a rhyming spell, Darrin made her pledge not to use her powers "except when absolutely necessary." And because he couldn't tell another living soul about Sam's "talent," he was forever having to deal with unexpected visitors (Julius Caesar, Napoleon) or outrageous circumstances (being turned into a goose, transported to 17th-century Salem) which were the result of one of Sam's mis-cast spells or interference from another member of her family—usually Endora, who insisted on calling her son-in-law "Derwood."

Samantha's incantations aside, the best magic on *Bewitched* was the blending of pure fantasy with well-grounded reality. In a lot of ways the Stephens' struggle to fit their extraordinary marriage into the narrow confines of everyday normalcy made them one of the most realistic couples on the tube. Darrin's never-ending battles with Endora and Uncle Arthur, the fuzzy absent-mindedness of Aunt Clara and the pressures of keeping Sam's powers a secret notwithstanding, they were down-to-earth homebodies who loved, argued and made up just like a real couple. Sam's bag of tricks never outshone the crazy collection of characters, and her understated sexiness never threatened to explode the myth of the magic. On all levels, *Bewitched* was truly a masterpiece of fantasy television.

Notable Quotable

"You're having a party? On Halloween? I never thought I'd see a daughter of mine condoning bigotry."

—Endora

My Living Doll

Series debut: Sept. 27, 1964 (CBS). Final telecast: Sept. 8, 1965 (CBS). 26 episodes.

Just 10 days after the debut of *Bewitched* on ABC, CBS launched this entertaining series about a curvaceous female robot (Julie Newmar), programmed for "absolute obedience" by her creator, Air Force scientist Dr. Carl Miller. Designated as "Top-Secret Project AF709," the robot possessed myriad extraordinary talents, including super-human strength, a computer brain and the ability to see and hear from great distances.

In the series' opening episode Dr. Miller was assigned to a special project in Pakistan, so he entrusted the robot to his colleague, psychologist Dr. Robert McDonald (Bob Cummings), who named her "Rhoda" and passed her off as Dr. Miller's niece. She moved into his home and spent the rest of the series learning how to be a "perfect woman," who never uttered a word until spoken to and did only what she was instructed to do. Dr. McDonald routinely had to fend off his neighbour Peter Robinson

(Jack Mullaney), who fell madly in love with Rhoda the first time he met her but never discovered her secret.

The appeal of *My Living Doll* was obviously the statuesque Newmar, who stood nearly six feet tall. Though she didn't have much to work with in the way of dialogue, Newmar's timing and delivery were a perfect complement for Cummings' harried style, and, as she was later to showcase as the original Catwoman on *Batman*, her seductive body language infused an otherwise one-dimensional character with a smoldering femininity rarely seen on any sitcom before or since.

I Dream of Jeannie

Series debut: Sept. 18, 1965 (NBC). Final telecast: Sept. 1, 1970 (NBC). 139 episodes.

What could be better than a gorgeous blonde who lives in a bottle, obeys your every command and calls you Master? Best-selling novelist Sidney Sheldon (*Master of the Game, The Other Side of Midnight, Windmills of the Gods*) tapped into the subconscious fantasies of millions of male viewers when he created this stylish hybrid of *My Living Doll* and *1001 Arabian Nights*.

In the debut episode, U.S. Air Force astronaut Capt. Anthony Nelson (Larry Hagman) failed to reach orbit in the Stardust 1 and crash-landed the space capsule off the coast of a deserted island in the South Pacific. After paddling ashore in a rubber raft, he found a mysterious bottle on the beach. When he uncorked it, a beautiful 2,000-year-old genie (Barbara Eden) emerged in a puff of smoke, babbling incoherently in ancient Arabic

A beautiful blonde who parades around in a harem outfit, blinks up gourmet meals and calls you Master? What was not to love about Barbara Eden on I Dream of Jeannie?

until Nelson muttered the words, "I wish you could speak English." The genie—who happened to be named Jeannie—expressed her undying gratitude for being set free and declared that henceforth the astronaut would be her Master and she would fulfill his every whim. By crossing her arms and blinking her eyes she conjured up a rescue helicopter, then returned to her bottle and stole away in Nelson's gear for the trip back to his home base in Cocoa Beach, Florida.

During the first season Nelson was engaged to Melissa Stone (Karen Sharpe), the shapely daughter of his commanding officer, Gen. Wingard Stone (Philip Ober). Trying to do his job while making wedding plans and keeping Jeannie a secret from Melissa, the general and snoopy Air Force psychiatrist Dr. Alfred Bellows (Hayden Roarke) made Tony a nervous wreck, to the point where the engagement was finally cancelled and Gen. Stone and his daughter were written out of the series. Eventually Tony revealed Jeannie to his best friend, fellow astronaut Capt. Roger Healey (Bill Daily), and most of the comedy over the next four seasons revolved around Tony and Roger's efforts to keep Jeannie a secret while trying to extricate themselves from the jams her magic inevitably created for them. Borrowing a plot staple from *Bewitched*, Barbara Eden periodically appeared in the dual role of her raven-haired evil twin sister—who was also named Jeannie—to wreak even more havoc.

In an unusual twist for a sitcom, there was a four-part *I Dream of Jeannie* mini-movie in the third season (episodes 77–80) built around a story line of Jeannie being accidentally locked in an explosives-lined safe filled with survival gear that's slated to be deposited on the moon. Tony and Roger enlist a pair of professional safecrackers to spring her (she couldn't blink her way out, just as she couldn't blink her way out of her bottle), but the crooks end up stealing the safe and selling it to a scrap yard to be crushed. After a

TeleTrivia

➤ Darren McGavin (*Kolchak: The Night Stalker*) and Robert Conrad (*The Wild, Wild West*) were both considered for the role of Tony Nelson before it was offered to Larry Hagman.

➤ Tony Nelson and Roger Healey were both promoted to the rank of major in episode 22, entitled How Lucky Can You Get?

➤ Jeannie was born in 64 B.C. She was imprisoned in her bottle for refusing to marry the Blue Djinn.

TeleTrivia

Jeannie's original sequined harem outfit was banned by NBC censors because her bellybutton was visible. The sexy costume was redesigned to cover up her navel, but eagle-eyed viewers caught a quick peak of it in episode 131, entitled Mrs. Djinn Djinn.

hilarious cat-and-mouse chase highlighted by the evil twin Jeannie shrinking Tony and Roger to the size of canaries and trapping them in a birdcage, the pair succeed in finally retrieving the safe (disguised as an ice cream cart) and getting it back to Tony's house. This four-parter also included several flashbacks to previous episodes, and set the stage for Tony's marriage proposal, which Jeannie enthusiastically accepted in episode 117.

Of all the fantasy sitcoms in TV history, *I Dream of Jeannie* gets my vote as the funniest and most charming, even if a lot of viewers figured Jeannie's powers were no match for Samantha Stephens on *Bewitched*. In 1994, the Nick at Nite cable station conducted a month-long poll that revealed 58 percent of the 1.4 million respondents felt Samantha's powers were greater. *TV Guide* responded to the survey with the following observation in its "Jeers" section, addressed to "the 810,939 Nick at Nite viewers who think Samantha has more power than Jeannie: In a viewers' poll to decide which sitcom sprite packs the most mystic muscle—*Bewitched* or *I Dream of Jeannie*—the Nick-at-nuts picked simpy Sam by about 200,000 votes. Are you crazy? Sam didn't even have enough wattage to keep the same Darrin for the run of her show! She also received frequent paranormal assists from Endora and the rest of her TV coven. Meanwhile, bottled beauty Jeannie not only kept Maj. Nelson in a trance for five seasons, she wed him, kept her evil sister in check and did it all with nothing but crossed arms. We think Tabitha was stuffing the ballot box."

TeleTrivia

I Dream of Jeannie creator Sidney Sheldon cut his TV teeth on *The Patty Duke Show*, which he created and wrote 78 episodes for. The world's most translated author (over 300 million copies of his books are in print) also created the '80s adventure drama *Hart To Hart*, starring Robert Wagner and Stefanie Powers.

'Nuff said!

The Flying Nun

Series debut: Sept. 7, 1967 (ABC). Final telecast: Sept. 18, 1970 (ABC). 83 episodes.

Sister Bertrille (Sally Field), the former Elsie Ethington, was a cute 90-pound novice nun at the ancient Convent San Tanco outside San Juan, Puerto Rico. One day while out for a walk she discovered the irrefutability of the physical law of aerodynamics that states "when lift plus thrust is greater than load plus drag, an object will fly." In Sister Bertrille's case, the lift was provided by the starched cornet worn by her order while the thrust came from any gust of wind into which she could position herself in order to become the "object" swept skyward. Of course, it wasn't an infallible equation. Occasionally she made uncontrolled landings in the ocean or some other unpleasant environment, and in one classic episode she was chased through the sky by a love-sick pelican looking for a pal.

The high-spirited Sister Bertrille's unusual mode of travel, combined with her rough-around-the-edges skills as a nun (she made a lot of rookie mistakes) were frowned upon by her strict Reverend Mother (Madeleine Sherwood) but were a source of great amusement for Sister Jacqueline (Marge Redmond) and Sister Sixto (Shelley Morrison), a Puerto Rican who routinely butchered the English language. The external focus of many of the plots was handsome playboy Carlos Ramirez (Alejandro Rey), the wealthy owner of a San Juan nightclub who had a soft spot for the convent because he'd been an orphan raised by nuns. Sister Bertrille often went to Carlos for help and guidance in dealing with the outside world, and he was always willing to lend a hand.

The Ghost and Mrs. Muir

Series debut: Sept. 21, 1968 (NBC). Final telecast: Sept. 18, 1970 (ABC). 50 episodes.

Based on the 1947 movie of the same name that starred Gene Tierney and Rex Harrison, this whimsical series is remembered for two things: Charles Nelson Reilly's manic characterization of Claymore Gregg, and the multi-talented Hope Lange's portrayal of classy Carolyn Muir, which earned her back-to-back Emmy Awards for best actress in a comedy in 1969 and 1970.

Carolyn was a widow looking for a quiet place to raise her young children Candice (Kellie Flanagan) and Jonathan (Harlen Carraher), along with their dog Scruffy and a housekeeper/nanny named Martha Grant (Reta Shaw). They finally found a cozy, opulently furnished house on a secluded stretch of New England coastline overlooking the hamlet of Schooner Bay. The only thing wrong with Gull Cottage, as it was called, was that it was haunted by the ghost of its original owner, a 19th-century sea captain named Daniel Gregg (Edward Mulhare). His nephew Claymore (Charles Nelson Reilly) was the landlord, but every time Claymore tried to rent the house to someone, Capt.

Notable Quotable

"It's time you got married and realized that happiness isn't the only thing in life."

—Carolyn Muir

Gregg scared him or her off. He tried doing the same to the Muirs—invisibly moving objects and making spooky sounds were two of his favourite tricks—but Carolyn and her kids were undeterred. Eventually the captain consented to make himself visible to them and they struck up a truce. By the second season he was almost a member of the family and was falling in love with the feisty Mrs. Muir.

During its first season on NBC the series got lost in the shuffle of Saturday night programming and was cancelled after 30-odd episodes. ABC picked it up and moved it to Tuesday night, where it consistently won its time-slot and gained enough exposure for Lange to win those two Emmys.

The Least You Need to Know

➤ Dick York, the first Darrin Stephens on *Bewitched*, had been one of TV's busiest actors through the 1960s before a serious illness forced him to retire in 1969.

➤ *My Living Doll* was the first TV series to star a robotic female—a device later used on *The Bionic Woman* and *Small Wonder*.

➤ *I Dream of Jeannie* was created by internationally renowned novelist Sidney Sheldon.

➤ *The Ghost and Mrs. Muir* was inspired by the 1947 hit movie of the same name.

Armed Farces

The most memorable military comedies of the 1960s were in stark contrast to the gritty war dramas airing on all three networks, which often utilized actual combat footage to heighten their realism (see Chapter 12). With memories of the Second World War still fresh in the minds of millions of viewers, TV took a calculated risk in wringing comedy out of something so horrible, but it ultimately proved to be a popular premise—particularly among veterans.

The 1955 Broadway smash *No Time For Sergeants*, starring Andy Griffith as a hillbilly simpleton drafted into the Air Force, helped inspire television's wave of military sitcoms, especially after the hit play was turned into an equally successful motion picture (also starring Griffith) in 1958. The movie later became the basis for both a short-lived sitcom of the same name and the hugely successful series *Gomer Pyle, USMC*.

In between Andy and Gomer, however, were two of the small screen's most inventive military farces, both of which helped pave the way for what to this day is still vilified in some quarters as the single most repugnant concept in the history of television comedy: milking laughs from a Nazi prisoner-of-war camp.

The Phil Silvers Show

Series debut: Sept. 20, 1955 (CBS). Final episode: Sept. 11, 1959 (CBS). 136 episodes.

Notable Quotable

Sgt. Sampson: "Gentlemen, you're looking at the only American soldier who took a Japanese prisoner and tried to hold him for ransom."

Bilko: "That's a lie. I was just trying to show the general staff how we could run the war at a profit."

Set in mythical Fort Baxter, Kansas, this brilliant series was originally titled You'll Never Get Rich, which remained a subtitle in the credits after it was renamed *The Phil Silvers Show* two months into its run. The star was Master Sgt. Ernie Bilko (Silvers), head of the Fort Baxter motor pool and the most notorious con man in the U.S. Army. He spent most of his time gambling, setting up elaborate sting operations or recruiting members of his platoon into outrageous money-making schemes—none of which ever seemed to pan out. Loud, bossy and resourceful, Bilko could also be disarmingly charming and had a knack for talking his way out of any situation. Base commander Col. John Hall (Paul Ford) was Bilko's regular foil, while the misfits in his platoon—Cpl. Rocco Barbella (Harvey Lembeck), Pvt. Duane Doberman (Maurice Gosfield), Sgt. Rupert Ritzik (Joe E. Ross) and Cpl. Henshaw (Allan Melvin)—were his usual partners in crime. For the first three seasons Bilko had a mild romance with Sgt. Joan

Fast Forward

In 1961 ABC used *The Phil Silvers Show* as the basis for the prime-time animated hit "Top Cat." The star—known as T.C. to his friends—was a sly con artist and leader of a gang of scruffy New York alley cats. Maurice Gosfield, who portrayed Pte. Doberman on *The Phil Silvers Show*, provided the voice of Benny the Ball on the cartoon.

The inimitable Phil Silvers was a scream as scheming Sgt. Ernie Bilko. The series was originally titled You'll Never Get Rich.

Hogan (Elisabeth Fraser), who worked in the base office, but she was gradually phased out.

As good as the supporting cast was, it was Silvers' towering comedic talent that vaulted this show into the upper echelon of Boomer classics. He could be roguishly dominant and self-effacing in the same scene, transformed from a bombastic blowhard to a heart-of-gold teddy bear in the blink of an eye. His shameless sycophancy and endless flattery of Col. Hall's wife ("Hello, miss...the Colonel didn't tell me his daughter was visiting. Why, it's *you* Mrs. Hall...") became Bilko trademarks, as did his patented wooing technique (known as the Bilko Blitz), "an unbeatable combination of moonlight, music and a man in a uniform." The many sides of Bilko were best showcased in the 1957 episode Rock 'n' Roll Rookie, a clever parody of the real-life drafting of Elvis Presley into the U.S. Army. Bilko's recruit, Elvin Pelvin, even warbles a song called "Bilko Is The Best" (to the tune of Presley's "Love Me Tender"), but in the end the sarge just can't bring himself to exploit the naive country boy for his own gain.

McHale's Navy

Series debut: Oct. 11, 1962 (ABC). Final telecast: Aug. 30, 1966 (ABC). 138 episodes.

"In the Pacific in 1943, the tide of battle had turned. The American forces, led by the largest navy in history, were preparing for an embattled enemy. Millions of men and thousands of ships readied for this great offensive, and on the island of Taratupa in the heart of the South Pacific, the PT73 under the command of Lt.-Cmdr. Quinton McHale had more than their share of hazardous missions...."

That was the stirring intro to the debut episode of *McHale's Navy*—just before the scene shifted from real-life footage of men and ships to a shot of McHale (Ernest Borgnine) water-skiing behind the PT73 in a placid, palm-lined lagoon. Like *The Phil Silvers Show*, this series revolved around a scheming lower-echelon commander and his merry band of cowardly misfits. Like Silvers, Borgnine was surrounded by an outstanding cast of wonderfully gifted comedic actors, which made for some truly memorable episodes. Leading the way was McHale's arch-enemy, Capt. Wallace "Leadbottom" Binghampton (Joe Flynn), who was stationed on a neighbouring island with his suck-up subordinate, Lt. Elroy Carpenter (Bob Hastings). On McHale's side were his good buddy Ensign Charles Parker (Tim Conway) and a motley crew of conniving goof-offs led by Lester Gruber (Carl Ballantine), Harrison "Tinker" Bell (Billy Sands), Happy Holmes (Gavin McLeod) and Takeo "Fuji" Fugiwara, an eager-to-please Japanese prisoner of war whom McHale and his men kept hidden from Binghampton because he also served as their cook.

Borgnine might have had the star billing, but Flynn ("Why me? Always me!") and Conway carried most of the comedy. The second-season episode The Day The War Stood Still brilliantly showcases the talents of both men. Binghampton discovers Fuji and has him thrown in the brig as a spy. In order to get their cook released, McHale uses Parker's impersonations of Franklin Roosevelt, Winston Churchill and General Tojo on the radio to broadcast that the war is over. The outbreak of peace relieves a lot of pressure and stress—especially for the high-strung Binghampton, who proceeds to tell a visiting admiral exactly what he thinks of the navy. After the plot is blown, just when everyone is facing a court martial, a top-secret Japanese patrol boat surrenders to McHale because its crew heard the fake broadcast. Naturally, all is forgiven.

In an unusual move, after three seasons of garnering respectable ratings with the show's South Pacific setting, the producers moved the action to Italy. McHale and his crew were assigned to a camp on the outskirts of the village of Voltafiore, and for the remainder of the series the comedy focused less on interaction between the regulars and more on situations involving the bizarre collection of characters living in the village.

Freeze Frame

At 138 episodes, *McHale's Navy* was the fourth-longest military sitcom in TV history, after *M*A*S*H, Hogan's Heroes* and *Gomer Pyle, USMC.* The series was also turned into two feature-length films—*McHale's Navy* (1964) and *McHale's Navy Joins the Air Force* (1965)—in which all the regulars reprised their TV roles.

Gomer Pyle, USMC

**Series debut: Sept. 25, 1964 (CBS). Final telecast: Sept. 9, 1970 (CBS).
150 episodes.**

By putting a military spin on *The Beverly Hillbillies* premise, *Gomer Pyle, USMC* quietly became one of CBS' biggest hits of the 1960s. The series starred horse-faced Jim Nabors as an inept and incredibly naive country bumpkin who enlists in the U.S. Marine Corps (or "corpse," as he says in the pilot episode), and some of the filming was done at real boot camps.

Pyle's home base was Camp Henderson, California, and his immediate superior was Sgt. Vince Carter (Frank Sutton), a barrel-chested old-school leatherneck with a penchant for screaming "I can't hear yooooo!" in response to anything his raw recruits had to say. Carter was crusty, abrasive and impatient, and initially thought Pyle's complete disregard for Marine propriety was a lame attempt to earn a discharge. Despite his tough exterior, Carter gradually warmed to Pyle's child-like innocence, and eventually became his friend and mentor. Other regular cast members included Pvt. Duke Slater (Ronnie Schell), Cpl. Chuck Boyle (Roy Stuart), and Carter's girlfriend, Bunny Olsen (Barbara Stuart), who adored Gomer's puppy-like devotion to his

Notable Quotable

"Shazzam!"

"Gollllly!"

—Gomer Pyle's favourite expressions

The antics of Gomer Pyle (Jim Nabors) and Sgt. Vince Carter (Frank Sutton) made a mockery of the U.S. Marine Corps.

99

sergeant. Semi-regulars were Pvt. Lester Hummel (William Christopher), Pvt. Frankie Lombardi (Ted Bessell) and Sgt. Hacker (Allan Melvin).

Gomer Pyle, USMC was inspired by the Broadway play (later a big-screen movie) *No Time For Sergeants*, starring Andy Griffith. Coincidentally, Gomer was first introduced on *The Andy Griffith Show* as the dimwitted proprietor of Wally's Filling Station in Mayberry (see Chapter 4), and the pilot episode for *Gomer Pyle* was in fact an episode of Griffith's series in which Gomer decided to join the service after reading the Marine hymn on the back of a calendar.

The best comedy on the show came from the interaction between Gomer and Sgt. Carter. Nobody, but nobody could portray a vein-popping, I'm-so-furious-I'm-shaking character better than Frank Sutton, and the smiley, child-like charm Nabors brought to his role was a perfect counterpoint. So good was the chemistry between the two actors that Nabors later made Sutton a regular on the *The Jim Nabors Variety Hour* (1969–1971). Sadly, Sutton passed away in 1974 at the age of 51.

F Troop

Series debut: Sept. 14, 1965 (ABC). Final telecast: Aug. 31, 1967 (ABC). 65 episodes.

Fort Courage, a remote cavalry outpost "somewhere west of the Mississippi" was the setting for this post–Civil War ensemble comedy, which starred Ken Berry as wimpy Capt. Wilton Parmenter and Forrest Tucker as his rough-around-the-edges adjutant, Sgt. Morgan O'Rourke. Parmenter had been promoted from private during the last days of action when, during a chaotic retreat, he inadvertently led a charge in the wrong direction—toward the hostile Hekawi Indians. Earlier, however, O'Rourke had negotiated a secret deal with the tribe for exclusive rights to sell their hand-made

Fast Forward

Larry Storch's talent for dialects made him one of Hollywood's most sought-after actors for voicing cartoons. In addition to providing the voice for Mr. Whoopee on *Tennessee Tuxedo & His Tales*, Storch also "starred" in the animated *Sabrina & The Teenage Goolies* and *Sabrina The Teenage Witch*. Years after *F Troop* had ridden into the sunset, he was reunited with Forrest Tucker in the live-action *Ghost Busters* (1975–1978) and in the made-for-TV movie *The Adventures of Huckleberry Finn* (1981).

trinkets to tourists, so the Hekawi passively "surrendered" after Parmenter's charge. As a reward for his gallantry, Parmenter was moved up in rank and given command of Ft. Courage, where he tried to maintain a semblance of military discipline over O'Rourke, Cpl. Randolph Agarn (Larry Storch), troopers Duffy (Bob Steele) and Vanderbilt (Joe Brooks) and whiny bugler Hannibal Dobbs (James Hampton). Wrangler Jane (Melody Patterson) was a wild cowgirl from a neighbouring ranch who was out to lasso Parmenter, while Chief Wild Eagle (Frank deKova) was the head of the Hekawi.

Silly, yes, but *F Troop* was also well written and fast paced. Storch was hilarious as Cpl. Agarn, bringing his trademark manic schtick to the role, which also periodically gave him a chance to showcase his considerable talent for mimicry and dialects. Tucker was almost as good as the crusty, conniving O'Rourke, and when the need arose to move the comedy out of Ft. Courage, there were plenty of memorable guest stars waiting in the wings. They included a wayward singing Mountie named Sgt. Ramsden (the irascible Paul Lynde), intrepid Indian detective Wise Owl (Milton Berle), hard-luck trooper Wrongo Starr (Henry Gibson) and 147-year-old Chief Flaming Arrow (Phil Harris).

Hogan's Heroes

Series debut: Sept. 17, 1965 (CBS). Final telecast: July 4, 1971 (CBS). 168 episodes.

One of the most amazing tidbits of Boomer TV trivia is that the six-year run of this notorious send-up of life in a Nazi POW camp lasted two full years longer than America's actual involvement in the Second World War. The fact that a show universally panned as the most offensive comedy concept in television history not only lasted that long but *thrived* before going on to become even more successful in syndication is still rather puzzling—until you watch it.

The original title for the series was Hogan's Raiders, and an early CBS publicity release described it as "the adventures of a glib and impudent ringleader of a zany band of Allied captives in a German prisoner-of-war camp." That was enough for most critics, who described the premise in less jocular terms after screening the pilot episode. One reviewer opined that "with all those swastika flags, Gestapo giggles and jokey references to the Nazi high command, CBS might as well go all the way and call the show Fuehrer Knows Best." Another accused the network of "crass exploitation of the

Freeze Frame

Hogan's Heroes was the ninth most popular program of the 1965–1966 season and for the remainder of its run consistently finished in the top 25. Within two years of its cancellation, reruns of the series were airing in every city in the United States with a population over 250,000, and by 1973 it was being aired in 47 different countries. Germany wasn't one of them.

most criminal regime in history," adding, "the motivation behind putting 'Hogan's Heroes' on the air could be summed up in just two words: Heil Nielsens!" But creator/producer Ed Feldman, who got the idea for the show after watching the William Holden movie *Stalag 17*, remained undaunted. He was convinced that outrageous stereotyping and clever dialogue could make even something as distasteful as a Nazi prison camp funny, provided the right actors could be recruited.

For the lead, Col. Robert Hogan, Feldman picked Bob Crane, a hugely popular L.A. radio host familiar to TV audiences as Dr. Dave Kelsey, the handsome next-door neighbour on *The Donna Reed Show*. Co-starring as the monocled, bumbling Col. Wilhelm Klink, commandant of Stalag 13, was Werner Klemperer, a distinguished stage actor. The "heroes" were Frenchman Louis LeBeau (Robert Clary), British airman Peter Newkirk (Richard Dawson) and American sergeants James Kinchloe (Ivan Dixon) and Andrew Carter (Larry Hovis), while porcine Sgt. Hans Schultz (John Banner) and sexy stenographers Helga (Cynthia Lynn) and Hilda (Sigrid Valdis) made up Klink's staff.

Under Hogan's direction the prisoners secretly had complete control of the camp, with everything from an elaborate system of tunnels (including one that came out under a guard dog's kennel) to sophisticated electronic bugs in Klink's office and a short-wave radio over which they received instructions from London (Hogan's radio code name was Goldilocks; his commander in London was Papa Bear). The prisoners also routinely sneaked out of the camp to meet with members of the underground in the nearby town of Hammelburg, but of course Klink and Schultz never caught on. Schultz's signature expression was "I know nussing, Col. Hogan...I zee nusssing...NUSSING!" while Klink, the self-proclaimed "Iron Colonel of the Third Reich," was content to delude himself into believing his genius alone was responsible for Stalag 13's reputation for being escape-proof.

Col. Wilhelm Klink (Werner Klemperer) fought a losing battle against Col. Robert Hogan (Bob Crane) in trying to maintain order at Stalag 13.

I have to confess, even as an adult I've never understood what fuelled all the fuss about *Hogan's Heroes*. Certainly the concept was bound to be offensive to some people—but that can be said about almost any television series in any era. The fact that three of the show's stars—Klemperer, Banner and Clary—had experienced real-life persecution at the hands of the Nazis only reinforces the theory that perhaps making a joke out of something tragic truly is the best form of catharsis. Klemperer's father, Otto, was a world-renowned symphony conductor who whisked his family out of Germany during Hitler's crackdown on the performing arts in 1935. Banner, born and raised in Vienna, fled Austria just months before the outbreak of the war, while Clary, born in Paris in 1926, spent 31 months in Nazi concentration camps. In 1982 he appeared as himself in the TV movie *Remembrance of Love*, about a real-life gathering of Holocaust survivors in Israel. None of the three men had any qualms about *Hogan's Heroes*; in fact, Klemperer, who won two Emmys for his work on the series, called it one of the highlights of his career. "The fame of the (Klink) character will remain always, and there's nothing wrong with that," he said in 1986. "I really think I did a good job. Klink was a well-conceived character, and I'm very proud of that show. It's timeless."

Freeze Frame

John Banner, the actor who portrayed rotund Sgt. Hans Schultz on *Hogan's Heroes*, had been a popular romantic lead on the stage in pre-war Germany and Austria. He moved to the United States in 1939 and appeared in several films, usually as an angry foreigner. He died on his 63rd birthday, Jan. 28, 1973. Werner Klemperer, the bumbling Col. Klink, passed away in 2000 at age 80.

Controversy continued to swirl around *Hogan's Heroes* for years after the show was cancelled, as such disparate groups as the Holocaust Memorial Society, the German-American Friendship League and the American Nazi Party continued to protest its continued presence on the air in reruns. A bizarre footnote: Bob Crane was bludgeoned to death in Scottsdale, Arizona, on June 29, 1978. The heinous crime was officially listed by the police as "unsolved" for more than 20 years before charges were finally brought against one of the actor's former associates, but the man was never convicted.

M*A*S*H

Series debut: Sept. 17, 1972 (CBS). Final telecast: Sept. 19, 1983 (CBS). 251 episodes.

The longest-running military sitcom started off as a $300-per-week "bonus" for a small-town doctor named Richard Hornberger, who also happened to be a part-time novelist. Under the pen name "Richard Hooker" he wrote the novel that became the 1970 hit movie *M*A*S*H*, starring Donald Sutherland and Elliott Gould as irreverent doctors in a mobile army surgical hospital (MASH) during the Korean War. When Twentieth Century Fox and CBS approached Hornberger about turning his book into a TV series, he accepted their offer of $300 per episode, believing it wouldn't last more than a month or two on the small screen. Eleven years and several renegotiations later, Hornberger still couldn't believe his good fortune.

The series revolved around day-to-day life in the 4077th MASH unit. Since the hospital was very close to the front lines there was never a shortage of patients, but rather than counterbalancing the humour with depressing depictions of battlefield surgery, producer Gene Reynolds initially concentrated on focusing on the characters and their relationships. And what an array of whackos they were! Capts. "Hawkeye" Benjamin Franklin Pierce (Alan Alda) and "Trapper" John McIntyre (Wayne Rogers) were topnotch surgeons who, when they weren't saving lives, could usually be found passed out next to their home-made still or peeking into the nurses' shower tent. Maj. Margaret "Hot Lips" Houlihan (Loretta Swit) and Maj. Frank Burns (Larry Linville) were lovers who despised Pierce and McIntyre, while Col. Henry Blake (MacLean Stevenson) was the unit's spineless commanding officer. Other regulars included the company clerk, Cpl. Walter "Radar" O'Reilly (Gary Burghoff); Cpl. Max Klinger (Jamie Farr), who dressed in women's clothing in hopes of snagging a Section 8 psychological discharge; and the 4077th's chaplain, Father Francis Mulcahy (William Christopher).

Freeze Frame

Gary Burghoff ("Radar" O'Reilly) was the only member of the *M*A*S*H* television cast who appeared in the big-screen version. He left the series in 1979 and was replaced as company clerk by Cpl. Max Klinger (Jamie Farr).

After *M*A*S*H* finished its first season mired in 46th place in the ratings, Reynolds retooled the series to give it more of an edge. When it returned in the fall of 1973 there was still broad humour and marvellous satire, but the show's story lines gradually became less jokey and started tackling taboo topics like homosexuality, interracial marriage, war crimes and adultery. The ratings climbed to the point where *M*A*S*H* soon occupied a permanent perch in the top 10. By the time the fourth season rolled around, not even major cast changes could slow the juggernaut. Rogers left the series and his character was replaced by Capt. B.J. Honeycutt (Mike Farrell). Next to go was Stevenson (Col. Blake was killed in a helicopter crash), which resulted in Col. Sherman Potter (Harry Morgan) taking over as commanding officer. Linville left after the fifth season and his character was replaced by Maj. Charles Emerson Winchester (David Ogden Stiers), but through it all the show's uncompromising devotion to absurdist "dramedy" remained intact.

Even in its waning years, when *M*A*S*H* overflowed with a kind of creeping nobility and came dangerously close to becoming a caricature of itself, the series remained very watchable. The terrific chemistry between Alda and Farrell gave even the preachiest offerings a cheeky sort of bite—including the last original episode in the series, which was telecast as a two-and-a-half-hour special on Feb. 28, 1982. Entitled Goodbye,

Farewell and Amen, it chronicled the end of the war and what finally going home meant to the men and women of the 4077th. The powerful and complex finale—highlighted by Hawkeye's mental breakdown when he tries to suppress memories of an atrocity—became the single highest-rated program in network television history, seen by an incredible 125 million viewers.

Right to the end, the formula that made *M*A*S*H* a ratings blockbuster for more than a decade—humour, pathos and a rollercoaster of emotions—was still working.

TeleTrivia

When Harry Morgan joined the cast of *M*A*S*H* as Col. Sherman Potter, it marked the eighth television series for the diminutive character actor from Detroit. His first forays into TV were on a couple of sitcoms, *December Bride* (1954–1959) and *Pete and Gladys* (1960–1962). He then co-starred on *The Richard Boone Show* (1963–1964) and *Kentucky Jones* (1964–1965) before launching a three-year run as Officer Bill Gannon opposite Jack Webb on *Dragnet* (1967–1970). That was followed by *The D.A.* (1971–1972) and *Hec Ramsey* (1972–1974) before a guest spot on *M*A*S*H* landed him the job of commander of the 4077th when MacLean Stevenson left the series. While he was playing Col. Potter, Morgan also appeared in two limited series—*Backstairs at the White House* (1979) and *Roots: The Next Generation* (1980)—and he later co-starred in *AfterMASH* (1983–1984) and *Blacke's Magic* (1986).

TeleTrivia

In the first half-dozen episodes of *M*A*S*H*, "Hawkeye" Pierce and "Trapper" John McIntyre shared their tent with a laconic black surgeon named "Spearchucker" Jones (Timothy Brown). He was intended to become a major character but was dropped after research revealed there were no black surgeons with the American forces during the Korean War.

The Least You Need to Know

➤ *The Phil Silvers Show* was the first sitcom to build an episode around a parody of Elvis Presley.

➤ In its final season *McHale's Navy* shifted locales from the sun-drenched South Pacific to a camp in Italy.

➤ The pilot episode of *Gomer Pyle, USMC* was an episode of *The Andy Griffith Show*.

➤ Larry Storch, who portrayed Cpl. Randolph Agarn on *F Troop*, provided the voice of worldly Mr. Whoopee on the cartoon hit *Tennessee Tuxedo & His Tales*.

➤ Three members of the *Hogan's Heroes* cast—Werner Klemperer, John Banner and Robert Clary—were real-life victims of Nazi persecution.

➤ The final episode of *M*A*S*H* was the most-watched single presentation in television history, attracting an incredible 125 million viewers.

Chapter 9

On the Job

In This Chapter

➤ Pathetic patrolmen: *Car 54, Where Are You?*

➤ Would you believe?: *Get Smart*

➤ Mind games: *The Bob Newhart Show*

➤ Looking good!: *Chico and The Man*

➤ Utter inn-sanity: *Fawlty Towers*

After home life and relationships, the most fertile ground for harvesting Boomer TV comedy was employment. That's only natural, since most of us have had jobs that could best be described as situation comedies. In my life there have been many—from that ill-fated effort to become the best darned shoe salesman in Victoria, B.C. (see *Family Affair* in Chapter 1) to a mercifully short stint as a professional chicken wrangler (you'd be surprised how ornery hens can get when they're awakened at 2 a.m. for that final ride to the poultry plant).

Of course, on television even the most mundane jobs always seem more interesting. Shirley Booth turned household drudgery into a hoot on *Hazel* (1961–1966), and Frank Aletter milked laughs from being an investment counsellor on *Bringing Up Buddy* (1960–1961), but the funniest work-oriented shows were those that opened our eyes to totally alien environments or shed light on some aspect of "regular" jobs that perhaps we hadn't considered.

In each of the following Boomer classics a unique job situation framed the comedy, but as with every other branch of the basic sitcom root, that frame was built on a rock-solid foundation of good writing and strong characters. From the adventures of a pair a bumbling Bronx cops to the escapades of a frenetic English innkeeper, these shows remain timeless and refreshing antidotes to the workday blues.

Car 54, Where Are You?

Series debut: Sept. 17, 1961 (NBC). Final telecast: Sept. 8, 1963 (NBC). 60 episodes.

It opened with a theme song that still echoes heroically in the subconscious of every true Boomer:

> There's a holdup in the Bronx,
>
> Brooklyn's broken out in fights,
>
> There's a traffic jam in Harlem
>
> That's backed up to Jackson Heights;
>
> There's a scout troop short a child,
>
> Khrushchev's due at Idlewilde—
>
> Car 54, WHERE A-A-A-RE YOU?

The reference to Soviet premier Nikita Khrushchev arriving at Idlewilde International Airport forever froze this show in a cocoon of Cold War trappings, but that hasn't stopped it from being one of the most fondly remembered comedies of the Boomer era. Indeed, for many of us, the adventures of Officers Gunther Toody (Joe E. Ross) and Francis Muldoon (Fred Gwynne) provided the first evidence that hey, maybe cops really were just as human as everyone else.

Notable Quotable

"If you really want to study police methods, do what I do: watch a lot of television."

—Officer Gunther Toody

Toody and Muldoon were assigned to New York's 53rd Precinct, deep in the heart of the Bronx. Toody was squat, cherubic and loveably stupid, and had a habit of exclaiming "Ooooo!...Ooooo!" every time an original thought popped into his head. Muldoon was tall, quiet and urbane—the voice of reason in the creeping chaos of the concrete jungle. Despite the wide intellectual rift between them, the partners got along famously—until there was someone else to talk to. On one memorable occasion the police force experimented with having three men in the patrol car, and the guy who joined Muldoon and Toody turned out to be a Harvard-educated snob. Feeling left out of the high-brow conversation, Toody stayed up all night memorizing the encyclopedia, beginning with the letter A. The next day, when his partners got in the car, his first comment was: "Ooooo! Oooooo! Did somebody mention aardvarks?"

When Toody and Muldoon weren't on patrol, most of the slapstick and pratfalls on *Car 54, Where Are You?* took place in the precinct squad room, where the supporting cast led by Officer Leo Schnauser (Al Lewis), Officer O'Hara (Nipsey Russell) and Capt. Block (Paul Reed) was usually ensconced. Bea Pons appeared as Toody's wife Lucille, while Charlotte Rae (later the matriarch on the '70s sitcom *The Facts of Life*) portrayed Schnauser's wife Sylvia.

TeleTrivia

Since *Car 54, Where Are You?* was shot on location in New York City and the patrol cars used in the show were the same make and model as the real ones, they were painted bright red and white to distinguish them from the dark green and white ones of the NYPD. On black-and-white TV, however, viewers couldn't tell them apart.

Get Smart

Series debut: Sept. 18, 1965 (NBC). Final telecast: Sept. 11, 1970 (CBS). 138 episodes.

Would you believe 57 million angry viewers fired off letters of protest when CBS cancelled *Get Smart* in 1970? Fifty-seven million!

Would you believe fifty thousand?

How about 19 diehard fans in Vegreville, Alberta?

Yes, it's been more than three decades since Maxwell Smart (Don Adams), Agent 99 (Barbara Feldon), The Chief (Edward Platt), Agent Larabee (Robert Karvelas), Hymie the Robot (Dick Gautier) and the rest of the intrepid CONTROL spy agency defended truth and justice from the nefarious forces of KAOS led by criminal mastermind Konrad Siegfried (Bernie Kopell), but the show is as fresh and funny today as when Max (code name: Agent 86) first answered his ringing shoe phone in the fall of 1965. After just a few weeks Smart's catch phrases were permanently etched in the North American lexicon, and over its five-year run the series blossomed into one of the cleverest and most parodied sitcoms of all time. Even 35 years later, any Boomer worth his or her P.F. Flyers can still mimic Max's best lines: "Sorry about that, Chief." "Missed it by *that* much!" And, of course, "Would you believe...," which always preceded some preposterous bluff when Smart and his cohorts were trapped in a seemingly hopeless situation:

Max (to enemy agent): "You'll never get away with this!"

Agent: "Why is that, Mr. Smart?"

Max: "Because at this very minute 25 of our finest commandos are surrounding this building. Would you believe it? Twenty-five commandos!"

Agent: "I find that hard to believe."

Max: "Would you believe two squad cars and a motorcycle cop?"

Agent: "I don't think so."

Max: "How about a vicious street cleaner and a three-legged police dog?"

Another Smart trademark was his blustery self-confidence.

Chief: "Now you realize, Max, that once KAOS learns of your mission they'll stop at nothing to get the information. You'll be in imminent danger and constant jeopardy, facing torture or death at every turn...."

Max: "And...*loving* it!"

But there was much more than silly slapstick and clever dialogue to sustain this madcap creation of Mel Brooks and Buck Henry. *Get Smart* was a brilliant spoof of all things "official" and featured an endless parade of gizmos and gadgets to pander to the James Bond generation. The cleverest props were always introduced by the old labelling-them-an-old-trick trick, as in "the old tiny tape recorder inside the French pastry trick," or "the old bullet-proof cummerbund in the tuxedo trick." My favourite was "the old lighter in the gun in the bunny trick." Then there was the infamous Cone of Silence at CONTROL headquarters that Max insisted on activating every time he had something confidential to tell The Chief. And the steering wheel telephone in his car. Smart also carried a pen with a built-in sleeping-gas discharger and a magnetic cigarette case that could catch bullets. Occasionally he made use of Inflato-Girl, a cheesy blow-up doll that helped him "blend in with the crowd" during stakeouts.

THAT FAT GENTLEMAN LOOKS FAMILIAR.

CONTROL'S TOP AGENTS

Maxwell Smart (Don Adams) and Agent 99 (Barbara Feldon) teamed up to defend the world from KAOS on Get Smart.

Freeze Frame

As dopey hotel detective Byron Glick on *The Bill Dana Show* (1963–1965), Don Adams perfected many of the phrases and mannerisms that became part of the character of Maxwell Smart—including "would you believe?" (conceived by Dana), and the trademark false bravado. At the same time as he was appearing on *The Bill Dana Show*, Adams provided the voice of wisecracking penguin Tennessee Tuxedo on the cult animated series *Tennessee Tuxedo & His Tales*.

Like James Bond and the boys on *The Man From U.N.C.L.E.* (see Chapter 16), Max also had a penchant for passwords and countersigns. He'd open a mailbox, for instance, and whisper: "Ricardo Montalban hates tortillas." A moment later, Agent 13 (David Ketchum) or Agent 44 (Victor French) would respond with "Herb Alpert takes trumpet lessons from Guy Lombardo." Agents 13 and 44 were officially designated as "deep plants" and might show up inside a laundromat dryer or hanging upside down in an elevator shaft, but Max and 99 could always count on them to pass along crucial information.

During the fourth season of *Get Smart*, Max and 99 were married, and after the series moved from NBC to CBS for season five, much of the comedy shifted away from the spy stuff to focus on their domestic relationship. In a two-part episode (Nov. 7 and Nov. 14, 1969), 99 gave birth to twins (a boy and a girl), but the final 18 "post-baby" episodes generally aren't as funny as the rest and aren't even included in most syndicated packages.

When Max's shoe phone rang for the last time on May 15, 1970, it brought down the curtain on one of the most cleverly crafted programs of the decade—and an unforgettable role that earned Don Adams three Emmy Awards for best lead character in a comedy series.

The Bob Newhart Show

Series debut: Sept. 16, 1972 (CBS). Final telecast: Aug. 26, 1978 (CBS). 142 episodes.

"Comedy," Bob Newhart once observed, "is my way of bringing logic to an illogical situation."

Freeze Frame

One of the funniest episodes during the final season of *Get Smart* was Ice Station Siegfried, which opens with Max standing in 12 feet of snow in Miami after KAOS activates a weather-altering ray at the North Pole. The Chief dispatches 99 to the Arctic, where she's shocked to discover that Siegfried and his lieutenant, Shtarker, have quit KAOS in order to join the Royal Canadian Mounted Police. It's a trap, of course, but 99 escapes from their clutches in time to activate an igloo-mounted giant electric fan that returns the planet's climate to normal.

The former accountant-turned-standup-comic first made a name for himself as a deadpan "man-on-the-street" interviewer for a Chicago TV station in the late 1950s. That job landed him a recording contract for an album entitled *The Button-Down Mind of Bob Newhart*, which promptly sold millions of copies and earned him a Grammy Award. The album's success paved the way for the first version of *The Bob Newhart Show*, a short-lived comedy-variety hour on NBC that won an Emmy Award for outstanding achievement in comedy in 1961–1962, but it was cancelled after just one season. Discouraged, Newhart went back to his roots. A master of flat delivery and the pregnant pause, Bob became so renowned on the night club circuit for his trademark one-way telephone conversations with the likes of Abraham Lincoln, Julius Caesar and Sir Walter Raleigh that before long *The Tonight Show* and *The Smothers Brothers Comedy Hour* were calling with offers for regular guest appearances. For the next decade Newhart appeared sporadically on TV during breaks from touring, but in 1972 he agreed to return to the weekly grind in what became one of the most beloved adult sitcoms of all time.

The second incarnation of *The Bob Newhart Show*, co-created by Lorenzo Music and David Davis, featured Bob in the role of Dr. Robert Hartley, a mild-mannered Chicago psychologist. Suzanne Pleshette portrayed his wife, Emily, while the inimitable Bill Daily (Roger Healey on *I Dream of Jeannie*) was their dimwitted next-door neighbour, airline pilot Howard Borden. The other regulars were Peter Bonerz as Dr. Jerry Robinson, a bachelor dentist whose office was on the same floor as Bob's, and Marcia Wallace, who played their receptionist, Carol Bondurant. Besides the outstanding primary cast, what elevated *The Bob Newhart Show* above most of its contemporaries was attitude. Like *The Mary Tyler Moore Show* (see Chapter 10) and *Barney Miller*, the series was populated by believably sincere characters doing their best to cope with the irrationalities of everyday life—but that's where the comparisons end. Even at their zaniest, *Mary Tyler Moore* and

Barney Miller were only mildly offbeat, with most of the comedy wrung from the characters' efforts to maintain a semblance of sanity in the chaos surrounding them. In marked contrast, Bob and Emily Hartley and the folks who populated their surreal world were unfettered by the conventional laws of sanity and logic. They wholeheartedly embraced absurdity as the key to conquering it— not unlike Newhart's real-life standup persona. The result was a consistently funny show that entertained on several different levels. The bizarre situations and quirky characters that Dr. Hartley encountered each day at work were exquisite—and all the funnier because his home life was so well grounded. Even so, Emily's unabashed sensuality was a hilarious counterpoint to her husband's prudish demeanour, so we were never quite sure what to expect next from prime-time's first forty-something couple to acknowledge a healthy, happy sex life.

Freeze Frame

The most memorable of Dr. Hartley's patients was Elliot Carlin (Jack Riley), who wore a bad hairpiece, had no self-esteem and suffered from an enormous persecution complex. One of his favourite expressions was: "It's hard to be natural when you're wearing a toupee, contact lenses and four-inch lifts."

Another secret to the success of *The Bob Newhart Show* was that it adhered to the star's lone request when he accepted the role: no kids. "I didn't want to do the same old wisecracking-kids-dopey-parents schtick that had been done to death on a hundred other shows," Newhart said at the time. "I'd been offered several series over the years, but this script was the first one I'd read where I didn't say 'It's a good idea, but what do

Notable Quotable

The following exchange is a sample of the inspired lunacy that became a hallmark of *The Bob Newhart Show*:

Jerry, as he's leaving on a trip to Mexico: "Howard, do you want me to bring anything back for you?"

Howard: "Padded coat hangers."

Jerry: "Howard, you can get those anywhere."

Howard (testily): "I don't care where you get them, just get them!"

we do for show number two?' It was grown-up comedy, and there was a certain charm and wit about it that really struck a chord."

After six years of dispensing advice to his patients for $40 per hour, Dr. Hartley took down his shingle for good in 1978. "We hadn't slipped in any way," Newhart recalled years later. "The show was still funny, so it was the right time to get off. I was very proud of our effort, but disappointed that the show and the people on it were never truly acknowledged by the TV industry. Not one Emmy! We had so many good people and they made it look so easy. Maybe that worked against us."

Bob employed the same winning formula of bizarre "button-down" humour when he returned to TV with another hit, *Newhart*, in 1982. He portrayed Dick Loudon, an author of "how-to" books who bought a rundown New England inn with his wife Joanna (Mary Fran). Over its eight-year run the show incorporated many of the hooks that made his first show so successful, and in the series' classic final scene, after being hit in the head by an errant golf ball, Bob woke up in bed—next to Suzanne Pleshette, on *The Bob Newhart Show* set—and explained how he'd had a "really weird dream" about owning a hotel and being married to a beautiful blonde who looked good in knitted sweaters (Fran). It was classic Newhart: once again bringing a twisted kind of logic to a completely illogical situation.

Chico and The Man

Series debut: Sept. 13, 1974 (NBC). Final telecast: July 21, 1978 (NBC). 88 episodes.

Set in a shabby service station in a crime-ridden corner of East Los Angeles, this blue-collar sitcom rejuvenated the career of former vaudeville hoofer Jack Albertson and—far too briefly—made a star out of Freddie Prinze.

Albertson, who was 67 when the series started, cut his TV teeth as host of a variety show called *Broadway Jamboree* in 1948 before co-starring opposite Peter Lawford in *The Thin Man* police drama a decade later. His show business career dated back to the 1920s, when he was a contract dancer on the vaudeville circuit, and he had several movies and dozens of television guest appearances on his resume by the time he took the role of crotchety garage owner Ed Brown on *Chico and The Man*. Prinze, who grew up in a poor Puerto Rican neighbourhood in New York City, had just turned 20 when the series began. He got the part of Chico Rodriguez after one of the show's creators saw him do a hip ethnic-oriented standup routine on *The Tonight Show*.

The premise behind *Chico and The Man* was simple: A grouchy, set-in-his-ways old widower reluctantly agrees to give a smooth-talking, happy-go-lucky street kid a job in his rundown garage after finding him asleep in an abandoned truck. It turned out to be a smart move, because Chico worked hard to clean up the place and brought in new business with his good looks and easy charm. Female viewers were especially receptive to the handsome, muscular Prinze, whose signature expression of "Looooooking good!" quickly became the year's hottest catch phrase. The show featured strong writing and thoughtful plots that inevitably revealed some greater truth behind the comedy, and the chemistry between Albertson and Prinze was obvious and genuine. While on the surface Ed whined and complained about Chico and his lifestyle or pretended to make token efforts to get rid of him, deep down there was a palpable respect and affection between the two characters that crossed over into real life. Other regulars in the cast through the first three years included garbage man Louie Wilson (Scatman Crothers), Mabel the letter-carrier (Bonnie Boland) and Chico's pal Mando (Isaac Ruiz). In 1976 old pro Della Reese joined the series as the owner of a neighbourhood diner and became a regular foil for Ed's anti-social antics.

Notable Quotable

"I am not a minority; I'm just an outnumbered majority."

—Ed Brown

Chico and The Man was an instant hit, winding up as the No. 3 show on network television in the 1974–1975 season. It remained in the top 25 for most of the next two years, until Jan. 25, 1977, when Prinze, despondent over the pressures of his sudden stardom and escalating drug dependency, shot himself in the temple during a meeting with his manager. Rushed to hospital for emergency surgery, the 23-year-old actor lingered on life-support for 33 hours before he died.

Prinze's death at the height of his fame sent shock waves through the entire TV community. Albertson and pop star Tony Orlando, a close friend of Prinze's, read touching eulogies at his funeral, which was attended by many of Hollywood's biggest names. NBC gave serious consideration to cancelling *Chico and The Man*, but by the following September the series had been retooled. In the opening episode of the 1977–1978 season, as Ed and Louie prepared for a fishing trip to Tijuana, it was revealed that Chico had left the garage to join his father in a business venture. When Ed and Louie returned from their trip they found a 12-year-old runaway named Raul Garcia (Gabriel Melgar) hidden in the trunk of their car. Once again Ed reluctantly agreed to take in a young roommate, and in a touching scene at the end of the episode, when Raul climbed into bed and said "Good night, Mr. Brown," Ed replied with: "Good night, Chico." Then he caught himself and quietly said: "You're all Chicos to me."

Freeze Frame

The catchy theme song for *Chico and The Man* was written and performed by Jose Feliciano.

The series limped through that final season with steadily dwindling viewership, and in a last-ditch effort to prolong the inevitable the producers cast sexy nightclub star Charo as Raul's long-lost aunt from Spain. The gimmick briefly improved the ratings, but not enough to stave off cancellation.

Fawlty Towers

Series debut: April 1975 (BBC in England), April 1976 (PBS in North America). Final telecast: July 1975 (BBC), July 1976 (PBS). 12 episodes.

The short-lived sitcom that in 2000 was voted the best series in the history of British television was actually a spinoff from an obscure British series called *Doctor At Large* (1973), but the original roots of *Fawlty Towers* can be traced to the real-life experience of members of the troupe from *Monty Python's Flying Circus* (see Chapter 10), who in early 1972 spent a few days ensconced at a seedy hotel in Torquay, England. One of those performers was John Cleese, who later wrote a comedy script for *Doctor At Large* set in just such a place. Along with his wife, Connie Booth, Cleese subsequently revamped the script, fashioning it into a short-run series about a pompous innkeeper named Basil Fawlty and his priggish wife, Sybil. Cleese cast himself in the starring role, with Prunella Scales as Sybil and Booth as the scatter-brained maid, Polly. The other regular cast member was an incompetent Spanish waiter named Manuel (Andrew Sachs), who butchered the English language and was forever being bullied by Basil. The diminutive Manuel's pat response to any question or order was "Que?," which inevitably prompted a smack or kick from Fawlty, followed by his explanation to onlooking guests: "You'll have to excuse him...he's from Barcelona."

Freeze Frame

When *Fawlty Towers* was sold to the national network in Spain, language dubbers transformed Manuel into an Italian waiter named Mario in order to avoid offending their viewers.

Although only 12 episodes of *Fawlty Towers* were produced, each is a masterpiece of comic timing and execution. Most of the plots revolve around ridiculous misunderstandings and Basil's exhaustive efforts to prove to everyone—especially Sybil—that he's in complete control of the chaos. In one of the funniest episodes a group of German tourists arrive at the hotel shortly after Basil has sustained a mild concussion. After exhorting Sybil, Polly and the rest of the guests to be on their best behaviour for the foreigners ("Don't mention the war!"), he proceeds to make a series of incredible gaffes, culminating in an exaggerated goose-step around the dining room while pressing a finger to his upper lip to imitate Hitler's moustache. In another classic, when Sybil storms out in a huff after her husband forgets their anniversary, Basil forces Polly to dress up as his wife and feign sickness to avoid having to greet friends who have dropped in for a drink. When the friends insist on looking in on poor bed-ridden Sybil, Basil goes to hilarious lengths to prevent them from discovering his ruse.

Tight writing and brilliant plots aside, the most enduring quality of *Fawlty Towers* is Cleese's overblown physicality. Though they always look spontaneous, every gesture and move Basil made was carefully and deliberately crafted by the star for maximum comedic effect. Everything from his trademark squirming at yet another dressing down from Sybil to the angle of those recurring smacks to Manuel's head was painstakingly choreographed in scripts that often topped 100 pages, whereas the norm for most half-hour sitcoms is around 70 pages. That meticulous attention to detail and the lengthy production schedule help explain why only a handful of episodes were produced, but the timeless quality of each and every instalment of *Fawlty Towers* more than makes up for the lack of quantity.

Fast Forward

The 2000 British Film Institute survey that named *Fawlty Towers* the all-time best British TV series included two other sitcoms among the top 10 vote-getters: *Monty Python's Flying Circus* (5) and *Yes, Minister* (9).

The Least You Need to Know

➤ Because *Car 54, Where Are You?* was shot on location in New York City, the producers had to use bright red police cars to distinguish them from the real thing.

➤ In his first regular TV role as bumbling store detective Byron Glick on *The Bill Dana Show*, Don Adams perfected many of the comic mannerisms he showcased as the star of *Get Smart*.

➤ Former accountant Bob Newhart was working as a man-on-the-street interviewer for a Chicago TV station when he recorded a hit comedy album in 1959.

➤ *Chico and The Man* star Freddie Prinze took his own life in 1977 at the age of 23.

➤ *Fawlty Towers* was named the best series in the history of British television in a survey conducted by the British Film Institute.

Chapter 10

Excellent Ensembles

In This Chapter

➤ Musical mayhem: *The Monkees*

➤ Lumberjacks in lingerie: *Monty Python's Flying Circus*

➤ Nutty newsroom: *The Mary Tyler Moore Show*

➤ School daze: *Welcome Back, Kotter*

➤ Sherwood be funny: *When Things Were Rotten*

While today's high-brow critics breezily dismiss the sitcom programming of the 1960s as trite and facile, the fact remains that most of the greatest comedies from the last two decades of the 20th century—everything from *Taxi* and *Cheers* to *Seinfeld* and *Friends*—can trace at least part of their success to the great ensemble efforts of the late '60s and early '70s, which themselves took a cue from Boomer classics like *The Andy Griffith Show*, *The Beverly Hillbillies*, *Gilligan's Island* and *Get Smart*.

Ensemble comedies represent the greatest challenge for writers, producers and actors because there has to be enough "meat" for everyone. What's more, the shows have to be crafted in such a way as to justify having more than one or two primary characters, and those characters have to be interesting enough for viewers to identify with and care about.

In their own way, each of the five ensemble series discussed in this chapter emerged as a precursor to the trends that shaped television situation comedy through the 1980s and '90s, and while you can agree or disagree with their inclusion on my list of Boomer favourites, each helped define the genre that has become a staple of post-2000 network fare.

The Monkees

Series debut: Sept. 12, 1966 (NBC). Final telecast: Aug. 19, 1968 (NBC). 54 episodes.

In early 1965, just months after The Beatles' *A Hard Day's Night* debuted on the big screen, a couple of young Hollywood producers named Bert Schneider and Bob Rafelson hit on the idea of designing a weekly TV series around the comic misadventures of an American equivalent of the Fab Four. Schneider and Rafelson placed a small ad in the trade papers inviting "insane boys, aged 17–21" to try out, and a few months later more than 500 applicants showed up to audition for The Monkees—pop music's first synthetic superstars.

From that hopeful horde the producers picked two youngsters with rudimentary acting experience and two who had some basic musical ability. The actors were Micky Dolenz and Davy Jones; the musicians were Peter Tork and Michael Nesmith. A decade earlier, at the age of 10, Dolenz (a.k.a. Micky Braddock) had starred in the adventure series *Circus Boy*, while English-born Jones had been a semi-regular child actor on *Coronation Street*. Tork and Nesmith had both dabbled in folk singing. The four were drilled and rehearsed for months until they had a passing familiarity with their instruments, then Schneider and Rafelson unleashed them on unsuspecting viewers in what quickly became the most talked about series of the 1966 season and winner of the Emmy Award as that year's best comedy.

In a strange way, the fictional antics of The Monkees on TV—whirlwind tours, gorgeous groupies, shady business advisers—became almost a mirror image of what happened to Peter, Micky, Mike and Davy in real life. To cash in on the show's popularity the band released several albums, but on the first few records the boys were limited to just supplying the vocals. Eventually they got to the point where they could play passable versions of million-selling songs like "Last Train to Clarksville" and "I'm a Believer" in front of live audiences, but for the most part The Monkees' sound relied heavily on studio musicians and behind-the-scenes production wizardry. Meanwhile, thanks largely to their TV show, the band's fame began to rival that of The Beatles and The Rolling Stones. "Monkeemania" was rampant in North America throughout 1966–1967, and with it came the prying eyes of the gossip media, legal hassles over songs and merchandising, and enough other problems to keep the band's management team working around the clock.

Freeze Frame

Before landing the role as The Monkees' diminutive lead vocalist and tambourine player, Davy Jones worked as a jockey in his native England.

None of those problems appeared to affect the series, however. From the outset all four of the boys showed a remarkable grasp for acting and innate comedic ability which, combined with such unconventional filming techniques as distorted focus, fast and slow motion and quick cuts, gave the show a look unlike anything else on TV. To top off each week's episode, The Monkees sang their latest hit in an extended forerunner to the modern music video, incorporating the same refreshingly quirky production techniques. The whole package had a hot, hip look about it, and for two seasons The Monkees were a bona fide pop culture juggernaut. Then, as quickly as it had come, the fame evaporated. NBC pulled the plug on the series in the summer of 1968, and a few months later the band released a feature-length film called *Head* that was a box-office flop. The touring and recording sessions ended shortly afterwards, and the band members went their separate ways. There was a brief (and moderately successful) reunion in the late 1980s, but it never came close to duplicating the "Monkeemania" of their TV heyday.

Fast Forward

Michael Nesmith, whose trademark with The Monkees was his ever-present woolen cap, won the first Grammy Award for video in 1982 for "Elephant Parts," which led to a short-lived 1985 series on NBC called *Michael Nesmith In Television Parts*. Nesmith's other claim to fame is that his mother made millions as the inventor of Liquid Paper correction fluid.

Monty Python's Flying Circus

Series debut: 1969 (BBC in England), 1972 (PBS in North America). Final telecast: 1974 (BBC), 1978 (PBS). 54 episodes.

According to one of the pioneers of the Python troupe, the BBC's penchant for penny-pinching nearly cost North Americans the opportunity to savour the delicious decadence of these misguided geniuses. Just imagine—had some cost-conscious bean-counter gotten his or her way, we'd never have split a gut over such unforgettable bits as The Academy of Silly Walks, The Dead Mother in the Sack, The Dead Parrot ("It's not dead, it's sleeping!") and those lumberjacks in lingerie. Not to mention the Upper Class Twit of the Year Award and Spam, Spam, Spam, Spam and Spam!

The Pythons' wickedly funny sketches made North American series such as Rowan & Martin's Laugh-In *and* The Carol Burnett Show *look tame by comparison.*

"When we first started, the BBC had a policy of erasing tapes after a certain period so they could be reused...especially light entertainment," Terry Jones recalled during a trip to the Just For Laughs festival in Montreal in 1999. "One of the production guys who liked what we were doing tipped us off that ours was going to be among the next batch of shows to get erased, so one night we smuggled out the tapes and got them copied. Shortly afterwards the series got sold in the States so the BBC didn't wipe them out after all, but it was a very close call."

Freeze Frame

According to a speech given by Graham Chapman at Indiana University shortly before his death, he and his comedy partners dreamed up "Monty Python" as the name of the fictitious weasel agent allegedly representing them. It sounded so cool that it was eventually incorporated into the group's name.

The Pythons—Jones, Eric Idle, John Cleese, Terry Gilliam and Graham Chapman—introduced North American viewers to an innovative brand of off-the-wall zaniness that made *Rowan & Martin's Laugh-In* look sophomoric and amateurish by comparison. The series created major stars out of its core performers, started trends in ensemble comedy that other shows rushed to copy and became the foundation for a very successful movie franchise, which included (among others) *And Now For Something Completely Different, Monty Python and The Holy Grail, Monty Python's The Life of Brian* and *Monty Python's Meaning of Life.*

This was a series that pushed all the envelopes and kept censors and church groups in a constant state of agitation. The core performers were its best asset, and the fact they wrote all the material themselves accounts for why the best sketches have, for the most part, withstood the test of time. Much like the core troupe on *Saturday*

Night Live years later, The Pythons wrote and perfected their comedy on the basis of mutual criticism. The end result was a synthesis of what they all thought was funny—but it had to be unanimous. "If there was a thing where it was a split, we didn't use it," recalled Jones. "But other times the skits came together very easily. For the Mr. Creosote bit, for instance (in which a hideously obese man goes on an eating binge in a restaurant, then vomits everything out, only to be offered an after-dinner mint at the end), I remember sitting down at my typewriter, not knowing what I was going to write, then just typing out a sketch in the worst possible taste. It sat on the shelf for a while, but we eventually used it."

Despite the enormous success of the movies and the continued popularity of the original series via the Internet and cable channels on both sides of the Atlantic, Jones doesn't see a reunion of Monty Python's Flying Circus happening any time soon. Chapman died a few years ago, Idle and Cleese turned to the big screen, while Jones himself has become a successful author of children's books. "You can't reunite what hasn't broken up, and we never broke up," he said. "We've all just moved on to the next stage of our lives, but Monty Python will always be with us."

The Mary Tyler Moore Show

Series debut: Sept. 19, 1970 (CBS). Final telecast: Sept. 3, 1977 (CBS). 168 episodes.

If imitation is the sincerest form of television, *The Mary Tyler Moore Show* ranks as one of the greatest hybrid sitcoms of all time—and arguably the funniest "soft" comedy ever made. By incorporating the best elements of three landmark predecessors—*I Love Lucy, The Honeymooners* and *The Dick Van Dyke Show*—Mary and her hubbie, producer Grant Tinker, created a series that was both compelling and compassionate, with enough gentle laugh-out-loud humour spread through the unusually large cast to keep everybody happy. From *I Love Lucy*, Moore and Tinker borrowed the idea of filming on simple, bare-bones sets. Whether it was the WJM-TV newsroom or Mary's apartment, this technique forced the actors to enrich their characterizations by concentrating on movement and projection, as in live theatre. Like *The Honeymooners*, the series was shot before a live audience, which charged each show with an undercurrent of spontaneity and exuberance. And like *The Dick Van Dyke Show*, on which Mary had become America's sweetheart by portraying Laura Petrie for five years (see Chapter 3), *The Mary Tyler Moore Show* gave the star's home and work environments equal billing, with a superbly talented supporting cast in both worlds.

Still, the girl "who could turn the world on with her smile" might never have returned to television if a smarmy movie entitled *Thoroughly Modern Millie* hadn't been such a bust. Made in 1967, it was a big-budget musical send-up of the Roaring Twenties, with Julie Andrews in the starring role. Moore, still basking in the glory of her success as Laura Petrie, made her movie debut with a meaty supporting role—a part she viewed as a stepping stone toward realizing her ultimate career goal of becoming a big-screen musical comedy star. When the movie flopped, Mary's career pretty much got stuck in neutral. She co-starred as a nun opposite Elvis Presley in *Change Of Habit* the following year and looked to be on the verge of never rising above such forgettable fare when, out of the blue, CBS came calling with an offer to reunite with Van Dyke for an hour-long special in the fall of 1969. The show scored mammoth ratings, and before long CBS execs were falling all over themselves to develop a suitable format that would return the perky Ms. Moore to prime time.

Freeze Frame

Mary Richards was a divorcee in the initial outline for *The Mary Tyler Moore Show*, but then was made "independently single" after network executives expressed concern that some viewers might believe Moore was really "divorced" from Dick Van Dyke, her previous TV husband.

TeleTrivia

John Amos, who portrayed WJM-TV weatherman Gordy Howard formerly played for the Victoria (B.C.) Steelers in the Continental Football League, and went on to portray James Evans, the father on the 1970s' sitcom *Good Times*.

The network suits needn't have bothered. After talking it over with Tinker, Mary decided the only way to ensure her triumphant return to TV was for the two of them to create, cast and produce the show themselves. They formed MTM Productions and immediately set out to hire the best writers, directors and performers they could find. *The Mary Tyler Moore Show* debuted a little more than six months later, and within weeks the series about single, career-minded Mary Richards, an associate producer at WJM-TV in Minneapolis, transformed a group of talented but largely unknown character actors into one of the most beloved ensemble casts in television history.

All the key secondary characters—gruff-but-good-hearted producer Lou Grant (Ed Asner), dimwitted anchorman Ted Baxter (Ted Knight), wisecracking news writer Murray Slaughter (Gavin MacLeod) and Mary's best friends, Rhoda Morgenstern (Valerie Harper) and Phyllis Lindstrom (Cloris Leachman)—were crucial to the success of the series, particularly in the first two seasons. When Betty White joined the cast as Sue Ann Nivens, the man-hungry host of WJM's Happy Homemaker Show in 1973, the core supporting cast was complete.

Rhoda and Phyllis, though often on opposite sides of an issue, provided the anchor for Mary's home life and helped steer her through the trials and tribulations of making it on her own, while Lou, Murray, Ted and Sue Ann provided the comedic counterpoint at the office. Georgia Engel joined the cast late in the 1973 season as Ted's ditsy girlfriend, Georgette Franklin Baxter, and after a two-year courtship they married. Sue Ann and Georgette became more important characters after Rhoda and Phyllis were written out in 1974 and 1975 respectively (Harper and Leachman each got their own series), but the quality of *The Mary Tyler Moore Show* never wavered. For many fans, the single best episode was Chuckles Bites The Dust

(Oct. 25, 1975), in which beloved WJM superstar Chuckles the Clown meets a tragic end when, dressed as a peanut, he is shelled by a rogue elephant. Much to Mary's horror, the newsroom gang can't help making jokes about the macabre nature of Chuckles' death, but at the funeral it's Mary who can't stop herself from cracking up during the solemn ceremony.

Through the first six of its seven seasons *The Mary Tyler Moore Show* never dropped out of the top 25 (it was No. 39 the final year), and earned a total of 27 Emmy Awards, including three each for Moore and Asner. Despite the dip in ratings, the series still had a large viewership when the star decided to pull the plug after the 1977 season. In the final episode, new managers took over WJM and decided the only way to boost the station's performance was to purge the newsroom staff—all except Ted, the bumbling anchorman. It was a fitting finale for a great ensemble series that right to the end stayed true to the elements responsible for that greatness: compassion, honesty and a subtle brand of gentle humour that has rarely, if ever, been duplicated.

TeleTrivia

Phyllis Lindstrom (Cloris Leachman) and her husband Lars owned the Minneapolis apartment building in which Mary Richards and Rhoda Morgenstern lived. Lars was never seen in the series, but he "died" in 1975, an event that prompted Phyllis to move to San Francisco—the setting for Leachman's spinoff series.

Welcome Back, Kotter

Series debut: Sept. 9, 1975 (ABC). Final episode: Aug. 10, 1979 (ABC). 95 episodes.

"Up your nose with a rubber hose!"

With that rallying cry, a rebellious band of bell-bottomed remedial students at Brooklyn's James Buchanan High School exploded on the consciousness of Middle America with all the subtlety of a hand grenade in a chicken coop. Known simply as Sweathogs, the roster included swaggering, pompadoured Italian Vinnie Barbarino (John Travolta); hip, black Freddy "Boom Boom" Washington (Lawrence Hilton Jacobs); a Jewish Puerto Rican con artist named Juan Luis Pedro Philippo de Huevos Epstein (Robert Hegyes) and class clown Arnold Horshack (Ron Palillo). Rookie teacher Gabe Kotter (Gabriel Kaplan) was assigned the task of instructing these teenaged misfits by vice-principal Michael Woodman (John Sylvester White) because Kotter had once been a Buchanan High Sweathog himself. That earned him grudging respect from the kids, and for the next four years his efforts to instil a semblance of "book learning" in his streetwise charges formed the basis for one of the unlikeliest hits of the decade. Other cast regulars included Kotter's wife Julie (Marcia Strassman), Rosalie "Hotsy" Totzy (Debralee Scott) and Verna Jean (Vernee Watson).

John Travolta became an overnight sensation as Vinnie Barbarino, leader of the rebellious Sweathogs on Welcome Back, Kotter.

Freeze Frame

Each of the four Sweathogs had a signature expression. For Barbarino, it was a suitably stunned "What? Where?" every time he was asked a question. Horshack's schtick was to get Kotter's attention by pleading "Oooh, oooh!" whenever he raised his hand, while Washington could disarm anyone with his resonant "Hi there!" Epstein didn't really have a trademark phrase—his gimmick was to present notes signed by "Epstein's Mother," excusing him for being absent, from taking exams, and even from participating in gang rumbles.

During the last two seasons the core group was joined by the first female Sweathog, Angie Globagoski (Melonie Haller) and a smooth Southerner named Beau De Labarre (Stephen Shortridge).

The appeal of *Welcome Back, Kotter* was that it deftly combined snippets of reality with broad slapstick to create what was essentially a half-hour standup routine, with Kotter as the Groucho Marx–like straight man. The hip, anti-establishment story lines were a hit with youngsters, but there was also an undercurrent of genuine affection, an "all-for-one, one-for-all" attitude among the Sweathogs and in their relationship with Kotter that struck a deeper chord with older viewers. The series was based on the real-life experiences of Kaplan, who had been a remedial student in high school before launching his career as a standup comedian, and he never missed an opportunity to inject some honest realism into the scripts.

Unfortunately, as often happens on hit shows, the harmony on *Welcome Back, Kotter* began to fray after one of its principals simply got bigger than the group and struck out on his own. By 1976 John Travolta, whose cocky portrayal of Barbarino made him the focal point of the cast almost from day one, had branched into popular music with several hit records then launched an enormously successful movie career by co-starring in *Carrie* and *Saturday Night Fever*. By 1978 he was seen only occasionally on Kotter, and despite the admirable efforts of the other regulars, Travolta's absence left a void that was never adequately filled. At the end of the 1976–1977 season Julie Kotter became pregnant, and the following fall gave birth to twins (Rachel and Robin), which moved the focus of the series to Kotter's home life. It was a good try, but the show's last two seasons pale in comparison to the first two. As the Sweathogs made room for a seemingly endless string of new students, it just wasn't very funny any more.

Freeze Frame

The theme song for *Welcome Back, Kotter* was written and performed by John Sebastian, formerly of The Lovin' Spoonful, and made the Billboard Top 10 in 1975.

Notable Quotable

"In the land of my ancestors Horshack is a very old and honoured name. It means 'the cattle are dying.'"

—Arnold Horshack

When Things Were Rotten

Series debut: Sept. 10, 1975 (ABC). Final episode: Dec. 24, 1975 (ABC). 13 episodes.

I know, I know. You're wondering how a series that lasted less than a full season can be considered a Boomer classic. In response, I can only point to *Fawlty Towers* and *Police*

Squad. The former, which makes my list as one of the top 10 greatest Boomer sitcoms (see Chapter 9 and Appendix 1) was largely ignored during its original 13-episode run and gained world-wide acclaim only years later. Ditto for the brilliant post-Boomer era *Police Squad*, which lasted just six episodes in 1982 but was such a terrific showcase for Leslie Nielsen's comedic genius that it served as a "prequel" for the enormously successful Naked Gun movies.

When Things Were Rotten was Mel Brooks' last foray into television, a clever spoof of Robin Hood and his Merry Men that saw the co-creator of *Get Smart* pull out all the stops. Dick Gautier (Hymie the Robot on *Get Smart*) starred as Robin, with another Smart alumnus, Bernie (Siegfried) Kopell, as Alan-a-Dale, a sort of minstrel narrator who sounded more like a game show host. Dick Van Patten was Friar Tuck, David Sabin was Little John and former *Hee Haw* regular Misty Rowe was the well-endowed Maid Marion. Richard Dimitri appeared in the dual role of Betram/Renaldo, while Henry Polic II was hysterical as the Sheriff of Nottingham. Ron Rifkin portrayed Prince John, while Jane A. Johnston rounded out the cast as his wife, Princess Isabelle.

In typical Brooks' style, the comedy came from overloaded sight gags, non sequiturs and historical anachronisms. In the debut episode, Prince John tricked Robin into entering an archery contest, then had him taken prisoner and locked in a dungeon. In order to rescue their boss, the Merry Men disguised themselves as a travelling conga band and sashayed their way into the castle to spring him. In another memorable episode Prince John contracted the fastest woodcutters in England to chop down all of Sherwood Forest in a single day to accommodate a new housing development. The inventive scripts, Gautier's over-the-top characterization and the solid comic timing of old pros Van Patten and Kopell permanently etched this outrageously irreverent series into the minds of those who took the time to savour it, but alas, because so few episodes were made, it's never resurfaced in syndication.

The Least You Need to Know

➤ *The Monkees* pioneered the filming techniques that paved the way for music videos.

➤ *Mary Tyler Moore* took the starring role in her long-running series after co-starring with Elvis Presley in *Change of Habit*.

➤ *Welcome Back, Kotter* was based on the real-life experiences of creator and star Gabe Kaplan.

➤ *When Things Were Rotten* reunited two former "foes" from *Get Smart*: Dick (Hymie) Gautier and Bernie (Siegfried) Kopell.

Part 3

Distinguished Dramas

While the golden age of television drama certainly extended well into the 1960s, it would be inaccurate to credit Boomers with the actual gilding of most of those classic shows. Network offerings at the beginning of the 1950s consisted mostly of news, sports, a handful of game shows and embryonic sitcoms like The Goldbergs *and* Amos 'n' Andy *(see Part 1), but by mid-decade live anthology "showcase" programs had given way to a bold new hybrid that combined the best of anthology and series programming. That formula—first presented on such forgotten gems as* Kraft Television Theatre *and* Goodyear TV Playhouse*—went a long way toward forging the dramas that to this day define Boomer TV.*

There were doctors, lawyers and cops on television almost from the beginning, of course, but not until the mid-1950s did the idea of creating episodic serials around those professions gain wide acceptance with the networks. Taking a cue from the success of the daytime soaps, the first great continuing story line prime-time dramas were medical and police shows that framed human interest stories within the context of their respective settings.

The Doctor, *a 1952–1953 anthology starring Warner Anderson in a series of mini-dramas that focused more on emotional stress than physical trauma was one of the earliest, as was* Dragnet, *arguably the most successful police show in television history. Starring Jack Webb as humourless Sgt. Joe Friday of the L.A. Police Department ("Just the facts, ma'am"),* Dragnet *debuted on NBC on Jan. 3, 1952, and remained near the top of the ratings until it was cancelled seven years later. It returned to the air in 1967 with Harry Morgan as Friday's new partner, Officer Bill Gannon, and lasted another three seasons. Another great early police anthology was* Gangbusters *(1952), which tracked the apprehension of major criminals "taken from actual police and FBI files." For the first few months of 1952 NBC alternated* Dragnet *and* Gangbusters *in the Thursday night time-slot until Webb's production company could crank out a weekly episode of his series, at which time the highly rated* Gangbusters *was abruptly cancelled.*

Other notable early efforts were Medic, *a stark drama starring Richard Boone as Dr. Konrad Styner (1954–1956) and* Dr. Hudson's Secret Journal *(1955–1957), staring John Howard and Cheryl Callaway.* Medic *was a breakthrough series that was filmed at real hospitals and clinics and often incorporated real footage of operations, while* Dr. Hudson's Secret Journal *was based on a character in Lloyd Douglas' best-selling novel* Magnifcent Obsession. *Both were huge ratings winners that helped pave the way for a quartet of Boomer hits:* Dr. Kildare, Ben Casey, Marcus Welby, M.D. *and* Medical Center *(see Chapter 17).*

While the dramas that helped make the 1950s, '60s and '70s the most diverse era in television history generally aren't as fondly remembered as their sitcom counterparts, the shows discussed in the following chapters were all distinguished enough to warrant recognition as enduring examples of the Boomer genre.

Avant-garde Adventure

From the earliest days of anthology programming writers and directors of TV drama recognized that conflict was the secret to creating story lines compelling enough to sustain viewer interest for a full hour. When the anthologies gave way to episodic series, conflict became even more important because the challenge became one of enticing viewers back next week and next month, rather than just holding on to them for one evening. Unlike most movies and stage productions, the earliest TV dramas relied heavily on cliffhanger endings (another nod to the daytime soaps), but by the mid-1950s most had evolved into a format of neatly resolving one main conflict each week in order to start a fresh adventure in the next episode.

While conflict was crucial in the maturation of Boomer TV dramas, character development quickly became equally important in creating shows that viewers cared enough about to continue following. Each of the series profiled in this chapter featured the best of both: external conflict manifested in a different situation each week, and a main character who evoked a strong emotional reaction in viewers.

Perry Mason

Series debut: Sept. 21, 1957 (CBS). Final telecast: Sept. 7, 1966 (CBS). 270 episodes.

One of the great mysteries in TV history is how District Attorney Hamilton Burger (William Talman) managed to keep his job for nine years, even though he lost every case to Perry Mason (Raymond Burr). It got to the point where you actually felt sorry for the craggy-faced D.A. and his equally inept pal, hard-boiled police lieutenant Arthur Tragg (Ray Collins). Week after week, case after case, they took it on the chin from the stocky, smooth-talking Mason, who was ably assisted by his super-efficient secretary Della Street (Barbara Hale) and intrepid private investigator Paul Drake (William Hopper). It was downright embarrassing. How did Burger explain that miserable record when he was running for re-election? Why wasn't Tragg reassigned to the park patrol?

The character of Perry Mason was created by lawyer-turned-novelist Earle Stanley Gardner in the late 1930s, and when the courtroom superstar's adventures moved to radio in 1943, the show became equal parts soap opera and detective drama. On TV the series followed a formulaic routine of "backtracking" to solve the crime (which was usually shown in the opening scene), but strong characterizations and clever plots managed to keep the show fresh and interesting. The high point of each episode was the dramatic courtroom confrontation between Mason and Burger, which usually culminated with Perry shredding one of the D.A.'s prize witnesses in a ruthless cross-examination. The drama was often heightened by Drake's timely appearance with some unexpected piece of "surprise" evidence, at which time the witness would break down

TeleTrivia

Raymond Burr got his start in Hollywood in the late 1940s, portraying cold-blooded villains. He was especially memorable as the crazed Thorwald in the Alfred Hitchcock classic *The Rear Window* (1954), and later starred in the cult favourites *Godzilla* and *Godzilla At Large*. He also appeared as Jack Webb's boss in the pilot episode of *Dragnet* in 1951, and landed the starring role in *Perry Mason* after auditioning for the part of detective Paul Drake.

Perry Mason (Raymond Burr) and his trusty secretary Della Street (Barbara Hale) always had the upper hand on hapless District Attorney Hamilton Burger (William Talman).

and confess. Each show wrapped up with Mason, Drake and Street back in the office, reviewing the case and congratulating themselves on yet another win—sometimes joined by the client they'd gotten off the hook. This had the dual effect of neatly resolving unanswered questions for confused viewers and clearing the slate for an entirely new adventure the following week.

After *Perry Mason* was cancelled, the Canadian-born Burr moved from the courtroom to the police station in 1967, starring for eight years as wheelchair-bound San Francisco detective Robert Ironside on NBC's *Ironside*. CBS launched *The New Adventures of Perry Mason* in 1973 with Monte Markham as Mason, Sharon Acker as Della Street and Albert Stratton as Paul Drake, but it was a flop. Twelve years later NBC aired a reunion movie entitled *Perry Mason Returns*, which brought back Burr to defend Hale, whose character had been

Freeze Frame

Devoted fans of the series will recall that Mason actually did lose one case early in the 1963 season when a female client refused to reveal a key piece of evidence that would have exonerated her. Later in the same episode Mason and Drake tracked down the real culprit and won the woman's freedom, despite her objections.

falsely accused of murder. The movie garnered enormous ratings and led to a highly successful series of TV movies through the rest of the 1980s.

Sea Hunt

Series debut: Jan. 10, 1958 (syndicated). Final (original) telecast: 1961. 156 episodes.

The story line for what became one of the most successful syndicated programs in television history was deceptively simple: Mike Nelson (Lloyd Bridges) was a former Navy frogman who quit the service to become a freelance underwater investigator. Hired by insurance companies, salvage firms and the U.S. government, he travelled the world to recover stolen goods, locate treasure and, occasionally, battle foreign agents. The abundance of underwater action sequences (including some great fight scenes) and the exotic sun-drenched locales made the show an instant hit for creator Ivan Tors, but it was also a surprisingly expensive production for its day: around $40,000 per episode, even though Bridges was the lone regular cast member.

Freeze Frame

Future movie star Beau Bridges, the real-life son of Lloyd Bridges, got one of his first acting jobs on his dad's landmark series.

Initially only about 25 percent of each episode of *Sea Hunt* took place underwater, but eventually, as Nelson's services were utilized less for civilian assignments and more for the government, more than half the show took place in the drink or on board his specially equipped boat, The Argonaut. The athletic Bridges did all his own diving and stunts, and filming was done at depths of between 20 and 40 feet. The real challenge for the producers was finding guest stars who didn't mind spending long hours in a wet suit or aboard the boat just to get a few minutes of watery adventure on film. "Most of them got seasick, and their faces got so green we just couldn't shoot close-ups," Tors recalled years later. "It would have been too ghastly to put those images on television."

Man With A Camera

Series debut: Oct. 10, 1958 (ABC). Final telecast: Feb. 29, 1960 (ABC). 29 episodes.

Charles Bronson, who went on to become one of Hollywood's quintessential big-screen action heroes, starred as a freelance photographer in this forgotten classic, which featured plausible plots that nicely complemented his portrayal of rough-around-the-edges former combat lensman Mike Kovac. During the course of carrying out assignments for newspapers, magazines and corporate clients, Kovac inevitably found himself in situations that required him to act more like a detective than a photographer, and there were plenty of opportunities for him to throw the odd punch or escape in a high-speed car chase. The other regular characters in this series, which was applauded for its decidedly "working-class" look, were Kovac's father Anton (Ludwig Stossel) and Lieut. Donovan (James Flavin), a sympathetic police officer who helped steer assignments Mike's way.

Man With A Camera was Bronson's first series after several years as a regular guest star on everything from *Treasury Men In Action* to *Have Gun, Will Travel* and *Alfred Hitchcock Presents*. In 1961 he received an Emmy Award nomination for a role on General Electric Theatre, and two years later he had supporting roles in a couple of short-lived westerns: *Empire*, which starred Richard Egan and Ryan O'Neal, and *The Travels of Jamie McPheeters*, starring Kurt Russell.

The Fugitive

Series debut: Sept. 17, 1963 (ABC). Final episode: Aug. 29, 1967 (ABC). 120 episodes.

Created by Roy Huggins, inspired by Victor Hugo's *Les Miserables* and often confused with the real-life case of Dr. Sam Sheppard, an Ohio physician accused of killing his wife in 1954, *The Fugitive*, starring David Janssen as Dr. Richard Kimble, gets my vote as the absolute best drama of the Boomer TV era. Here was a genuine television first: a hero who was a loser. He had no place to go, no one to ask for help and was totally powerless against the forces conspiring against him. From a dramatic standpoint it was one of the all-time most difficult series to write and act in because it focused on a protagonist whose every instinct told him to run, to get away, before he got emotionally involved in each week's adventure.

As revealed in the introduction to each episode by sonorous narrator William Conrad, Kimble, a pediatrician in Stafford, Indiana, was "an innocent victim of blind justice," tried, convicted and sentenced to die for the high-profile murder of his wife Helen—a crime he didn't commit. Escorted by implacable Lieut. Philip Gerard (Barry Morse), Kimble was being transported to his date with the electric chair when the train they were riding derailed and he escaped. For the next four years he crisscrossed the United States, taking odd jobs and assuming new identities while constantly at risk of being recognized and recaptured. And always, always, the relentless Gerard was hot on his trail.

Kimble's only hope for clearing himself was to find the real killer, a one-armed man named Fred Johnson (Bill Raisch) whom the good doctor had glimpsed fleeing from the scene on the night Helen was bludgeoned to death. At his trial nobody believed Kimble's story about the one-armed man, but after escaping he set out to hunt him down, following the slimmest leads. The search took him to big cities and tiny hamlets, and several times he and Johnson met face to face, but the killer always managed to slip away. The other semi-regular character in this taut, brilliantly crafted series was Kimble's

Freeze Frame

Voiced over a scene of a train moving through the darkness, William Conrad's famous introduction to the pilot episode for *The Fugitive* went as follows:

"Name: Richard Kimble. Profession: doctor of medicine. Destination: death row, state prison.

"Richard Kimble has been tried and convicted for the murder of his wife, but laws are made by men, carried out by men. And men are imperfect. Richard Kimble is innocent. Proved guilty, what Richard Kimble could not prove was that moments before discovering his wife's body, he encountered a man running from the vicinity of his home. A man with one arm. A man he had never seen before. A man who has not yet been found.

"Richard Kimble ponders his fate as he looks at the world for the last time and sees only darkness. But in that darkness, fate moves its huge hand...."

In all subsequent episodes an abbreviated version of this introduction re-established the fact of Kimble's innocence in order to set the stage for the story that followed.

TeleTrivia

➤ Richard and Helen Kimble resided in a small town in Wisconsin in the original outline for *The Fugitive*, but the setting was moved to Indiana when the producers found out there was no death penalty for capital murder in Wisconsin.

➤ Over the four-year run of the series, Dr. Kimble used the aliases "Carter" four times and "Parker" three times. His quest for the one-armed man, which started in Tucson, Arizona, in the pilot episode, took him to 37 states as well as to Mexico (three times) and Washington, D.C. He was employed as a chauffeur six times, as a truck driver five times and as a construction worker four times. Two of his strangest jobs were serving as a cut man for a professional boxer in Los Angeles (episode 6) and as a cranberry bog labourer in New England (episode 87).

sister, Donna Taft (Jacqueline Scott), who was convinced of her brother's innocence and served as the lone link to his previous life.

Janssen's haunted, anguished characterization tops the list of what made *The Fugitive* so great. A healer by profession and a humanitarian by nature, TV's first chain-smoking doctor invariably followed his instinct to do what was right, even when it meant compromising his very survival. That inner conflict surfaced time and again throughout the series and was the crux for many of its most memorable episodes. Morse was equally brilliant as Gerard, even though the taciturn lieutenant appears in less than one-third of the 120 episodes. His single-minded obsession with being "an instrument of the law" and carrying out his duty no matter what the cost made him frightfully omnipresent. Even when he didn't make an appearance for long stretches, his dark shadow fell across every move Kimble made. The scariest thing about Gerard was that he

TeleTrivia

If you carefully watch the fight sequence during scene IV of the pilot episode, you'll notice David Janssen wince very convincingly when he's thrown against the bus by Ed Welles (Brian Keith). Keith threw him so hard that Janssen sustained three broken ribs—but he continued the scene to its conclusion.

didn't care one way or the other about his quarry's innocence. As he tersely stated in the pilot episode, Fear In A Desert City: "Let others debate and conclude. I'm just an instrument of the law."

Another enduring plus for the series is its dual continuity. While each episode involved Kimble in a tense self-contained story with its own unique plot twists, there was the week-to-week suspense of the bigger picture. Would he find the one-armed man? Would this be the job that gives away his identity? Would Gerard finally corner him? Add an impressive list of guest stars (Robert Duvall, Kurt Russell, Telly Savalas, Leslie Nielsen, Charles Bronson and Mickey Rooney were just a few) and it had all the ingredients for richly textured, timeless television.

In an historic move, the premise behind *The Fugitive* was unexpectedly resolved in a special two-part presentation in the summer of 1967 entitled The Judgment. Kimble finally tracked down Johnson in Los Angeles, only to be arrested by Gerard, who was following the same lead. In the final scene of Part One, Gerard looks genuinely uncomfortable taking Kimble into custody, and for the first time in the series he mutters an apology for carrying out his duty. That snippet of humanity carries over to Part Two, which sees Kimble convince Gerard that Johnson is headed back to Stafford to kill a man who actually witnessed the murder of Helen. Gerard grudgingly grants his long-time nemesis a 24-hour reprieve, and they too return to Stafford. Upon their arrival Kimble learns that Johnson is meeting the witness the next day at an abandoned amusement park to receive $50,000 in exchange for the man's life, and under Gerard's watchful eye he moves in to intercept them. In a climactic exchange atop a water tower,

Freeze Frame

On the night a record audience tuned in for the final episode of *The Fugitive*, David Janssen was in Georgia filming *The Green Berets* with John Wayne. Thirty minutes after the episode ended, Janssen appeared via live satellite feed on Joey Bishop's late-night talk show on ABC and cracked everyone up by shouting into the camera: "I killed her, Joey! She just talked too much!"

Johnson admits beating Helen to death, but just as he's about to finish off the doctor, Gerard shoots him. The very last scene of the series shows Gerard and Kimble exchanging a wordless handshake outside the courthouse after Kimble has been exonerated, and as the camera pulls away narrator William Conrad solemnly intones: "Tuesday, August 29—the day the running stopped."

Part Two of The Judgment was watched by the largest audience ever for a single television program to that time: an astounding 72 percent of all TV owners in the United States were tuned in. That record stood for 13 years, until the infamous Who Shot J.R.? episode of *Dallas*.

Flipper

Series debut: Sept. 19, 1964 (NBC). Final telecast: Sept. 1, 1968 (NBC). 88 episodes.

Creator-producer Ivan Tors put a new spin on the formula that made *Sea Hunt* such a huge success to turn this gentle adventure series about two boys and their pet dolphin into a surprise hit that won rave reviews from educators and youth organizations for its wholesome content.

Widower Porter Ricks (Brian Kelly) was the head ranger at Florida's Coral Key Park, responsible for protecting the fish and wildlife as well as campers and hikers. He lived with his two sons, 15-year-old Sandy (Luke Halpin) and 10-year-old Bud (Tommy Norden) in a seaside cottage, and during the first season they were often visited by Happy Gorman (Andy Devine), a jovial handyman who enthralled the boys with his tall tales of adventure on the high seas. But the real star of the show was Flipper, an incredibly intelligent dolphin that would come when called, did tricks on command and served as a friend, playmate and protector for the boys as they explored the park's bays and channels in their small boat. As he did with *Sea Hunt*, Tors made sure each episode included plenty of underwater action and once in a while Flipper even had to fight off a shark or a "bad guy" diver in order to save the day.

The character of Happy Gorman was written out of the series after the first season replaced by an oceanographer named Ulla Norstrand (Ulla Stromstedt), who provided a platonic romantic interest for Ranger Ricks.

Freeze Frame

Ivan Tors made a career out of filming fish and wildlife. In addition to creating and producing *Sea Hunt* and *Flipper*, he developed the TV adventure series Daktari! (1966–1969), about an American physician (Marshall Thompson) living in Africa, and produced several successful movies, including *Clarence The Cross-Eyed Lion*.

TeleTrivia

Flipper was in fact a highly trained dolphin named Suzy, who got the full "star" treatment during filming of the series. She was transported between locations in a specially built tank, got regular snack breaks and had a personal trainer with her at all times. That role was filled by veteran Hollywood animal trainer Ricou Browning, who played the monster in the motion picture *The Creature From the Black Lagoon*.

The Life and Times of Grizzly Adams

Series debut: Feb. 9, 1977 (NBC). Final episode: July 26, 1978 (NBC). 42 episodes.

This engaging drama about an animal-loving loner was sort of a wilderness equivalent of *The Fugitive*, but unlike Dr. Richard Kimble, Grizzly Adams (Dan Haggerty) didn't have to worry about a relentless cop shadowing his every move. He did, however, have to worry about blizzards, disease, wildfires, hostile Indians, snakes and quicksand. The series was set in the late 1800s in the Sierra Nevada region of the western United States, where Adams had fled to start a new life after being wrongly accused of murder. He built a cabin deep in the forest, made friends with a wandering trapper named Mad Jack (Denver Pyle) and an Indian scout named Nakuma (Don Shanks) and devoted his energies to learning all he could about nature and people's place in it.

In the pilot episode Adams rescued a starving orphaned bear cub from a mountain ledge and brought it back to his cabin. He named the bear Ben, and after nursing it back to health the two became inseparable companions, roaming the wilderness and finding adventure in whatever Mother Nature threw at them. Most of the "drama" was pretty tame, which allowed the series to showcase some spectacular scenery and wildlife, but occasionally Adams' insular world was invaded by outsiders, which generated some genuinely tense episodes. The other semi-regular character was young Robbie Cartman (John Bishop), whose family owned a nearby ranch. He visited periodically to play with Ben and was always enthralled by the tall tales spun by Grizzly and Mad Jack.

Haggerty, who was an accomplished animal trainer before he turned to acting, had previously starred in a big-screen version of *Grizzly Adams* and another similar motion picture called *The Adventures of Frontier Freemont*, both of which also featured his TV co-star Denver Pyle. Ben the bear was also an old hand at acting, having co-starred with Dennis Weaver and Clint Howard in the 1967–1969 series *Gentle Ben* on CBS.

The Least You Need to Know

➤ En route to compiling the most enviable case record of any lawyer in television history, Perry Mason lost only one case in nine years.

➤ Despite having just one regular cast member, *Sea Hunt* averaged $40,000 per episode in production costs.

➤ Future Hollywood heavyweight Charles Bronson made his TV series debut as the star of *Man With A Camera*.

➤ David Janssen broke three ribs during a fight scene in the pilot episode of *The Fugitive*.

➤ Dan Haggerty was a professional animal trainer before he starred in *The Life and Times of Grizzly Adams*.

Whirled War, Too

In retrospect, the idea of building dramas around fictional war at the same time Americans were seeing the awful cost of the Vietnam War on the six o'clock news every night seems absurd. But in the mid-1960s all three networks correctly deduced that the same folks horrified by the body counts from Southeast Asia might still watch Uncle Sam kick some Nazi butt.

It was pretty much a no-brainer. After all, war has all the ingredients for terrific television drama: endless conflict, strong characters, heroic story lines. Just add the Nazis and stir. Even at the height of the Vietnam conflict it was acceptable to use the Second World War as the setting for "fake" war on TV for the simple reason that we all knew the ultimate outcome. The godless Nazis might win the odd skirmish, but in the end truth and freedom would prevail—just as it was supposed to in Vietnam.

For many Boomers—myself included—the quartet of war dramas outlined in this chapter provided a rudimentary introduction to real-world history and our first exposure to such memorable expressions as *"Achtung!"* *"Schnell!"* and *"Nicht schiessen!"* Who said TV doesn't teach?

Combat!

Series debut: Oct. 2, 1962 (ABC). Final episode: Aug. 29, 1967 (ABC). 152 episodes.

Hands-down the best war series ever made and a show that ranks right behind *The Fugitive* on my personal list of the greatest Boomer dramas (see Appendix 1), *Combat!* was a hit because it succeeded on so many levels. As straight drama, this series about a U.S. Army platoon fighting its way across 1944 France excelled in telling stories that shed light (or cast dark shadows) on the frailty of ordinary men caught up in extraordinary circumstances. As pure escapism it often morphed into allegorical plays that could just as easily apply to the situation in Vietnam. There was also an occasional dose of humour, and the cast exuded a genuine sense of camaraderie. There was no phony esprit de corps or puffed-up jingoism here; just a kind of numbing awareness that no matter how many missions these guys completed, the war would go on and on and on.

That was a big part of the appeal, of course. For the first time ever on TV, the squad on *Combat!* looked and talked and acted like real soldiers. They were dirty, tired, cranky and often confused, yet they came across as heroic pawns to the whims of distant commanders who had no regard for the human cost of implementing their orders. *Combat!* also devoted a lot of time to showing how war impacts on the lives of helpless

Vic Morrow starred as rugged Sgt. Chip Saunders on Combat!, *while the "guest Nazis" included the likes of Richard Basehart.*

civilians caught in the crossfire. There was an underlying sense of solemnity to the series, but it was never allowed to get too preachy. Another plus was the "look"—particularly in the 127 black-and-white episodes (only 25 were shot in colour). Smoke, fog and mud were used a lot, as was actual Second World War film footage. The mortar and grenade explosions were among the most realistic ever seen on television, and the pioneering use of a roving cameraman offered up a gritty, unpolished perspective.

Vic Morrow and Rick Jason, who starred as Sgt. Chip Saunders and Lt. Gil Hanley respectively, both displayed an on-screen intensity that gave their characters an edgy command presence. The supporting cast was equally excellent: Pvt. Paul "Caje" Lemay (Canadian-born Pierre Jalbert), a quiet, efficient Cajun; Pvt. William G. Kirby (Jack Hogan), the squad's temperamental hothead; hulking Pvt. Littlejohn (Dick Peabody), the proverbial "gentle giant"; and Doc Walton (Steven Rogers), the melancholy medic. Comedian Shecky Greene portrayed Pvt. Braddock in 1962–1963, and the following year Pvt. Billy Nelson (Tom Lowell) signed up for one season. In 1963 Conlan Carter replaced Rogers as the medic, and over the course of the series there were literally dozens of other personnel changes as guest stars came and went. The fresh faces only added to the sense of realism as the squad's half-dozen core members constantly broke in new replacements.

TeleTrivia

Before *Combat!* went into production, all the cast members prepared for their roles by completing a gruelling week-long "boot camp" at a real U.S. Army training base.

As with all great shows, the writing on *Combat!* remained strong throughout the entire run of the series, and the producers explored many non-conventional story lines. One of the best episodes was The Glory Among Men (1964), in which a new replacement named Mason (Eddie Ryder) gets off on the wrong foot by cheating the other squad members in a poker game. The animosity only worsens when they go on patrol and Mason's irresponsibility gets another soldier killed. As Saunders tries to maintain discipline, the squad comes under attack from a German machine gun nest and Mason is wounded, trapped in "no-man's land" halfway between his own troops and the enemy. When the Germans don't pick him off right away, hoping to lure more of the squad into the killing zone, Saunders and his men are forced to face the ultimate moral dilemma: risk almost certain death to save someone they've come to hate, or abandon him to save themselves. It's an intense, unpredictable episode that plays out almost like a religious allegory, with Mason trapped between heaven and hell. Another quirky episode that strikes a similar chord is The Farmer (1965), featuring guest star Dennis Weaver as Pvt. Noah, a gentle pacifist who "snaps" and takes up arms only after watching an enemy patrol needlessly shoot a cow that has just delivered a calf. It's another example of a strong script and the right actor putting a human face on the insanity of war without getting overly righteous about it—a formula that became a *Combat!* hallmark.

Freeze Frame

While the producers of *Combat!* went to great lengths to recreate the authenticity of war-ravaged France, they weren't able to get their hands on any authentic German tanks. Instead, they substituted American M-42s, suitably camouflaged and adorned with Nazi insignia.

TeleTrivia

Twelve O'Clock High was loosely based on the novel of the same name by Beirne Lay and Sy Bartlett, which was also made into a hit movie starring Gregory Peck in 1949.

Combat! was still notching very respectable ratings when it was cancelled after five years (the last episode aired on the same night and network as the finale of *The Fugitive*), and despite the phenomenal popularity of the series most of the core cast drifted into relative obscurity. Jack Hogan (Kirby) spent one year as Sgt. Jerry Miller on *Adam 12* (1969) and later had a recurring role on the wilderness adventure series *Sierra*, while Pierre Jalbert (Caje), Dick Peabody (Littlejohn) and Rick Jason (Lieut. Hanley) all but vanished from the airwaves. Vic Morrow concentrated on directing and movie work until the mid-'70s, when he returned to television in the drama *Captains and the Kings* and the landmark mini-series *Roots*. His last TV role was as Capt. Eugene Nathan on the short-lived *B.A.D. Cats* (1980), which also starred a young Michelle Pfeiffer.

Morrow was killed in a freak helicopter accident during the filming of *The Twilight Zone* movie in 1982. He was 51. His old *Combat!* commander, Rick Jason, committed suicide at his home near Los Angeles in 2000. He was 74.

Twelve O'Clock High

Series debut: Sept. 16, 1964 (ABC). Final telecast: Jan. 13, 1967 (ABC). 78 episodes.

Unlike *Combat!*, which focused on the front-line "grunts," *Twelve O'Clock High* chronicled the adventures of a brigadier general. It was a bit of a stretch to believe such a high-ranking officer would be permitted to consistently place himself in such risky situations, but thanks to believable scripts and strong casting, this Quinn Martin-produced series emerged as one of the surprise hits of the 1964–1965 season.

Robert Lansing was wonderful as Brig.-Gen. Frank Savage, commander of the 918th Bombardment Group of the U.S. Eighth Air Force, stationed outside London. Savage personally led his squadron on bombing missions over Germany, much to the chagrin of his direct superior, Maj.-Gen. Wiley Crowe (John Larkin) and his ground-bound adjutant, Maj. Harvey Stovall (Frank Overton).

Savage was steely-eyed and somewhat caustic, but he never asked his men to perform a duty he wouldn't take on himself. His daring and coolness under fire were legendary, and even seasoned cohorts like Maj. Joe Cobb (Lew Gallo) and Maj. "Doc" Kaiser (Barney Phillips) never ceased to be amazed by the general's courage.

In the opening episode of the second season, entitled Loneliest Place In The World, what was thought to be a straggler B-17 from another squadron was granted permission to join the 918th en route back to England. Once in formation, however, the Flying Fortress turned out to be filled with Germans, who opened fire on the other bombers. Savage's plane sustained multiple hits and went down behind enemy lines. That was the end for Robert Lansing, whose character was written out of the series after being officially listed as missing in action. Col. Joe Gallagher (Paul Burke) assumed command of the outfit for the duration, and while he it gave it the old college try, the show was never as good from that point on. Gallagher had appeared in the pilot episode as a brash airman who believed he deserved special treatment because his father was a Pentagon general, and as he gradually worked his way up from captain to major to colonel under Savage's command, his metamorphosis from goof-off to leader made for an interesting sub-plot. Brig.-Gen. Ed Britt (Andrew Duggan) replaced Crowe as the unit's overall commanding officer after Savage was written out, and Sgt. Sandy Komansky (Chris Robinson) joined the cast as Gallagher's wisecracking flight engineer and tail gunner.

Twelve O'Clock High took a cue from *Combat!* by switching to colour episodes for the last season, but it turned out to be an annoying distraction because all the stock footage of air battles and bombing runs was in black and white. Still, the series managed to maintain the strong story lines right to the end, and discerning Boomers fondly recall it as one of the underrated gems in the pantheon of small-screen war dramas.

Freeze Frame

A quartet of future stars had recurring roles as support players during the first season of *Twelve O'Clock High*: Tom Skerritt (Lt. Ryan), Sally Kellerman (Lt. Libby MacAndrews), Burt Reynolds (Tech.-Sgt. Chapman), and Bruce Dern (Lt. Michael).

The Rat Patrol

Series debut: Sept. 12, 1966 (ABC). Final telecast: Sept. 16, 1968 (ABC). 58 episodes.

If the idea of having a brigadier general lead bombing missions on *Twelve O'Clock High* was a bit far-fetched, the premise behind *The Rat Patrol*—three Yanks and a Brit in a couple of souped-up jeeps keeping the entire German Afrika Korps at bay—was full-blown fantasy.

Not that this show wasn't entertaining in an *A-Team* kind of way. Sgt. Sam Troy (Christopher George), Sgt. Jack Moffitt (Gary Raymond) and Pvts. Mark Hitchcock

TeleTrivia

Each member of *The Rat Patrol* wore distinctive headgear. Sgt. Troy opted for an Aussie field cap, while Moffitt, the Brit, wore a commando-style beret. Hitchcock looked rather silly decked out in a bright red Civil War–style kepi, while Pettigrew wore the traditional steel helmet.

(Lawrence Casey) and Tully Pettigrew (Justin Tarr) managed to cram an awful lot of demolition and derring-do into each half-hour instalment—and that was good, because all that action tended to distract viewers from the general lameness of the plots. In most episodes it was painfully obvious that Hitchcock and Pettigrew were only there to drive the jeeps, because they had very little dialogue and were rarely seen in close-up shots. During the second season, in fact, Tully was cut loose and his spot on the team was taken by another character who wasn't even acknowledged in the credits!

The real stars of *The Rat Patrol* were the jeeps, which were each equipped with a .50-calibre machine gun mounted on a swivel. The fact that the recoil of a real .50-cal would make a Second World War vintage jeep nearly impossible to drive didn't seem to bother the producers, and in scene after scene Troy and Moffitt both proved deadly accurate when it came to wiping out whole columns of German trucks during the team's lightning-quick ambushes. And even though they were often hundreds of miles behind enemy lines, the boys always managed to have enough gas and water to make a speedy escape after completing their mission.

Sgt. Sam Troy (Christopher George, right) outlines a plan to Pvt. Mark Hitchcock (Lawrence Casey). Pvt. Tully Pettigrew (Justin Tarr) was all but mute during his time with The Rat Patrol.

Considering its other implausiblities, it's fitting that *The Rat Patrol* was also the only Boomer war drama to give one of the "bad guys" star billing in the credits. That honour went to the inscrutable Hauptman (Capt.) Hans Dietrich, portrayed by Hans Gudegast. Dietrich spoke flawless English and often displayed unexpected humanity as his troops hounded the Rat Patrol back and forth across the desert. After the series was cancelled the actor who portrayed Dietrich changed his name to Eric Braeden and joined the cast of the daytime soap *The Young and The Restless* as the suave and sophisticated Victor Newman.

TeleTrivia

Most of the desert sequences on *The Rat Patrol* were filmed in Spain and utilized buildings and equipment left over from the big-screen epic *The Battle of the Bulge*.

Garrison's Gorillas

Series debut: Sept. 5, 1967 (ABC). Final telecast: Sept. 17, 1968 (ABC). 26 episodes.

TV's version of the *The Dirty Dozen* wasn't nearly as exciting as the hit movie, but it had its moments. Lt. Craig Garrison (Ron Harper) was a no-nonsense West Pointer hand-picked by the brass to mold a motley collection of misfits into a crack commando unit to carry out "suicide" missions behind German lines. His four top recruits—Casino (Rudy Scolari), Actor (Cesare Danova), Goniff (Christopher Gray) and Chief (Brendan Boone)—all faced death sentences in military stockades when Garrison came calling with the promise of a presidential pardon if they signed on. For the duration of the series they bickered among themselves with almost the same intensity with which they battled the Germans, but when it came time to go into action they were a well-oiled machine.

The unit was headquartered at a secluded estate in the English countryside, where they trained and holed up between missions. Actor was the boisterous, smiling con man of the crew, Casino was a safecracker, Goniff an accomplished thief and Chief was an American Indian who had mastered the fine art of the switchblade. When they weren't trying to rescue captured Resistance operatives or steal information on the Nazi rocket program, the men kept Garrison on his toes by constantly using their "talents" to improve their chances of waiting out the war in secluded comfort.

Freeze Frame

Although it lasted only one season, *Garrison's Gorillas* was a magnet for past and future stars from other military series. The episode entitled Black Market featured former *McHale's Navy* regular Gavin MacLeod along with future *M*A*S*H* stars Jamie Farr and Mike Farrell, while The Magnificent Forger starred *F Troop* alumnus Larry Storch. Jack Hogan from *Combat!* was the guest star in War Games, while Hans Gudegast of *The Rat Patrol* showed up in The War Diamonds.

The Least You Need to Know

➤ *Combat!* star Vic Morrow was killed during the filming of *The Twilight Zone* movie in 1982.

➤ Robert Lansing's character was written out of *Twelve O'Clock High* when he went "missing in action" in the opening episode of the second season.

➤ Hans Gudegast, who portrayed German captain Hans Dietrich on *The Rat Patrol*, later changed his named to Eric Braeden and became a star on the daytime soap opera *The Young and The Restless*.

➤ *Garrison's Gorillas* was TV's answer to the hit movie *The Dirty Dozen*.

Home and School

One of the things that distinguishes classic Boomer dramas from those of the post-1980 era is their level of intensity. Where series like *Perry Mason, Grizzly Adams* and *Combat!* relied on strong characterizations and well-crafted plots to gradually heighten their dramatic impact, even the best from the past 25 years—*The Equalizer, Beauty and The Beast, NYPD Blue, The X-Files*—invariably were forced to introduce new cast members, gimmicky story lines or bizarre plot twists to sustain viewer interest. Granted, the TV landscape has become more crowded and the audience more fragmented, but is it mere coincidence that shows like *Sea Hunt* and *The Fugitive* continue to be held in such high regard today? I don't think so. When was the last time you heard anyone excitedly recount a plot from *Moonlighting* or *Miami Vice*?

While each of the shows profiled in this chapter could rightfully be described as "soft" drama, what elevates them to the status of classic Boomer fare is their uniform attention to character development and consistently strong writing.

Lassie

Series debut: Sept. 12, 1954 (CBS). Final telecast: Sept. 12, 1971 (CBS). 186 episodes.

Sundays were special when I was a kid because I was allowed to stay up past my usual 8 p.m. bedtime in order to watch *Lassie*. There was never any dog as great as that magnificent collie—not even Rin Tin Tin—and all week long I waited impatiently to see what new adventure Lassie and young Jeff Miller (Tommy Rettig) would be involved in. Like most 10 year olds, I also secretly envied that Miller kid. He lived on a farm, never seemed to go to school, and he trained Lassie to do things like make the bed, milk the cow and open the fridge door. Okay, I made up the part about milking the cow, but Lassie was extraordinarily intelligent—especially when it came to saving injured "city folks." A driver would be knocked unconscious in a car crash or a hiker would break his leg miles from nowhere, but good ol' Lassie could always find a way to summon help.

This long-running series was inspired by Eric Knight's best-selling novel *Lassie Come Home* (1940), which, a few years later, was made into a hit movie starring a couple of kids named Roddy McDowall and Elizabeth Taylor. In the original TV version, Jeff and his widowed mom Ellen (Jan Clayton) lived on the farm with "Gramps" (George Cleveland). In 1957 an orphan named Timmy (Jon Provost) joined the family, and

Lassie's courage and smarts put Rin Tin Tin to shame.

shortly afterwards Gramps died. Ellen sold the farm to Paul and Ruth Martin (Jon Shepodd and Cloris Leachman), and Lassie was left in the care of Timmy, whom the Martins eventually adopted. In 1958 June Lockhart and Hugh Reilly replaced Leachman and Shepodd as the Martins, and over the next six years Timmy and Lassie shared an amazing series of adventures, coping with everything from tornadoes and chicken thieves to forest fires and floods.

In 1964 the Martins moved to Australia to become homesteaders, but Lassie couldn't accompany them because of quarantine restrictions. The dog was left with Cully Wilson (Andy Clyde), an old-timer who lived on a nearby ranch. After Wilson died from a heart attack, Lassie was adopted by forest ranger Corey Stuart (Robert Bray), and the focus of the series shifted to more exotic settings as Stuart travelled all over the country as a troubleshooter for the U.S. Forest Service. By the fall of 1968, when Bray's character was written out of the series after sustaining serious injuries in a forest fire, Lassie became a loner, roaming the countryside with only infrequent pit-stops to visit two of Stuart's friends, rangers Scott Turner (Jed Allan) and Bob Erickson (Jack De Mave). During a seven-part story to open the series' final season (1970–1971), Lassie finally met a soul mate and bore a large litter of puppies.

Although no longer airing on CBS, *Lassie* remained in production as a syndicated series for three more years—the last of which saw the wonder dog join the Holden family on a ranch in California.

Fast Forward

Actor Tommy Rettig, who portrayed Lassie's original master, was arrested in 1975 on charges of smuggling cocaine into the United States. He was convicted and sentenced to five years in prison, but the sentence was overturned and the charges dropped after he won the appeal.

TeleTrivia

When Lassie "gave birth" to a litter of pups in the 1970–1971 season it was quite a startling feat, considering that all 10 of the dogs who portrayed television's most heroic pooch were male!

Room 222

Series debut: Sept. 17, 1969 (ABC). Final telecast: Jan. 11, 1974 (ABC). 112 episodes.

What makes this drama about day-to-day life at Walt Whitman High School so memorable is that it was one of the very few "serious" shows from the Boomer era that was produced in half-hour episodes. The condensed time frame, however, didn't prevent the series from exploring relevant themes like racism, poverty and drug abuse, and thanks to strong performances from a supporting cast made up largely of untried student actors, *Room 222* became the benchmark for all future school-based dramas—including the critically acclaimed *Boston Public* more than 30 years later.

The series focused on the trials and tribulations of history teacher Pete Dixon (Lloyd Haynes), a liberal who went out of his way to listen to the suggestions and concerns of his students. His girlfriend Liz McIntyre (Denise Nicholas) was the school counsellor, while Seymour Kaufman (Michael Constantine) was the principal and Alice Johnson (Karen Valentine) was the flighty, exuberant student teacher. Helen Loomis (Judy Strangis) was the adorably cute, incredibly bright kid who excelled at everything, while Bernie (David Joliffe), Jason (Heshimu) and Richie (Howard Rice) were other prominent students.

TeleTrivia

Lloyd Haynes, who starred as history teacher Pete Dixon on *Room 222*, was cast as Lt. Alden in *Where No Man Has Gone Before*, the second pilot episode for *Star Trek*. The character was subsequently rewritten to be a woman, which resulted in Nichelle Nichols joining the permanent cast as Lt. Uhura (see Chapter 18). Judy Strangis, who portrayed Mr. Dixon's star pupil Helen Loomis, went on to star in the '70s Saturday morning live-action series *Dyna-Girl*.

Room 222 was filmed on location at the 3,000-student Los Angeles High School, which certainly added to the realism, and as a result of its willingness to showcase issues like teen pregnancy, civil rights and gang violence, the series received dozens of awards from educational and civic organizations—as well as Emmys in 1970 for Karen Valentine and Michael Constantine.

The Waltons

Series debut: Sept. 14, 1972 (CBS). Final telecast: Aug. 20, 1981 (CBS). 220 episodes.

Arguably television's all-time best family-oriented saga, *The Waltons* was created and narrated by novelist Earl Hamner Jr., who based the series on recollections of his own Depression-era childhood in the Blue Ridge Mountains region of Virginia.

Told through the eyes of 17-year-old John-Boy (Richard Thomas), the stories focused on the family's day-to-day struggle of making ends meet, dealing with minor crises like a lost dog or a wounded bear, and coping with all the other peaks and valleys you'd expect from an extended family of 11. Ralph Waite and Miss Michael Learned portrayed John and Olivia Walton, and the primary cast was rounded out by Grandpa Zebulan Walton (Will Geer), his wife Esther (Ellen Corby) and the six other kids: Mary-Ellen (Judy-Norton Taylor), Jason (Jon Walmsley), Ben (Eric Scott), Erin (Mary-Beth McDonough), Jim-Bob (David W. Harper) and Elizabeth (Kami Cotler). Ike and Corabeth Godsey (Joe Conley and Ronnie Edwards) ran the dry-goods store in the fictional hamlet of Walton's Mountain, and Epp Bridges (John Crawford) served as sheriff. The neighbours included elderly sisters Mamie and Emily Baldwin (Helen Kleeb and Mary Jackson), who brewed moonshine called "the recipe" from a still in their mansion, and Yancy Tucker (Robert Donner), a likeable loser who lived with his chickens, hogs and geese in a rundown shack. Dozens of other semi-regulars came and went over the course of the series, including young Rev. Matthew Fordwick (John Ritter), schoolteacher Rosemary Hunter (Mariclare Costello) and feisty octogenarian Maude Gormsley (Merle Earle).

Simplicity was the foundation of *The Waltons*, and most of the stories during the first three seasons focused on the children. While Olivia and Esther were kept busy in the kitchen and John and Zeb earned a meagre income from their home-based lumber mill, the kids' lives revolved around school, social activities and their individual interests. John-Boy was determined to become a professional writer, while Mary-Ellen had her heart set on a career in medicine. Jason was an aspiring musician, Ben showed a talent for his father's business and Erin wanted to be a movie star. Jim-Bob dreamed of becoming a pilot and Elizabeth was content just to be "daddy's little girl."

Freeze Frame

CBS didn't expect *The Waltons* to survive when the series went head-to-head against NBC's No. 1–rated *Flip Wilson Show* on Thursday nights in 1972, but to everyone's surprise the saga of John-Boy and his family quickly became a hit in rural America and by season's end had forced *Flip Wilson* off the air.

Notable Quotable

"Goodnight Mama. Goodnight Daddy."

"Goodnight John. Goodnight Livvy."

"Goodnight Grandma. Goodnight Grandpa."

"Goodnight John-Boy. Goodnight Mary-Ellen. Goodnight Jason. Goodnight Erin. Goodnight Ben. Goodnight Jim-Bob. Goodnight Elizabeth."

—Lights-out at the Walton house (combining 11 different voices)

Freeze Frame

The Walton kids had their fair share of pets over the life of the series, including Old Blue (mule), Reckless (dog), Nick (pup), Chance (cow) and Rover (Jim-Bob's peacock).

Notable Quotable

"When you come to a mountain there's two things you can do: go around it, or go over it. The first way's the easiest, but you miss the view from the top."

—Grandpa Zeb Walton

John-Boy was still in school when the series started, but by the start of the 1976–1977 season he'd graduated, won an academic scholarship to Boatwright University and started publishing a local newspaper, The Blue Ridge Chronicle. The following year, as war clouds gathered over Europe, he moved to New York and became a foreign correspondent (Richard Thomas made only sporadic appearances over the next two seasons) while Mary-Ellen got engaged to Dr. Curtis Willard (Tom Bower), who enlisted in the Army Medical Corps shortly afterwards. Those events heralded several other major changes in the months ahead, including the deaths of Zeb (Will Geer passed away in the spring of 1976) and Curtis, who was killed in the Japanese attack on Pearl Harbor. If that wasn't enough, Olivia discovered she had tuberculosis and was sent to a sanitarium in Arizona (Michael Learned asked to be written out of the show), which paved the way for her cousin Rose Burton (Peggy Rea) to move in and run the household. Rose brought along her two grandchildren, Serena (Martha Nix) and Jeffrey (Keith Mitchell), so once again the Walton house was filled to capacity.

By the time the series ended, all the Walton boys had done their patriotic duty by serving in the armed forces, and Ben and Jason had both gotten married. Ben's wife Cindy was played by Leslie Winston while Jason's wife Toni was Jon Walmsley's real-life bride, Lisa Harrison. The final season also featured two bizarre twists: Robert Wightman appeared occasionally as the "second" John-Boy after the character was reported missing in action in Europe, then resurfaced in a London hospital. Later, Mary-Ellen learned that Curtis hadn't been killed at Pearl Harbor after all, but by that time she was hopelessly in love with medical student Arlington Westcott Jones (Richard Gilliland). She went on to wed "Jonesy" in one of the five made-for-TV reunion movies shot after *The Waltons* ceased production as a weekly series.

The White Shadow

Series debut: Nov. 27, 1978 (CBS). Final telecast: Aug. 12, 1981 (CBS). 62 episodes.

Never a big ratings winner, this series about an unconventional white basketball coach at an inner-city Los Angeles high school was nonetheless one of the most realistic portrayals of student life ever shown on television and won numerous awards from educational organizations for its straight-forward and mature treatment of controversial subject matter.

Ken Howard, who co-created the series based on his own high school experiences, starred as Ken Reeves, a former second-stringer with the Chicago Bulls who was forced to retire from pro ball after sustaining a serious knee injury. Persuaded by his college pal turned principal Jim Willis (Ed Bernard) to give coaching a shot, Reeves signed on with Carver High. The tough, lower-middle-class environment was about as far from the glamour of pro hoops as he could get, and Reeves initially had difficulty getting through to his players, most of whom attended school only because it was their lone alternative to "the street." Reeves' unorthodox methods often got him into hot water with vice-principal Sybil Buchanan (Joan Pringle), but he persevered and eventually won the kids over to his way of thinking. While basketball was the thread that stitched together each episode, the series was more a study of the choices, conflicts and resolutions familiar to everyone who attended high school in the 1970s. Issues like drugs, crime, bullying, racism and sex all became fodder for the writers, and the young cast did a magnificent job of bringing the stories to life.

The Carver squad was led by star centre Warren Coolidge (Byron Stewart) and his supporting cast included Morris Thorpe (Kevin Hooks), Curtis Jackson (Eric Kilpatrick), Milton Reese (Nathan Cook), Mario "Salami" Pettrino (Timothy Van Patten), Abner Goldstein (Ken Michelman) and Ricky Gomez (Ira Angustain). In the spring of 1980 Jackson was shot to death after witnessing a liquor store robbery shortly before the team won the L.A. city championship. Several of the players then graduated and were seen only sporadically in the 1981 season as coach Reeves began to build a new team from scratch.

TeleTrivia

Byron Stewart, who portrayed hulking Warren Coolidge on *The White Shadow* from 1978 to 1981, used the same name for his character when he joined the cast as an orderly on the hospital drama *St. Elsewhere* in 1984.

The Least You Need to Know

➤ Ten different dogs appeared in the starring role on the long-running series *Lassie*—and all of them were males.

➤ *Room 222* star Lloyd Haynes was cast as the communications officer in the second pilot episode for *Star Trek*.

➤ Two actors portrayed John-Boy on *The Waltons*, at different times.

➤ *The White Shadow* was co-created by actor Ken Howard, who based the series on his own high school experiences in New York.

BOOK 'EM DANNO!

CALL BOX 5-0

Chapter 14

The Right to Remain Violent

In This Chapter

➤ Straight shooters: *The Untouchables*

➤ Perilous paradise: *Hawaii Five-O*

➤ Quite con-trary: *The Rockford Files*

➤ Maximum firepower: *S.W.A.T.*

➤ Takin' it to the streets: *Starsky and Hutch*

Cop shows have been a staple of television drama since the medium's infancy, when *Dragnet, Gangbusters* and the original *Police Story* first focused on the day-to-day activities of law enforcement officers. It didn't take long for the networks to realize they had a winning formula on their hands, and by 1954 there was at least one prime-time police drama airing every night of the week.

In 1957 Darren McGavin put a new spin on the cop show format by becoming TV's first blood-and-guts private investigator in *Mickey Spillane's Mike Hammer* (*Variety* labelled it "a repulsive mixture of blood, violence and sex"), and the following year *The Naked City* debuted on ABC as the first police series shot on location in New York. With a signature opening that intoned "There are eight million stories in the Naked City...," it was a gritty, realistic drama starring John McIntire, James Franciscus and Horace McMahon, and its success paved the way for the likes of *Brenner*, starring Edward Binns and James Broderick as father-and-son cops (1959), and Leslie Nielsen's *The New Breed* (1961).

Despite their proliferation in the mid-1950s, cop shows—with the exception of *Dragnet*—were relegated to the middle of the ratings, largely because they all looked pretty much the same. But at the end of the decade a new entry grabbed a huge audience, beginning with its debut episode and remained popular for four straight years. Unlike its relatively staid contemporaries, this series about the exploits of an elite crime-fighting unit in Depression-era Chicago was filled with gunplay and graphic violence—a winning combination that set the standard for police dramas for the next 20 years.

The Untouchables

**Series debut: Oct. 15, 1959 (ABC). Final telecast: Sept. 10, 1963 (ABC).
114 episodes.**

TV Guide succinctly (and unintentionally) summed up the appeal of *The Untouchables* in its initial review of the series, stating: "In practically every episode a gang leader winds up stitched to a brick wall and full of bullets, or face down in a parking lot and full of bullets, or face up in a gutter and full of bullets, or hung up in an ice box, or run down in the street by a mug at the wheel of a big black Hudson touring car."

Critics whined about the "mindless" violence, educators and public officials were furious over the "romanticized" depiction of bloodthirsty gangsters, and the Italian-American community complained about so many of the hoods having Italian names, but, like *The A-Team* a quarter-century later, this bullet-riddled series was an instant hit.

Freeze Frame

The Untouchables was a spinoff from a two-part dramatization about the fall of Al Capone, which aired on Desilu Playhouse in the spring of 1959.

Set in Chicago in the early 1930s and starring Robert Stack as Treasury Department crime-buster Eliot Ness, *The Untouchables* was the first series supervised by a young producer named Quinn Martin, who went on to develop some of the greatest dramas of the 1960s and '70s, including *The Fugitive, Twelve O'Clock High, The Invaders, The F.B.I.* and *The Streets of San Francisco*. The use of staccato-voiced narrator Walter Winchell to bridge the action and prolonged machine gun shootouts (sometimes three or four in an episode) quickly became hallmarks of *The Untouchables*, and those elements—combined with Stack's wonderfully wooden characterization and the uniform stoicism of his squad of "G-men"—breathed new life into the cop show format that had grown weary after seven years of *Dragnet*.

Agents Martin Flaherty (Jerry Paris), William Youngfellow (Abel Fernandez), Enrico Rossi (Nick Georgiade), Cam Allison (Anthony George) and Lee Hobson (Paul Picerni) made up Ness' squad of "untouchables," so named by a newspaper reporter because they couldn't be bribed or influenced at a time when police corruption was rampant. Another agent named Jack Rossman (Steve London) was a semi-regular, as was notorious mobster Frank "The Enforcer" Nitti (Bruce Gordon), who assumed control of Al Capone's Chicago crime empire in the pilot episode, entitled The Empty Chair. In addition to Gordon, the impressive list of guest stars appearing as thugs included Neville Brand, Nehemiah Persoff, Lloyd Nolan, Clu Galager, William Bendix, James Caan and Peter Falk.

While the series was based on the autobiography of the real-life Eliot Ness, in order to sustain the story line (and maintain the body count) a certain amount of dramatic licence was employed, including having Ness and his crew collar high-profile crime lords like Ma Barker, Dutch Schultz and Bugs Moran—which Stack's real-life counterpart never did. In a two-part episode that really stretched the limits of credibility, Ness and his boys even intervened in the 1933 attempted assassination of President Franklin Roosevelt in far-off Miami! Occasionally these flights of fantasy elicited official protests, as when the FBI complained their agents weren't given proper credit for apprehending Barker and when the estate of Al Capone sued the producers for $1 million for profiting from the use of Big Al's name and image. As a result, during the second season a disclaimer was flashed at the end of each episode stating that some of what the viewer had just seen was "fictionalized." Even with that, controversy dogged the series for the rest of its run, culminating in a threatened advertiser boycott by Italian-American groups if something wasn't done to homogenize the bad guys. That explains why in episodes from the third and fourth seasons there are more hoods named "O'Malley" and "Svenson" than "Petrone" or "Savelli."

It's sad to realize that political correctness was raising its ugly head even way back then.

Notable Quotable

Defiant hood: "I got nothin' to say to you, Ness."

Eliot Ness: "Hmmm...the code of bums...lips sealed tight. You stick to that code and your lips will be sealed tight forever."

Fast Forward

Thirty years after winning an Emmy Award for his unflinching portrayal of Eliot Ness (1960), Robert Stack returned to television as the erudite host of the reality-based crime series *America's Most Wanted*.

Hawaii Five-O

Series debut: Sept. 26, 1968 (CBS). Final telecast: April 26, 1980 (CBS). 270 episodes.

The '70s' equivalent of *The Untouchables* was this solidly written saga of an elite unit of the Hawaiian State Police that answered directly to the governor. Led by unflappable

Freeze Frame

Hawaii Five-O star Jack Lord, who died in 1998 at age 78, previously starred as a rodeo cowboy in the short-lived western *Stoney Burke* (1962–1963). Lord was an accomplished artist and his paintings and sketches are in the permanent collections of more than 40 museums and galleries around the world.

TeleTrivia

The Iolani Palace, which housed the *Five-O* offices during filming of the series, was actually a museum that at one time housed the Hawaiian Legislature.

Steve McGarrett (Jack Lord), the Five-O team also featured detectives Danny "Danno" Williams (James MacArthur), Chin Ho Kelly (Kam Fong), Kono Kalakaua (Zulu) and Ben Kokua (Al Harrington). Che Fong (Harry Endo) was the forensics guru, while Duke Lukela (Herman Wedemeyer) started the series as a uniform cop before graduating to detective. Hawaii Governor Philip Grey (Richard Denning) was the other regular cast member through the duration of the series, and in the final season three new detectives joined the unit: James "Kimo" Carew (William Smith), Truck Kealoha (Moe Keale) and Lori Wilson (Sharon Farrell).

On the way to becoming the longest continuously running police drama in the history of television, *Hawaii Five-O* shattered a trio of long-standing network myths about the genre. First and foremost, it proved that violence ranks a distant second to well-crafted scripts and powerful characters as a hook for viewers. Second, the gorgeous scenery and perpetual sunshine (the series was filmed entirely on location) punctured the belief that police dramas are best set in oppressive, inner-city gloom. Third, the series became the first successful cop show to continue to score big ratings after killing off one of its principal characters (Kam Fong quit at the end of the 1977–1978 season). Another important factor in *Five-O's* success was its methodical approach to presenting ingenious crimes, then neatly meshing the team's equally ingenious methods of solving them.

With the possible exceptions of McGarrett's bullet-proof hair and his trademark expression of "Book 'em, Danno!" at the end of each episode (until MacArthur left the show in 1979), the periodic appearances of Wo Fat (Khigh Dhiegh) rank as the quintessential *Five-O* memory for many Boomers. For 10 years the portly criminal genius eluded McGarrett while building an empire that encompassed everything from prostitution to Cold War military secrets, but in the third-to-last episode, on April 5, 1980, McGarrett posed as a scientist to spring a trap that finally sent Wo Fat to the slammer for good.

The Rockford Files

Series debut: Sept. 13, 1974 (NBC). Final telecast: July 25, 1980 (NBC). 113 episodes.

Everyone remembers two things about this peerless PI series: It's probably the only show in TV history to open with a recording from a telephone answering machine ("This is Jim Rockford. At the tone leave your name and message. I'll get back to you..."), and Rockford charged his clients $200 a day "plus expenses."

In the starring role was handsome James Garner, winner of two Purple Hearts in the Korean War, who parlayed his rugged good looks and easy charm into the lead on the hugely successful western *Maverick* (see Appendix 2) before appearing in several hit movies, including *The Great Escape* and *The Americanization of Emily*. On *The Rockford Files* he portrayed an ex-con who specialized in cracking cases the cops had already closed the book on. He had a talent for digging up evidence that could reverse a verdict or force a file to be reopened, and even though he relied on his friend Det. Dennis Becker (Joe Santo) to provide him with inside information, his investigations often resulted in Becker and the L.A. Police Department being put in an embarrassing situation.

Rockford lived and worked out of a beach-front trailer and his two closest confidants were his father Joe—a.k.a. "Rocky" (Noah Beery Sr.)—a retired truck driver, and his former cell mate, Evelyn "Angel" Martin (Stuart Margolin). One of TV's all-time great weasels, Angel often used his underworld connections to try to help solve Jim's cases but invariably ended up causing more harm than good. Rockford's girlfriend, lawyer Beth Davenport (Gretchen Corbett), was another ally, and when he got beaten up or arrested during the course of his investigations she was always there to nurse his wounds or bail him out of police custody.

What's often overlooked when fans recall the humour and creative plots in this series is that Rockford was a damn fine detective. He didn't like using his gun (he kept it in a cookie jar), but he wasn't shy about getting into fights or engaging in high-speed car chases in his gold Pontiac Firebird. He was a master at talking himself in and out of

TeleTrivia

The theme song for *The Rockford Files*, composed by Mike Post and C. Carpenter, went to No. 10 on Billboard's Hot 100 chart in mid-1975.

Freeze Frame

For his portrayal of "Angel" Martin on *The Rockford Files*, Stuart Margolin won back-to-back Emmy Awards for best supporting actor in a drama in 1979 and 1980. James Garner took the Emmy for outstanding lead actor in a drama in 1977.

situations, and he had enough phony identification and cheesy disguises to cover any contingency. During the final season a cocky PI named Lance White (Tom Selleck) appeared semi-regularly as Rockford's main competition for business, but what might have been an interesting rivalry between the two was never fully explored because Garner abruptly quit the series due to lingering leg injuries caused by doing his own stunts.

S.W.A.T.

Series debut: Feb. 24, 1975 (ABC). Final telecast: June 29, 1976 (ABC). 43 (?) episodes.

Okay, I'll be blunt about it. If you didn't like *S.W.A.T.* you probably were (and possibly still are) a communist sympathizer who thinks there's nothing wrong with spending an evening tuned into vapid crap like *Will and Grace* or *Ally McBeal*. When I think of *S.W.A.T.*, I think of the first time I ever played paint-ball with my brother-in-law Ron "Mad Dog" Flett. We flipped our hats backwards, positioned ourselves high in the windows of a rickety old barn and pretended our air rifles were M-16s so we could pick off the enemy players when they unknowingly stepped into our "kill zone." What a rush!

An acronym for special weapons and tactics, the S.W.A.T. unit, headed up by Lieut. Dan "Hondo" Harrelson (Steve Forrest), brought military-style firepower to the streets of Los Angeles in this action-packed series, which quickly developed a cult following. In theory the S.W.A.T. squad was supposed to be summoned only in situations when the police were outgunned or otherwise couldn't cope, but as the series evolved Harrelson and his fellow black-clad Vietnam vets were almost on regular patrol, prowling the streets in a rolling arsenal and dispatching killers, kidnappers and drug dealers with lethal panache.

Harrelson's second-in-command was Sgt. David "Deke" Kay (Rod Perry), who served as the team's observer and communications specialist. Officer Dominic Luca (Mark Shera) was the ace sniper, while Officer Jim Street (Robert Urich) was the scout. T.J. McCabe (James Coleman) served as an all-purpose backup, and usually got the call to accompany the team on especially dangerous missions.

ABC took a lot of heat over the level of violence on the show, especially in the wake of newspaper reports from all over the country that kids were tape recording the catchy theme song and playing it over and over again as they re-enacted the shoot-outs. The gunplay was cut back considerably in the second season, and along with it went any reason for continuing to tune in.

Fast Forward

Two members of Hondo Harrelson's *S.W.A.T.* unit went on to portray private investigators in successful series of their own. Mark Shera (Luca) co-starred with Buddy Ebsen on *Barnaby Jones* (1976–1980), while Bob Urich (Street) played the lead role of Dan Tanna in *Vega$* and later starred in *Spenser: For Hire.*

Starsky and Hutch

Series debut: Sept. 3, 1975 (ABC). Final telecast: Aug. 21, 1979 (ABC). 88 episodes.

Take two hip bachelors, a gas-guzzling muscle car and humour-laced scripts overflowing with car chases, gun fights and babes (not to mention the bell-bottom pants and a guy named Huggy Bear) and you've got the recipe for *Starsky and Hutch*, the best-loved and worst-acted cop show to ever crack the Nielsen ratings top 10.

A big part of the charm of this series was the chemistry between the two leads. Det. Dave Starsky (Paul Michael Glaser) was a streetwise practical joker who loved junk food almost as much as he loved his cherry-red 1974 Torino. Det. Ken "Hutch" Hutchinson (David Soul) was more refined, preferred health food and had an ear for classical music. Starsky carried a Colt .45 automatic; Hutch's weapon of choice was a .357 Magnum. Together they worked undercover in the scunggiest neighbourhoods of Los Angeles, apprehending dope dealers, pimps, gang leaders and other criminals. Their boss was Capt. Harold Dobey (Bernie Hamilton), and their most reliable informant was Huggy Bear (Antonio Fargas), a former small-time hood who fantasized about being a detective. In the course of their investigations Starsky and Hutch often donned unlikely disguises (once they went to work as hairdressers, another time they were dance instructors), but when they hit the street with guns blazing, the bad guys were mowed down with amazing regularity.

Notable Quotable

Starsky: "You know, I almost quit the police force once."

Hutch: "Why didn't you?"

Starsky: "The only other job I could find was as a defensive end on a Canadian Football League team."

Hutch: "Ouch!"

TeleTrivia

One of David Soul's earliest TV appearances was as the alien Makora in the *Star Trek* episode The Apple (1967). From 1968 to 1970 he co-starred as Joshua Bolt in the adventure series *Here Come The Brides,* and at the peak of his fame on *Starsky and Hutch* he released several successful records, including the top 10 single "Don't Give Up On Us, Baby."

The violence that helped account for the show's astronomical ratings during the first season was so relentless that the U.S. National Parent-Teacher Association organized a nationwide protest that eventually included dozens of churches and youth groups. In Britain, the chief constable of Merseyside complained that on days after the program aired, "police on duty are showing up with sunglasses and wearing their shirts with the cuffs turned up. They've also started driving like bloody maniacs." As a result of the uproar, beginning in the third season the series focused more on the relationship between Starsky and Hutch and less on their shoot-first-ask-questions-later approach to crime-solving. That pretty much sounded a death knell for the show, and by the fourth and final year it was a hollow imitation of its former blood-and-guts glory.

The Least You Need to Know

➤ The estate of Al Capone sued the producers of *The Untouchables* for $1 million in 1960 for profiting from the gangster's name and image.

➤ *Hawaii Five-O* star Jack Lord was an accomplished painter, and his work is exhibited in several galleries and museums around the world.

➤ James Garner, star of *The Rockford Files,* won two Purple Hearts in the Korean War before turning to acting.

➤ The violence on *Starsky and Hutch* was dramatically curtailed following a national protest organized by the American Parent-Teacher Association.

Brains Over Brawn

Just as the tough, no-nonsense modus operandi of Eliot Ness and Steve McGarrett helped pave the way for shows like *Mannix, Kojak* and *Barretta*, there was a comparable parallel for the kinder, gentler police and private-eye dramas that popped up on network television between 1967 and 1976.

The trend toward a less violent approach to solving TV crime actually started at the end of the '50s with the emergence of a slew of detective series in which the heroes relied more on guile than guns to get the job done. The relatively pacifistic tone on shows like *Peter Gunn* (Craig Stevens) and *Checkmate* (Anthony George, Doug McLure) certainly influenced the likes of *T.H.E. Cat* (Robert Loggia), *Burke's Law* (Gene Barry) and *Honey West* (Anne Francis), but it wasn't until the mid-1970s that a hit series built on the premise of feminizing law enforcement brought a whole new meaning to the term "soft" drama.

77 Sunset Strip

Series debut: Oct. 10, 1958 (ABC). Final telecast: Sept. 9, 1964 (ABC). 205 episodes.

This hip, humorous series was the first in a string of glamorous "buddy" private-eye shows—a lineage that included *Hawaiian Eye, Surfside 6* and *Bourbon Street Beat*—but today it's remembered mostly for its cool theme song and Edd Byrnes' goofy portrayal of Gerald Lloyd Kookson III, or "Kookie" for short. Originally scripted as a minor character, Kookie was the teenage parking lot attendant at Dino's, a swank Hollywood eatery. His real goal, however, was to become a P.I., and he eagerly volunteered his services to Stuart Bailey (Efrem Zimbalist Jr.) and Jeff Spencer (Roger Smith), two dashing investigators who worked out of an office next door to Dino's at 77 Sunset Strip.

Bailey was a smooth, sophisticated former army intelligence office who spoke six languages and was a judo expert. Spencer was a lawyer with connections to government intelligence circles, and he too had mastered judo. Together they tackled investigations that took them all over the world, but they always returned to the California sun for some well-deserved R-and-R after a case was solved. Other regulars included a well-connected racetrack tout named Roscoe (Louis Quinn), police lieutenant Gilmore (Byron Keith) and, during the third season, a partner named Rex Randolph (Richard Long). Sexy switchboard operator Suzanne Fabray (Jacqueline Beer) also had a recurring role, but it was the duck-tailed, hip-talking Byrnes who really stole the show with colourful Kookie-isms like "a dark seven" (a bad week), "the ginchiest" (the greatest), "piling up the Zs" (catching some sleep) and "headache grapplers" (aspirin).

In the opening episode of the second season Kookie helped Bailey and Spencer nab a jewel thief by staging a talent show in which he sang a little ditty called "Kookie, Kookie, Lend Me Your Comb." A few weeks later Byrnes teamed up with Connie Stevens to release the song as a single, and it promptly rocketed into the top 10 on the pop

TeleTrivia

In an embarrassing attempt to duplicate Edd Byrnes' musical success, both Roger Smith and Efrem Zimbalist Jr. ventured into the recording studio in 1960. Smith's album was titled *Beach Romance*, while Zimbalist cut a single of *Adeste Fidele*'s. Both bombed. However, the finger-snapping theme for *77 Sunset Strip* became a top 10 hit for composers Mack David and Jerry Livingston.

music charts. When Kookie's role on the show wasn't expanded to keep pace with the character's enormous popularity, Byrnes briefly resigned and was replaced by Troy Donahue. He returned in 1961 when Kookie was made a full partner in the detective agency, and J.R. Hale (Robert Logan) subsequently became the new lot boy at Dino's.

In 1963, when the premise behind *77 Sunset Strip* was showing signs of stagnation, Jack Webb (*Dragnet*) was brought in as producer and the entire cast—with the exception of Efrem Zimbalist Jr.—was fired. Over the last two seasons Zimbalist was featured as a globetrotting freelancer who took on only the toughest international cases, but the ratings continued to plummet.

Freeze Frame

77 Sunset Strip was created by producer-writer Roy Huggins, who also created *The Fugitive* a few years later. The series was introduced in two pilot movies that aired on ABC in 1957–1958, *Anything For Money* and *Girl On The Run*.

The Mod Squad

Series debut: Sept. 24, 1968 (ABC). Final telecast: Aug. 23, 1973 (ABC). 123 episodes.

For a show that was supposed to metaphorically represent the struggle of youth against The Establishment, this action series about three young "hippies" turned undercover cops in Los Angeles quickly morphed into a mainstream police drama that managed to consistently rate among the top 25 network programs—quite a feat, considering the temper of the times.

Each member of the squad—Pete Cochran (Michael Cole), Linc Hayes (Clarence Williams III) and Julie Barnes (Peggy Lipton)—had dropped out of "straight" society and been involved in minor scrapes with the law. Pete, who came from a white, wealthy Beverly Hills family, had been arrested for stealing a car. Linc, big and black, came from the Watts ghetto, where he was arrested during a race riot. Julie was picked up for vagrancy after running away from San Francisco, where her mother was a hooker. Capt. Adam Greer (Tige Andrews) came up with the idea of moulding them into a special unit to infiltrate the counterculture and put the finger on criminals preying on youth and he oversaw their training as auxiliary police officers.

TeleTrivia

The Mod Squad was based on the real-life experiences of series creator Bud Ruskin, a former officer in the L.A. Sheriff's Department who in the 1950s had been part of an undercover narcotics squad made up of young volunteers.

The most interesting thing about this series was watching the three principal characters mesh as a team. Initially there was lot of hostility and mistrust, but as the weeks went by and the tough-but-fair Capt. Greer continued to cut them some slack, the trio gelled as an effective undercover task force. In fact, they got so good at the job that by the final season it was difficult to differentiate between them from the regular cops—except for Linc's huge 'fro. Man, it was solid!

Notable Quotable

"You can't let a job stifle your mind, buddy boy. You've got to keep yourself free for cultural pursuits, you know. Good reading, good music...bowling."

—Det. Mike Stone

The Streets of San Francisco

Series debut: Sept. 16, 1972 (ABC). Final telecast: June 23, 1977 (ABC). 120 episodes.

In much the same way that *The Naked City* elevated the foreboding concrete canyons of New York to star status, this beautifully filmed series turned the hilly highways and byways of the city by the bay into a moody, powerful character. Tautly written and exceptionally well acted, *The Streets of San Francisco* also offered a compelling study in character contrasts within the larger framework of police drama. Det.-Lt. Mike Stone (Karl Malden) was a hard-boiled widower, a 23-year veteran of the San Francisco Police Department assigned to the Bureau of Inspectors Division. His partner was earnest young Insp. Steve Keller (Michael Douglas), an ambitious college grad who sometimes put too much stock in going "by the book" and not enough in what Stone like to call "cop's instinct."

The relationship between Stone and Keller became almost like that of a father and son as the series moved along. The crusty old vet hovered over his protégé like a mother hen, encouraging and scolding with equal conviction, but always with affection. For his part, Keller was able to teach the old guy a thing or two about "new fangled" policing

TeleTrivia

Michael Douglas left *The Streets of San Francisco* to work as a producer on the Oscar-winning film *One Flew Over The Cukoo's Nest*, then went on to become one of the busiest and most respected big-screen actors in the business. One of his finest performances was in *Basic Instinct*—portraying a San Francisco cop!

techniques, while at the same time respecting the value of his partner's considerable life experience. It was a winning formula—but never quite the same after Douglas left the series in 1976 to pursue his movie career. His character was replaced by Insp. Dan Robbins (Richard Hatch).

The Streets of San Francisco was adapted from a highly rated TV movie of the same name that aired in the spring of 1972. Both the movie and the series were based on characters from Carolyn Weston's best-selling novel *Poor, Poor Ophelia*.

Charlie's Angels

Series debut: Sept. 22, 1976 (ABC). Final telecast: Aug. 19, 1981 (ABC). 109 episodes.

"Once upon a time there were three little girls who went to the police academy—and they were each assigned very hazardous duties. But I took them away from all that, and now they work for me. My name is Charlie...."

That's how the voice of Charlie Townsend (John Forsythe) introduced each episode of this series, which opened with scenes of uniform-clad Sabrina Duncan (Kate Jackson), Jill Munroe (Farrah Fawcett) and Kelly Garrett (Jaclyn Smith) performing "hazardous" duties like crosswalk patrol, clerical work and writing up traffic tickets. It was never revealed exactly how Charlie was able to persuade the sexy trio to quit the force and join his private detective agency, but at some point during almost every episode his assistant, John Bosley (David Doyle), would present Sabrina, Kelly and Jill with perfume, jewelry or some other gift as "a small token of Charlie's appreciation." Hmmmmm.

Right from the start the show was chastised for its blatant exploitation of the Angels as sex objects, and there were howls of protest about "jiggle-vision" and "tasteless titillation." But to their credit, creators Ivan Goff and Ben Roberts and executive

TeleTrivia

John Forsythe starred in four series—*Bachelor Father, The John Forsythe Show, To Rome With Love* and *The World Of Survival* (narrator)—before becoming the off-camera voice of Charlie, but he's probably best remembered as suave Blake Carrington on the 1980s' prime-time soap *Dynasty*. Before turning to acting Forsythe performed in radio serials and served as the public address announcer for baseball's Brooklyn Dodgers at Ebbets Field.

Farrah Fawcett and Jaclyn Smith helped put the bounce in Charlie's Angels.

producers Aaron Spelling and Leonard Goldberg never caved to the critics and continued to come up with plots that involved the Angels working undercover as strippers, showgirls, dancers or at any other job that required them to show a lot of skin. There were also plenty of costume changes (lots of bikinis, miniskirts and short shorts) and enough phony stunts set to Henry Mancini's theme music to give the show an undeniably campy look, but in its own way, *Charlie's Angels* was a pretty decent action series.

Sabrina was the "brains" of the team, cool and multi-lingual. Kelly, a former showgirl, exuded a smouldering sexiness that could melt metal, while fresh-faced Jill was the athlete. On most cases they worked undercover, each assuming a "role" that suited her particular talents. Their assignments came from Bosley, who relayed orders received in telephone conversations with Charlie. If they happened to all be in his office, Bosley sometimes put the boss on the speaker phone so the girls could ask questions, but Charlie was never seen during the entire run of the series.

Although *Charlie's Angels* was originally envisioned as a vehicle for Kate Jackson, it quickly became apparent that Farrah Fawcett was the big draw. Virtually overnight, an entire industry sprang up to cash in on her gorgeous blonde mane, perfect smile and voluptuous figure. Everything from T-shirts and bedspreads to shampoo bottles and change purses was adorned with her image, and one particularly alluring cheesecake pose became the biggest-selling celebrity poster of all time. Hoping to parlay that adulation into a movie career, Fawcett walked out on the series after the first season despite having signed a long-term contract. When the smoke from the ensuing lawsuits cleared, she agreed to a make a limited number of guest appearances over the next three seasons, but other actresses were brought in to maintain the three-heroine format. The first "new" Angel was Jill's kid sister, Kris Munroe (Cheryl Ladd), who lasted four years (1977–1981). In 1979 Sabrina left and was replaced by Tiffany Welles (Shelley Hack), the daughter of a Connecticut police chief. Tiffany got the boot after just one year and was replaced by curvaceous Julie Rogers (Tanya Roberts). When the series was cancelled in the summer of 1981, Jaclyn Smith, David Doyle and John Forsythe were the only original cast members left.

TeleTrivia

Kate Jackson's first exposure to episodic TV was in the role of a ghost on the daytime chiller *Dark Shadows* (see Chapter 20). She later had a recurring role as the wife of a young police officer on *The Rookies*, and after *Charlie's Angels* she co-starred with Bruce Boxleitner in *Scarecrow and Mrs. King*.

The Least You Need to Know

➤ Edd Byrnes parlayed his portrayal of Kookie on *77 Sunset Strip* into a hit novelty song in 1960.

➤ *The Mod Squad* was based on the real-life police experience of series creator Bud Ruskin.

➤ Michael Douglas became one of Hollywood's hottest movie stars after leaving the role of Insp. Steve Keller on *The Streets of San Francisco*.

➤ John Forsythe, who provided the voice of Charlie on *Charlie's Angels*, once served as the public address announcer for baseball's Brooklyn Dodgers.

International Intrigue

The Cold War played a dominant role in shaping public attitudes in the 1950s and '60s, so it's not surprising that our ideological struggle with the big, bad Bolsheviks became the foundation for so many series during that era. Still, the networks were pretty selective about whom they cast in a bad light, even in fictitious drama. The unwritten rule was that it was okay to portray Third World terrorists as Marxist pawns or characterize the inhabitants of generic eastern European nations as enslaved automatons, but rarely did any series specifically mention Russia or China. Indeed, on most of the shows discussed in this chapter, the bad guys were merely "the other side," or "our enemies" or, in the case of *The Man From U.N.C.L.E.*, a vaguely foreign organization of murderous psychos who threatened decent folk all over the globe.

By neatly meshing the mythos of the recalcitrant loner of the Old West with the verve and gadgetry of contemporary sci-fi and comic book heroes, espionage shows were the

1960s' lone contribution to original dramatic programming. And thanks to the Cold War overtones, they struck a responsive chord in viewers who needed to be reassured that "our" spy guys were smarter and more courageous that "theirs." As it turned out, it was a recipe for ratings success.

Danger Man/Secret Agent

Series debut: April 5, 1961 (CBS). Final telecast: Sept. 10, 1966 (CBS). 39 half-hour episodes as *Danger Man*, 45 one-hour episodes as *Secret Agent*.

It's only fitting that the star of the television series that helped ignite North America's fascination with James Bond was the actor who turned down an opportunity to portray 007 in the movies before the role was offered to Sean Connery. Patrick McGoohan, though American-born, was the quintessential image of a cool, calculating British agent, and his portrayal of suave loner John Drake in *Danger Man* and *Secret Agent* made him an international superstar. He later parlayed his spy persona into a third series, which ranks as a genuine Boomer classic: *The Prisoner* (see Chapter 19).

On *Danger Man*, Drake was a NATO security investigator assigned to the U.S. Secret Service in Washington, D.C., but since his duties took him all over the world, most of the half-hour episodes were filmed in exotic European locations. Unique among fictional spies of the time, Drake neither carried a gun nor got involved with women. If the need arose he was an expert at boxing and judo, but he usually found ways to solve his cases without resorting to excessive violence. As for falling victim to feminine charms, forget it. He had a deep-rooted sense of ascetic professionalism and conducted himself as a gentleman at all times.

Patrick McGoohan was the quintessential British espionage operative in three series: Danger Man, Secret Agent *and* The Prisoner.

In 1964, after Drake was transferred to the M-19 branch of the British Secret Service, *Danger Man* was expanded to hour-long episodes and the name of the series was changed to *Secret Agent* in the U.S. The longer time-slot allowed the writers to weave more intricate plots around Drake's mission to "preserve world peace and promote brotherhood and better understanding between peoples and nations," but the superior look and quality of the series remained intact.

The Man From U.N.C.L.E.

Series debut: Sept. 22, 1964 (NBC). Final telecast: Jan. 15, 1968 (NBC). 105 episodes.

TeleTrivia

In 1966 singer Johnny Rivers scored a top 10 hit with "Secret Agent Man," the theme song for *Secret Agent*. It was written by Phil Sloan and Steve Barri.

NBC made no secret about the fact that *The Man From U.N.C.L.E.* was rushed into production to cash in on the James Bond craze that swept North America following the release of 007's first movie, *Dr. No*. What's not so well known is that Bond creator Ian Fleming played a role in launching this enormously successful series.

Fleming was having lunch with veteran producer Norman Felton one day in 1963 when Felton brought up the idea of developing a TV series that would combine the look of Alfred Hitchcock's 1959 big-screen spy thriller *North by North-West* with the cool sophistication of the Bond film. It would be an action-adventure series focusing on the exploits of a dashing, handsome hero who worked for a private international anti-crime organization. Fleming thought it sounded good, and even came up with a name for the

TeleTrivia

In the original outline for *The Man From U.N.C.L.E.* drawn up by Norman Felton and Ian Fleming, Napoleon Solo was a Canadian who attended Oxford University on a Rhodes scholarship before joining the intelligence community. Fleming later gave the character a military background with service in the Canadian Highland Regiment, but when the outline was revised under producer Sam Rolfe, Solo's history was rewritten and he became an American operative.

lead character: Napoleon Solo. Felton pitched the idea to NBC and got the green light to proceed, but Fleming was forced to drop out of the project by Eon Productions, the company making the Bond movies. Eon was understandably upset about the similarity of the TV show to their movie franchise, and subsequently tried to block Felton from using any name that included "Solo" because it was used by a minor character in *Goldfinger*. Eventually the hassle was settled, but even as late as 1966 all *U.N.C.L.E.* scripts were scrutinized by NBC's legal beagles to make sure no story line too closely mirrored anything in a Bond novel.

By the time *The Man From U.N.C.L.E.* finally aired, Felton's original concept had been reworked and refined by producer Sam Rolfe and the end result was a show that immediately captured the public's imagination. Robert Vaughn was cast as Napoleon Solo, with blonde-haired Brit David McCallum as his partner, a Russian named Ilya Kuryakin. They worked out of the secret headquarters of the United Network Command for Law and Enforcement (U.N.C.L.E.), located behind Del Floria's tailor shop in New York, and took orders from tweedy Alexander Waverly (Leo G. Carroll). Their cases usually involved ordinary people who suddenly found themselves caught in the middle of international intrigue, and in order to extricate the innocents Solo and Kuryakin employed an endless supply of gadgets and techno-hardware, including tiny two-way transmitters disguised as fountain pens that were voice-activated by the command "Open channel D!" One of their coolest pieces of equipment was a sky-blue, two-seat Piranha sports coupe, outfitted with rocket launchers hidden in the wheel wells and machine guns that popped out of the front and back grills. When Solo and Kuryakin battled agents from T.H.R.U.S.H. (supposedly an acronym for technological hierarchy for the removal of undesirables and subjugation of humanity), they had the latest in state-of-the-art firepower, including the famous "U.N.C.L.E. Special," a plain-looking pistol that could be transformed into several other weapons merely by adding a few attachments.

Freeze Frame

The Man From U.N.C.L.E. was originally developed as a one-star show, because the producers couldn't find an actor with the right "look" to be Napoleon Solo's partner. Robert Vaughn was cast as Solo only after the role was turned down by both Harry Guardino and Robert Culp, and David McCallum, a virtual unknown at the time, landed the part of Ilya Kuryakin when he was spotted wandering around the studio lot with his pal Charles Bronson.

During the first couple of seasons most of the episodes (or "Affairs," as they were designated) were solid adventure yarns that featured an impressive list of guest stars, including Vincent Price, Boris Karloff, Sharon Tate, Jill Ireland, William Shatner and Leonard Nimoy (the last two appeared together in The Project Strigas Affair two years before co-starring in *Star Trek*). Beginning in the fall of 1966, however, *The Man From U.N.C.L.E.* took a cue from *Batman* and became a full-blown exercise in camp, a move that signalled the beginning of the end. The plots got progressively dumber, and when a spinoff series called *The Girl From U.N.C.L.E.* (starring Stephanie Powers as agent April Dancer and Noel Harrison as agent Mark Slade) was introduced midway through the season, it only served to underline just how far this once-respectable show had fallen. In the final season, Lisa Rogers (Barbara Moore) joined the cast as Mr. Waverly's secretary, but the move did nothing to improve the show's ratings. After *The Man From U.N.C.L.E.* was cancelled, its Monday night time-slot was taken up by *Rowan & Martin's Laugh-In* (see Appendix 2), which went on to become one of the biggest comedy hits of the decade.

Fast Forward

In 1983 Robert Vaughn and David McCallum reprised their series roles in the made-for-TV movie The Return of the Man From U.N.C.L.E.: The Fifteen Years Later Affair. Leo G. Carroll had passed away by the time the movie was made, so Patrick Macnee, late of The Avengers, stepped in as the new head of U.N.C.L.E., Sir John Raleigh.

I Spy

Series debut: Sept. 15, 1965 (NBC). Final telecast: Sept. 2, 1968 (NBC). 82 episodes.

Considering the racial climate in the United States at the time, this was truly a landmark series. Kelly Robinson (Robert Culp) and Alexander Scott (Bill Cosby) were globetrotting undercover agents who specialized in sniffing out and defusing threats to American security in foreign countries. Their cover was unique: Robinson, a former Princeton law student, posed as a top-ranked tennis professional while Scott, a multi-lingual Rhodes scholar, was his trainer. While not quite as dashing or mysterious as John Drake or Napoleon Solo, these guys were dedicated and resourceful—and not above having a little fun while on a case.

Fast Forward

Bill Cosby won three Emmy Awards for his role as Alexander Scott, then went on to star as Cliff Huxtable on *The Cosby Show* 20 years later. To true Boomers, however, he'll always first and foremost be TV's all-time most annoying huckster of instant

Because *I Spy* was the first network series to give a black star equal billing with a white counterpart, NBC fretted over such details as showing the two men sharing a meal or a hotel room or going out together on a double date. To soften the impact of the breakthrough concept, particularly in the Deep South, most of the stories were set in foreign lands and Culp's character was clearly portrayed as being in charge. Still, *I Spy* was the first of a long line of black-white "buddy" shows that shattered the master/servant image of Jack Benny and Rochester, and the series paved the way for minority actors to land prominent roles on the likes of *Mission: Impossible, The Green Hornet, Star Trek* and *Mannix*.

The Avengers

Series debut: Sept. 1961 (BBC in Britain), March 28, 1966 (ABC in the United States) Final telecast: Sept. 15, 1969. 161 episodes.

Talk about lasting impressions! To this day, reruns of *The Avengers* air in France under the title *Chapeau melon et Bottes de Cuir* (Bowler Hat and High Leather Boots). In Germany, the series is called *Mit Schirm, Charm und Melone* (With Umbrella, Charm and Bowler Hat). And on the Internet, vintage posters of lithe, leggy, leather-clad Diana Rigg are prized collectors' items.

Wry and sophisticated, *The Avengers* was a very British spy fantasy that in many ways out-Bonded the venerable Mr. Bond. There was a stylish cheekiness about this show that

John Steed (Patrick Macnee) and Emma Peel (Diana Rigg) put some elegance into espionage as The Avengers.

lent charm to even the most outrageous story lines, which encompassed everything from man-eating plants to giant robots. As co-producer Brian Clemens observed: "We admit to only one class...and that is the upper. Because we are a fantasy, we have not shown women being killed, nor have we shown policemen in uniform or coloured men. And you will not see anything as common as blood-spilling. We have no social conscience at all...."

When the series was launched in 1961, John Steed (Patrick Macnee) was a mere sidekick for Dr. David Keel (Ian Hendry), but when Hendry left after the first season and the debonair Macnee moved into the starring role, Honor Blackman joined the cast as Steed's partner, widowed anthropologist and judo expert Cathy Gale. Her trademark wardrobe—a form-fitting leather jumpsuit and high boots—quickly became a sensation, and along with Steed's bowler hat, ever-present umbrella and Savile Row suits, the "look" of *The Avengers* was permanently established. Beneath the veneer of professionalism (Steed always addressed her as "Mrs. Gale") there was also a hint of sexual attraction between the partners, and it only intensified after Blackman left in 1964 to pursue a movie career and was replaced by Diana Rigg. When the producers met to come up with a name for the new character somebody suggested it should be one that reflected the statuesque Rigg's "obvious man appeal." In the transcript from that meeting the suggestion was noted as "Diana's m-appeal"— which became Emma Peel. Like Cathy Gale, "Mrs. Peel" was sexy, sophisticated and a widow—at least she thought so until March 20, 1968, when her long-lost husband was found alive in the Brazilian jungle. The episode that saw her bid a bittersweet farewell to Steed (The Forget-Me Knot) also introduced voluptuous young Tara King (Linda Thorson) as his new partner, and "Mother" (Patrick Newell) subsequently joined the cast as the duo's wheelchair-bound boss.

The original run of *The Avengers* ended in 1969, but six years later a retooled version of the series returned as *The New Avengers*, with Macnee reprising his role as Steed but leaving most of the action to his younger assistants, Mike Gambit (Gareth Hunt) and the lovely Purdy (Joanna Lumley).

TeleTrivia

In a case of life imitating art, Honor Blackman's first major film role after quitting *The Avengers* was as Pussy Galore in the James Bond thriller *Goldfinger*.

Freeze Frame

Future *Monty Python* alumnus and *Fawlty Towers* creator John Cleese shows up as the guest star in a comical episode of *The Avengers* with the rather unlikely title of Look (Stop Me If You've Heard This One), But There Were These Two Fellers....

TeleTrivia

The Green Hornet was renamed *The Kato Show* when it was sold into syndication in the Far East, and his exposure in the series helped Bruce Lee become a huge star in Asia. Lee later had a recurring role as James Franciscus' self-defence instructor on *Longstreet* (1971–1972), but he died in 1973 while filming an action movie in Hong Kong.

TeleTrivia

According to George Trendle, who created both characters, *The Green Hornet* is a direct descendant of *The Lone Ranger*. In the original radio version of the Hornet, Britt Reid was the son of Dan Reid, whose uncle John was "the Masked Rider of the Plains."

The Green Hornet

Series debut: Sept. 9, 1966 (ABC). Final telecast: July 14, 1967 (ABC). 26 episodes.

With a mandate "to protect the lives and rights of decent citizens," the Green Hornet (Van Williams) and his trusty driver/sidekick Kato (martial arts master Bruce Lee) prowled the streets in a hopped-up '66 Chrysler Imperial called Black Beauty in this prime-time adaptation of the exploits of George Trendle's radio hero. The Hornet's alter-ego was handsome young Britt Reid, owner of a TV station and publisher of The Daily Sentinel. Only Kato and District Attorney Scanlon (Walter Brooke) knew of his dual identity, and they were sworn to secrecy because the police considered the Hornet a criminal. Crusty investigative reporter Mike Axford (Lloyd Gough) and Reid's secretary, Lenore Case (Wende Wagner), were likewise convinced the emerald enforcer was a bad guy and they were constantly pushing for the newspaper to take an anti-Hornet editorial stand.

The Green Hornet was produced by William Dozier and looked very much like his other series, *Batman*, minus the campiness. He succeeded in creating an edgier, more menacing look, but the story lines were weak and formulaic. Even with an awesome arsenal that included a nifty non-lethal gas gun, a "stinger" sound weapon that utilized high-pitched echoes to immobilize opponents and a bunch of equally cool gadgets aboard Black Beauty, the Green Hornet and Kato were usually limited to battling petty criminals like bank robbers and jewel thieves, and the highlight of most episodes was Bruce Lee's incredible fight scenes.

"I think a major mistake was that the network didn't give the show an hour-long time-slot," Williams recalled in an interview years later. "They could have done so much more with it, like having the Hornet fight crime on an international scale like James Bond. Instead, they just set up a very simple plot a very simple introduction of the Green Hornet to that plot and the rest of the show was spent figuring out how to solve the crime using all the gimmicks...basically because they wanted to sell the merchandising."

Mission: Impossible

**Series debut: Sept. 17, 1966 (CBS). Final episode: Sept. 8, 1973 (CBS).
168 episodes.**

Set to one of the most recognized instrumental themes in television history, episodes of this ground-breaking series opened with a hand striking a match and lighting a fuse. That was the signal to override all other thought processes for the next 60 minutes, because the plots on *Mission: Impossible* were so intricately woven, so deliciously textured, that they required total concentration to follow. Acting out those plots were people who would lie, cheat, steal, subvert—even kill—to achieve their goals...and they were the good guys! I always loved this show because it had the balls to show that the end justified the means—at least on TV. It was cold and calculating, with no hint of remorse or redeeming social values. It was strictly about getting the job done, any way you could. It was wonderful.

In an early outline for the series he originally called Briggs' Squad, creator Bruce Geller summed up the concept: "[The team] was formerly a Special Forces group that performed wartime missions, often incredibly hazardous and totally without reward because the government of the United States must disavow any knowledge of these particular activities. Once, in a country in a crisis, the group of men were pulled together to do a job. It was only the first job of five years' work under the leadership of Lt.-Col. David Briggs, for what had come to be known, unofficially, as Briggs' Squad."

After extensive revisions and a couple of name changes, first to IMF (for "Impossible Missions Force") then finally to Mission: Impossible, Geller got the green light from CBS to shoot a pilot episode. However, when it came time to choose between his show and a police drama called *Nightwatch* (starring Carroll O'Connor), CBS was leaning heavily toward the latter—especially since *Mission* came with an "astronomical" price tag of $170,000 per episode. In the end, it took a veiled threat from Lucille Ball to finally get the network to acquiesce. *Mission* was being produced at Ball's Desilu Studios, so when CBS waffled on picking up the series, the flamboyant redhead speculated in a newspaper interview that she might pull the plug on *The Lucy Show*, one of the network's highest rated programs. Not surprisingly, within days of Ball's announcement, a deal was struck.

Each episode of *Mission: Impossible* opened with Briggs receiving a recorded message outlining the top-secret assignment and providing background information on the "target." The message concluded with the voice (Bob Johnson) stating: "Your mission, Dan, should you decide to accept it, is to——————. As always, should you or any member of your I.M. Force be caught or killed, the secretary will disavow any knowledge of your actions. This recording will self-destruct in five seconds...." After watching the message go up in a puff of smoke, Briggs would open his briefcase and leaf through dossiers of prospective operatives, but he invariably picked the same four: master of disguise Rollin Hand (Martin Landau); electronics wizard Barney Collier (Greg Morris); strongman Willie Armitage (Peter Lupus); and the beautiful and versatile Cinnamon Carter (Barbara Bain).

TeleTrivia

Mission: Impossible returned to the airwaves in 1988, with a made-in-Australia version starring Peter Graves, Terry Markwell, Tony Hamilton, Thaa Penghlis and Phil Morris—the real-life son of Greg Morris. The disappointing effort was cancelled after 35 episodes.

After the first season Steven Hill was cut loose and the character of Dan Briggs was replaced by Jim Phelps (Peter Graves), but the basic format was unchanged. In the early years there was a definite political tone to the series, as almost every week the team was entrusted with saving a tiny (fictitious) nation from the clutches of communism. The plots were always incredibly complex and required split-second timing, and as more cast changes took place it was interesting to see how each new character filled the bill. The real-life husband-and-wife team of Landau and Bain quit over a contract dispute in 1969, and over the last four years of the show the new faces included Paris (Leonard Nimoy), Doug (Sam Elliott), Dana Lambert (Lesley Ann Warren), Casey (Lynda Day George) and Mimi Davis (Barbara Anderson). Willie and Barney stuck it out for the entire run, but by the final season, when the team was concentrating more on domestic crime, the need for their special talents had been drastically reduced.

The Saint

Series debut: May 21, 1967 (NBC). Final telecast: Sept. 12, 1969 (NBC). 118 episodes.

Roger Moore, who succeeded Sean Connery as the big-screen James Bond, portrayed "international adventurer" Simon Templar in this tongue-in-cheek series, which was basically a hybrid of *The Man From U.N.C.L.E.* and Robin Hood. Dashing, urbane and wealthy, Templar was also a thief—but he used his talent only to avenge lesser mortals who had been swindled, cheated or otherwise taken advantage of by powerful criminal adversaries. His calling card—a stick-figure man with a halo—was as well known to international police forces as it was to the crime syndicates, but he was often contracted by the "good guys" to right a wrong...even if it meant breaking a few laws along the way.

Freeze Frame

The character of The Saint was first introduced by author Leslie Charteris in his 1928 novel *Meet the Tiger*. The TV role was offered to both David Niven and Patrick McGoohan before Roger Moore was cast as Simon Templar.

Moore was a perfect choice to play Templar, imbuing the character with the same unflappable coolness and dry wit he later brought to 007. He was often accompanied by a beautiful girl (Honor Blackman and Julie Christie were two of them) while zipping around in a yellow Volvo P1800 (licence plate ST1), and he routinely dispatched kidnappers, thieves and blackmailers with a stylish kick to the gut or a left hook to the head.

The Saint wasn't a particularly violent show, but the exotic settings and pricey props made it one of the most expensive productions of the era. Joining Moore as the only other regular cast member was Ivor Dean, who portrayed Chief Inspector Teal of Scotland Yard.

TeleTrivia

Roger Moore was no stranger to American audiences when NBC imported *The Saint*. In 1959–1960 he co-starred as suave Silky Harris on the adventure series *The Alaskans*, and the following year he had a recurring role as Cousin Beauregard on James Garner's hit western *Maverick* (see Appendix 2).

The Least You Need to Know

➤ John Drake didn't carry a gun on *Danger Man*.

➤ In the original outline for *The Man From U.N.C.L.E.*, Napoleon Solo was a Canadian Rhodes scholar.

➤ Bill Cosby won three Emmy Awards for his portrayal of Alexander Scott on *I Spy*.

➤ *Green Hornet* co-star Bruce Lee died while making a martial arts movie in Hong Kong in 1973.

➤ A veiled threat from Lucille Ball helped persuade CBS to purchase *Mission: Impossible*.

➤ The starring role in *The Saint* was originally offered to David Niven.

Heroic Healers

Similar to the way shows about cops and spies had their roots in radio serials and pioneering video anthologies, the medical dramas that would become a cornerstone of Boomer TV evolved from the earliest forays into what today would be called reality-based programming.

Richard Boone's *Medic* (1954–1956) dramatized actual case histories from the Los Angeles County Medical Association in order to give viewers an inside look at the workings of a major metropolitan hospital (Boone's intro to each episode included this solemn description of the doctor: "Guardian of birth, healer of the sick and comforter of the aged..."), while *Medical Horizons*, hosted by Quincy Howe and Don Goddard (1955–1956) was billed as a "public affairs" program to keep viewers abreast of the latest scientific advancements. But the earliest entry on the medical show menu was *The Doctor* (1952–1953), an obscure, unadorned anthology hosted by Warner Anderson that focused on the ways in which physical and mental ailments can impact everyday life. In what was hailed as a revolutionary move at the time, Anderson appeared as The Doctor at the beginning and end of each dramatized segment to set the scene and discuss the outcome—often advising viewers who were experiencing anything similar to what they'd just watched to "make an appointment with a real medical professional."

These earliest of medical shows were popular because they helped demystify the roles of doctors and nurses in society, but it wasn't until two young surgeons on rival networks grabbed the public's attention in the fall of 1961 that programming honchos recognized the correlation between higher pulse rates and higher ratings, especially among female viewers. It was a prognosis the networks took to heart, and one that continues to be just as applicable today.

Dr. Kildare

Series debut: Sept. 28, 1961 (NBC). Final telecast: Aug. 30, 1966 (NBC). 200 episodes (142 one-hour episodes, 58 half-hour episodes).

Dr. James Kildare (Richard Chamberlain) was a studious young intern honing his craft at Blair General Hospital in this immensely popular series, which was based on the dozen or so Dr. Kildare movies from the 1930s and '40s. Showing him the ropes was Dr. Leonard Gillespie (Canadian-born Raymond Massey), while Kildare's colleagues from med school, Dr. Simon Agurski (Eddie Ryder) and Dr. Tom Gerson (Jud Taylor), were also along for the ride. Receptionist Susan Deigh (Joan Patrick) tried unsuccessfully to get any of the trio of intense young doctors to notice her during the first season, but her character was written out (along with Argurski and Gerson) when the focus of the show shifted away from the hospital and onto the personal lives of the patients and their families.

Produced by Norman Felton, who went on to create *The Man From U.N.C.L.E.*, *Dr. Kildare* took a realistic approach to its subject matter, with dramatic freeze-frame titles and lots of close-up photography of real medical procedures. The program raised a few eyebrows when the odd patient was "lost" in the early years, but by the 1965–1966 season, when the series was airing twice a week and Kildare had been promoted to resident surgeon (specializing in internal medicine), it had become more of a soap opera, with a heavy emphasis on overdramatized story lines and fewer scripts exploring the student-teacher relationship between Kildare and Gillespie, which was largely responsible for the show's initial appeal.

At the peak of its five-year run, *Dr. Kildare* routinely grabbed a weekly audience of 20 million viewers, and Chamberlain averaged more than 50,000 fan letters per month—mostly from adoring females. So closely did the actor become identified with the role that strangers often approached him for advice about real medical problems. After leaving the series Chamberlain concentrated on reviving his stage and big-screen career (*Hamlet*, *The Three Musketeers*), but in the late 1970s and early '80s he returned to television as the king of the mini-series, starring in epic dramas like *Centennial* and *Shogun* and made-for-TV movies like *The Count of Monte Cristo* and *The Man In The Iron*

Mask before notching his greatest success as the tragic Father Ralph de Bricassart in *The Thorn Birds*.

In 1972 a short-lived (and highly forgettable) remake called *Young Doctor Kildare* was syndicated, starring Mark Jenkins in the title role and Gary Merrill as Dr. Gillespie.

Ben Casey

Series debut: Oct. 2, 1961 (ABC). Final telecast: March 21, 1966 (ABC). 153 episodes.

"Man...Woman...Birth...Death...Infinity!"

Those five words opened each episode of *Ben Casey*, spoken over dramatic scenes of the wards and operating room at County General Hospital. Like *Dr. Kildare*, much of the success of this series was due to the chemistry between the handsome lead (Vince Edwards) and his wise old mentor, Dr. David Zorba (Sam Jaffe), but in terms of pure medical drama, *Ben Casey* was by far the better show, and after the first season it consistently ranked higher in the ratings. Right from the start it tackled controversial subjects like abortion, drug dependency and euthanasia, and the stark photography and no-frills production values gave it a relentless edginess that was never matched on Richard Chamberlain's show. As one review in *Time* magazine noted: "[*Ben Casey*] accurately captures the feeling of sleepless intensity of a major metropolitan hospital."

At the beginning of the 1965–1966 season the demands of playing Dr. Zorba forced 74-year-old Sam Jaffe to quit the series, and Dr. Daniel Freeland (Franchot Tone) replaced him as County General's chief of surgery. Also joining the cast was a beautiful young patient named Jane Hancock (Stella Stevens), who awoke from a 13-year coma to fall in

Handsome Dr. Ben Casey (Vince Edwards) could always count on sage advice from County General Hospital's chief of surgery, Dr. David Zorba (Sam Jaffe).

Freeze Frame

Ben Casey was the first medical show to be widely merchandised. Fans could buy ultra-cool Casey surgical shirts, which featured a trendy off-centre row of buttons, and Edwards even recorded a best-selling album, *Vince Edwards Sings*. The rivalry between Drs. Casey and Kildare also inspired a 1962 novelty song called "Dr. Kildare! Dr. Casey! You Are Wanted for Consultation," which became a minor hit.

love with Ben. Her arrival on the scene put an end to any lingering hint of romance between Casey and Dr. Maggie Graham (Bettye Ackerman), but it also opened up a love triangle between Casey, Hancock and ambitious young Dr. Mike Rogers (Ben Piazza). Albeit unintentionally, all those elements combined to give the show the same demeaning soap opera look as *Dr. Kildare*, and the audience responded by changing channels.

Four years after *Ben Casey* was cancelled, Edwards returned to series TV as a hip, young psychiatrist running a crisis centre for inner-city teens on *Matt Lincoln* (1970–1971), but his subsequent acting endeavours were mostly limited to guest appearances and made-for-TV movies. In a 1988 interview he recalled how unprepared he was for the runaway success of *Ben Casey*. "My picture was on the cover of *Look* and *Life* magazines," he said. "I went from obscurity to fame literally overnight. What a cultural shock that was. It just exploded. I was living in a room at a friend's house, and I was totally unprepared for everything that happened."

Edwards died of cancer in 1996 at age 68.

Marcus Welby, M.D.

Series debut: Sept. 23, 1969 (ABC). Final episode: May 11, 1976 (ABC). 172 episodes.

After starring for eight years as prime-time's favourite dad on *Father Knows Best* (see Chapter 1), Robert Young came out of retirement to bring the same warm empathy and folksy charm to the lead role on this series about a veteran general practitioner in Santa Monica, California. Assisting him was Dr. Steve Kiley (James Brolin), a rather somber recent medical graduate who during the first season contracted to work with Welby for one year before resuming his training as a neurologist. He ended up staying, of course, and for seven years the tandem of Welby and Kiley dealt with an astonishing variety of ailments and situations that must have made them the envy of every other G.P. in America—everything from leukemia and autistic children to LSD paranoia and faith healing. Role reversal is what made them interesting. Dr. Welby was the more daring of the two, often resorting to radical methods of "whole patient" treatment, much to the chagrin of his young by-the-book colleague. Nurse-receptionist Consuelo Lopez (Elena Verdugo) often found herself caught in the middle, as did Nurse Kathleen Faverty (Sharon Gless), who joined the cast in 1974.

During the first season dapper Dr. Welby was wooed by Myra Sherwood (Anne Baxter), but the romantic undertones didn't really jibe with his grandfatherly image and she soon departed. Dr. Kiley, on the other hand, was a veritable chick magnet and in the episode that aired on Oct. 21, 1975, he married Janet Blake (Pamela Hensley), the public-relations director at Hope Memorial Hospital.

In its time, *Marcus Welby, M.D.* was the biggest hit in the history of the ABC network, and became the first ABC series to be ranked the No. 1 prime-time program for an entire season (1970–1971). Held in high esteem by viewers and competitors alike, it was also regularly saluted on the series that succeeded it at the top of the ratings. Between 1972 and 1976, Edith Bunker (Jean Stapleton) made numerous references to *Marcus Welby* on the mammoth CBS hit *All In The Family*.

Medical Center

Series debut: Sept. 24, 1969 (CBS). Final telecast: Sept. 6, 1976. 178 episodes.

The youth vs. experience tension on this fast-paced drama was provided by Dr. Joe Gannon (Chad Everett) and Dr. Paul Lochner (James Daly), chief of staff at the generic Medical Center, attached to a large university complex in Southern California. Lochner was a pedantic, compassionate perfectionist, while Gannon, an associate professor of surgery, was more apt to follow his instincts. Though they were close friends as well as colleagues, those traits often put them on opposite sides of an issue. In the second season Dr. Gannon also became director of the university's student health service, which provided more fodder for the youth-vs.-experience story lines. Several secondary female characters came and went over the first few seasons, including Nurse Chambers (Jayne Meadows), Nurse Courtland (Chris Hutson) and Nurse Bascomb (Louise Fitch), but when Nurse Wilcox (Audrey Totter) joined the cast in 1972 she became a permanent fixture and eventually achieved co-star status.

Emergency!

Series debut: Jan. 22, 1972 (NBC). Final telecast: Sept. 3, 1977 (NBC). 134 (?) episodes.

The day-to-day activities of Squad 51 of the Los Angeles County Fire Department's Paramedical Rescue Service was the focus of this venerable Jack Webb–produced series, which won a loyal audience thanks to strong acting and an imaginative semi-documentary look. Each episode included at least three and sometimes as many as five interwoven incidents, most of which required the attention of paramedics Roy DeSoto (Kevin Tighe) and John Gage (Randolph Mantooth). Serious cases were transferred to the emergency staff at Rampart Hospital, headed by Dr. Kelly Brackett (Robert Fuller), Dr. Joe Early (Bobby Troup) and Nurse Dixie McCall (Julie London). Fireman Chet Kelly (Tim Donnelly) was a regular at the Squad 51 response station, along with the unit's

Freeze Frame

Julie London was married to co-star Bobby Troup on *Emergency!*, which was produced by her former husband, Jack London.

mascot, a scruffy pooch named Boots.

Like *Adam-12*, another Webb production, *Emergency!* offered an interesting study in contrasts. Gage was quiet, cool and meticulous, while DeSoto was a boisterous take-charge type. Back at the hospital, Dr. Brackett's icy calm provided a nice counterpoint to the more outgoing Dr. Early, who was a neurosurgeon, and vivacious Nurse McCall. The overall tone of the show was serious and fast-paced, but it still allowed room for comic interplay between the characters, which helped break up the tension.

After the weekly series was cancelled, special two-hour movie versions of *Emergency!* were aired on NBC in 1978, and from 1973 to 1976 an animated spinoff titled *Emergency +4* aired on Saturday mornings.

The Least You Need to Know

➤ At the peak of his popularity as the star of *Dr. Kildare*, Richard Chamberlain averaged 50,000 fan letters per month.

➤ During the final season of *Ben Casey*, the lead character's love interest was a woman (Stella Stevens) who woke up from a 13-year coma.

➤ *Marcus Welby, M.D.* was the first series in the history of the ABC network to be ranked No. 1 through an entire year.

➤ *Emergency!* was spun off into a Saturday morning animated series.

Part 4
Superb Sci-fi

TV science fiction can trace its lineage back to Captain Video and His Video Rangers, *which debuted on the DuMont network June 27, 1949, and aired an astounding 1,427 episodes before it was cancelled on April 1, 1955. Even though nearly one-third of those shows were only 15 minutes in length (the rest were a full half-hour), that's still a production record that will never be equalled outside daytime soap operas.*

As the self-styled "Guardian of the Safety of the Universe," Capt. Video (Richard Coogan, later Al Hodge) was a 21st-century scientific genius who operated out of a secret mountain hideaway with his trusty sidekick, The Ranger (Don Hastings). Their headquarters was stocked with all the futuristic gizmos and gadgetry required to thwart adversaries like Mook the Moon Man, Kul of Eos and Dr. Pauli (Bran Mossen, Hal Conklin), evil head of the Astroidal Society, and when the need arose they could summon their army of Video Rangers by sending a message through the opticon scillometer or signalling via the remote carrier beam, which allowed the Captain to "see" who was out there. The props and special effects were terrible (the Opticon Scillometer was just a hunk of tubing with some cheesy knobs attached, and most of the controls aboard Capt. Video's space ship,

The Galaxy, were painted on flimsy cardboard panels), but the show was so popular that within two months the live episodes were airing five nights per week. Captain Video *also spawned TV's first line of mail-in viewer premiums, including plastic replicas of weapons and helmets, secret decoder rings, and star maps of the far reaches of the galaxy.*

CBS took a cue from the success of DuMont's star-faring hero to launch Tom Corbett, Space Cadet *on Oct. 2, 1950, and the series about a teenage student at the World Space Academy promptly rocketed to the top of its (three-nights-per-week) 7 p.m. time-slot, thanks in no small part to a generous budget that allowed for realistic effects like blastoffs and weightlessness. A few months later ABC unveiled* Space Patrol, *starring Ed Kemmer as Commander Buzz Corey of the United Planets of the Universe and Lyn Osborn as his exuberant pal, Cadet Happy ("Smokin' rockets, Commander!"). While all these shows were targeted at kids, it quickly became apparent the escapist "space operas" were also attracting a lot of older viewers, so in the summer of 1951 ABC committed the 9:30–10 p.m. time-slot on Friday nights to* Tales Of Tomorrow, *network television's first science-fiction anthology series for adults.*

Tales Of Tomorrow *was an immediate hit, attracting name performers like Lon Chaney Jr., Boris Karloff, Rod Steiger, Leslie Nielsen and Lee J. Cobb to perform both classic and modern stories of the strange, the supernatural and the unexplained. Episodes with titles like* The Monsters From Mars *and* The Flying Saucer *painted a decidedly darker portrait of the future than viewers were accustomed to seeing on* Captain Video *or* Space Patrol, *but the "what if?" format proved to be an audience magnet. Before long the other networks were experimenting with so-called "speculative" sci-fi, and the groundwork was laid for the rapid onslaught of some of the greatest and most thought-provoking series in the realm of Boomer TV.*

(For a refresher course on the classic openings for several of the shows discussed in this section, see Appendix 3.)

Chapter 18

The Sky's No Limit

In This Chapter

➤ Cosmic calamity: *Lost In Space*

➤ The final frontier: *Star Trek*

➤ Aliens among us: *The Invaders*

➤ Interstellar soap opera: *Battlestar Galactica*

Television's fascination with space exploration certainly predated the launch of *Sputnik 1*, but it wasn't until the Russian satellite became the first man-made object to orbit the Earth on Oct. 4, 1957, that millions of viewers woke up to the realization that hey, maybe the stuff we'd been watching on *Space Patrol* and *Tales Of Tomorrow* wasn't so far-fetched after all. The glut of manned missions that started a couple of years later only underlined what TV had been telling us all along: there was a whole big universe out there, just waiting for us to plunder and pollute with human pride and prejudice.

Although the concept of exploring "out there" was probably the most overworked plot device in TV's first tentative forays into science fiction, viewers never tired of it. Borrowing heavily from the schlocky paranoia movies of the day, formulaic depictions of courageous Americans single-handedly rescuing the planet from the nightmare of alien attack were oddly uplifting during a period when the Soviets were winning the space race and the Red Chinese were engaged in sabre-rattling in Korea and Southeast Asia.

TeleTrivia

Al Hodge was a struggling journeyman actor when he was chosen to replace Richard Coogan on *Captain Video and His Video Rangers* in 1951, but overnight he became a major star. So closely did Hodge become associated with the role of the clean-cut defender of truth and freedom that when he testified before the U.S. Congressional Committee on Television Violence in 1954, the senators routinely addressed him as "Captain." In later years Hodge blamed the show for stereotyping him, and claimed he couldn't even appear in a cigarette commercial "because nobody wants to believe the great Capt. Video enjoys a smoke." He died bitter and broke in 1979 at the age of 66.

Television sci-fi might have ridden that one-dimensional course for a lot longer had it not been for two visionaries: Irwin Allen and Gene Roddenberry. Both were blessed with a talent for crafting the kind of imaginative drama that forced viewers to sit up and notice, yet both were also chastised by critics for bucking what had become a predictable (and profitable) trend. No matter. When Boomers wax nostalgic about the science-fiction programs that echo loudest in their collective consciousness, what the critics had to say means nothing. The respective creations of Allen and Roddenberry will be no less intriguing a generation from now than when they first put pen to paper all those years ago.

Notable Quotable

"Danger! Danger, Will Robinson!"
—The robot's standard warning to the youngest member of the Jupiter II expedition

"There is nothing you can do with a really dedicated misfit."
—The robot again, sizing up Dr. Smith

Lost In Space

Series debut: Sept. 15, 1965 (CBS). Final telecast: Sept. 11, 1968 (CBS). 83 episodes.

Due to overpopulation, by 1997 Earth was rapidly running out of food, water and living space. From two million volunteer applicants an American family was selected by an international committee to embark on a five-year voyage aboard the Jupiter II. Their mission was to survey a planet on the perimeter of the Alpha Centauri star system for eventual human colonization. Astrophysicist John Robinson (Guy Williams) headed the expedition, along with his wife Maureen (June Lockhart) and their children, 20-year-old Judy (Marta Kristen), 11-year-old Penny (Angela Cartwright) and 9-year-old Will (Billy Mumy). Also aboard was handsome geologist/pilot Maj. Don West (Mark Goddard) and a seven-foot robot programmed to control the ship's navigational controls.

Unbeknownst to the Robinsons and West, the snivelling, weasely Dr. Zachary Smith (Jonathan Harris) had snuck aboard the ship prior to blastoff and hidden in the lower decks, where he attempted to reprogram the robot to kill the family—presumably so he could deliver the Jupiter II to a foreign power. Smith's sabotage backfired when the ship blasted off prematurely, but by the time the others regained control and captured him, they were far off course—hopelessly lost in space.

Notable Quotable

"Have no fear, Smith is here!"
—Dr. Smith

"You bubble-headed booby! I should turn you into a cosmic can-opener!"
—Dr. Smith again, sizing up the robot

After some initial soul-searching about what to do with their unwanted stowaway, the Robinsons cut an uneasy truce with Smith, and for the remainder of the series his attempts to undermine the expedition and return to Earth provided the secondary story line in what became progressively campier weekly adventures. Drifting from planet to planet (all of which seemed to have an oxygen-based atmosphere), the space family Robinson made contact with dozens of bizarre alien life-forms, battled a colourful assortment of monsters and survived everything from time warps to marauding bands

TeleTrivia

Lost In Space was the second of four sci-fi shows created and produced by Irwin Allen during the 1960s (see Chapter 19) and the first to use "recycled" monsters as a budget-saving measure. During a brief period when *Lost In Space*, *Voyage To The Bottom of the Sea*, *The Time Tunnel* and *Land of the Giants* were all in simultaneous production, it was possible to see a slightly revamped version of the same Allen creature on two or three shows within the span of a couple of weeks!

of "space pirates." The low point came in the third-to-last episode (The Great Vegetable Rebellion), when they sought haven on a lush planet, only to be captured by giant carrots who spoke flawless English and threatened to transform them into plants.

They just don't make 'em like that any more.

Star Trek

Series debut: Sept. 8, 1966 (NBC). Final telecast: Sept. 2, 1969 (NBC). 79 episodes.

I could easily fill the rest of this book with pithy commentary on how and why *Star Trek* has become the most revered of all Boomer classics. The original series spawned the most successful franchise in entertainment history, with movies, merchandising, conventions, cast reunions—you name it and somebody, somewhere, has put a *Star Trek* spin on it and made a buck. Hundreds of books have already been written about the phenomena and what it all means, so suffice it to say here and now that Boomer TV just doesn't get any better. This series is at the top of the heap. Period. Numero uno. The champ. Done deal.

Amazingly, when creator Gene Roddenberry, a former military aviator and L.A. cop, sat down to write what he envisioned as "a *Wagon Train* to the stars," he wasn't thinking long-term. All he wanted was to create something with humanity, a show that could address some of the issues that were important in his life and project his vision of a better future. "I realized that by creating a separate world, a new world with new rules, I could make statements about sex, religion, Vietnam, unions, politics and the arms race," Roddenberry once observed. "Indeed, we did make them on *Star Trek*...we were sending messages, and fortunately most of those messages got past the network brass."

Notable Quotable

➤ "Live long and prosper."
—Vulcan greeting

➤ "We're a killer species...it's instinctive, but the instinct can be fought. We're human beings with the blood of a million savage years on our hands, but we can stop it. We can admit that we're killers, but we're not going to kill today. That's all it takes—knowing that we're not going to kill...today."
—Capt. Kirk (A Taste of Armageddon)

Set in the 23rd century, the series followed the exploits of the commander and crew of the *United Star Ship Enterprise*. Its mission, which was stated by Capt. James T. Kirk (William Shatner) at the beginning of each episode, was "to explore strange new worlds, to seek out new life and new civilizations...to boldly go where no man has gone before." Rounding out the command crew was First Officer/Science Officer Spock (Leonard Nimoy), an emotionless half-human, half-alien (his father was from the planet Vulcan) with pointed ears and green blood; Chief Medical Officer Leonard "Bones" McCoy (DeForest Kelley), a wry Southerner; and Chief Engineer Montgomery "Scotty" Scott (James Doohan). Other principal crew members included the communications officer, Lt. Uhura (Nichelle Nichols); Lt. Hikaru Sulu (George Takei), who served as navigator; Ensign Pavel Chekov (Walter Koenig) and Nurse Christine Chapel (Majel Barrett, who was married to Roddenberry). During the first season Yeoman Janice Rand (Grace Lee Whitney) had a recurring role as Capt. Kirk's assistant, but when the focus of the series shifted to the relationship between the "big three" of Kirk, Spock and McCoy, Rand was written out.

While many *Star Trek* characters bordered on stereotypes and some of the plots were surprisingly dumb (the worst was when Spock's brain was stolen by a race of helpless women and Dr. McCoy managed to "re-install" it without even trimming the Vulcan's hair!), at the end of the day the series was more about hope and the resilience of the

TeleTrivia

➤ The middle initial in Capt. Kirk's name stood for Tiberius.

➤ The character of Chekov was added to the crew during the second season, after a caustic review of the series in the Soviet newspaper *Pravda* pointed out that the first nation into space had somehow been overlooked when the "international" crew of the *U.S.S. Enterprise* was selected.

➤ The first inter-racial kiss in U.S. network history took place in the episode Plato's Stepchildren, when Capt. Kirk was forced by aliens to embrace Lieut. Uhura. The scene was deleted by some NBC affiliates in the Deep South during its original airing.

➤ Aluminium dust sprayed into a bright beam of light was the simple but memorable special effect employed to enhance the transporter device aboard the *Enterprise* that dematerialized people and objects and then re-animated them.

Freeze Frame

Star Trek was a dismal failure in the ratings during its original network run, peaking at No. 52 in 1966–1967. It was slated for cancellation after its first season, but a massive letter-writing campaign from devoted fans convinced NBC to renew it. The show's worldwide popularity exploded only after it went into syndication in the 1970s—a move that eventually led to six motion pictures featuring the original cast, and four spinoff series: *Star Trek: The Animated Series* (1973–1975); *Star Trek: The Next Generation* (1987–1993); *Star Trek: Deep Space Nine* (1992–1999) and *Star Trek: Voyageur* (1995–2001).

human spirit than anything else, and that's why it continues to hold up so well. It showed us an enlightened vision of a united Earth and a society free of hate and prejudice, and by incorporating (mostly) thoughtful story lines—two of the best showcased murderous aliens who were half black and half white (Let That Be Your Last Battlefield) and a planet that evolved as another Nazi Germany after getting "help" from an Earth historian (Patterns of Force)—*Star Trek* really did convey some relevant messages.

The Invaders

Series debut: Jan. 10, 1967 (ABC). Final telecast: Sept. 17, 1968 (ABC). 43 episodes.

"How does a nightmare begin? For David Vincent, architect returning home from a business trip, it began a few minutes past four on a lost Tuesday morning, looking for a shortcut that he never found. It began with a welcoming sign that gave hope of black coffee. It began with a closed, deserted diner, and a man too long without sleep to continue his journey. In the weeks to come, David Vincent would go back to how it all began many times...."

The familiar look and tone of that opening scene in the debut episode of *The Invaders* is thanks to producer Quinn Martin and narrator William Conrad, who previously teamed up on *The Fugitive* (see Chapter 11). Indeed, from story concept to the casting of Roy Thinnes for the starring role, this underrated series bears a striking resemblance to the odyssey of Dr. Richard Kimble. Unlike *The Fugitive*, however, tough competition in a difficult timeslot (Tuesday night at 8:30, opposite the top-rated *Red Skelton Show* on CBS) prevented *The Invaders* from gaining a large enough share of the audience to warrant strong promotion by the network.

The premise was simple: David Vincent's nightmare was being the lone eyewitness to the landing of a spacecraft from a dying planet. The aliens aboard were a scouting party sent to Earth in search of the chemicals they needed to survive. They assumed human form by "absorbing" host bodies from the Earthlings they murdered, and except for inexplicably being unable to bend their pinkie fingers and the lack of a heartbeat, they were indistinguishable from the rest of us. Adding to the cat-and-mouse tension was the fact the aliens could be killed just as easily as their human hosts (they glowed when they expired), and while they were aware of Vincent's efforts to warn humanity of their presence, they chose not to eliminate him because his untimely death might lend credence to his story. Over the 43 episodes several familiar faces guest-starred as aliens, including Gene Hackman (The Spores), Suzanne Pleshette (The Mutation, The Pursued) and Ed Asner (The Miracle).

Thinnes, who could strike a grim, hunted countenance every bit as convincing as David Janssen's, brought a quiet desperation to the role that was genuinely depressing. No matter how many aliens David Vincent hunted down and vapourized, you knew there was another pack of 'em lurking around the next bend or in the next town. In the second season he was helped in his lonely crusade when a small group called The Believers got involved, but even with the resources of wealthy businessman Edgar Scoville (Kent Smith) to finance their fight, Vincent and his allies were constantly out-manoeuvred by the aliens and the series was cancelled before we learned if he ever succeeded in trying (cue William Conrad) "to convince a disbelieving world that the nightmare has already begun."

TeleTrivia

In series creator Larry Cohen's original outline for *The Invaders*, the aliens could be identified by a disappearing eye centred in the palm of each hand of the human bodies they inhabited. ABC rejected the notion as "too frightening" and countered with the unbendable pinkie gimmick.

Fast Forward

In 1995, 27 years after the original series was cancelled, *The Invaders* returned in a four-hour mini-series. Thinnes made a cameo appearance as David Vincent, while Scott Bakula starred as alien-chaser Nolan Wood. In a radical change from his usual "good guy" roles, Richard Thomas (John-Boy from *The Waltons*) was the alien leader posing as a car mechanic.

Battlestar Galactica

Series debut: Sept. 17, 1978. Final telecast: Sept. 10, 1979. 24 episodes.

Hyped as the most expensive series in television history to that point (in excess of $1 million per episode), *Battlestar Galactica* opened with an intriguing premise: humanity was all but wiped out in a 1,000-year war with a race of androids called Cylons, and now, in the seventh millennium A.D., the mile-wide Galactica was mankind's last battlestar-class warrior vessel. Escorted by a rag-tag assortment of 220 smaller craft containing the survivors of the 12 colonial tribes of humans that had populated the cosmos, and with the Cylons in hot pursuit, the Galactica headed off into deep space in search of the "lost" 13th colony—a distant, unknown world called Earth.

Commanding the Galactica was Adama (Lorne Greene), ably assisted by Col. Tigh (Terry Carter). Adama's daughter Athena (Maren Jensen) was in charge of communications, while his son Capt. Apollo (Richard Hatch) led the battlestar's fighter fleet. Ace pilot and dashing womanizer Capt. Starbuck (Dirk Benedict) was Apollo's best friend, and sexy Cassiopeia (Laurette Sprang) was Starbuck's main squeeze. Other notables in the large cast included Apollo's adopted son Boxey (Noah Hathaway) and his mechanical dog Muffit; fighter pilot Lieut. Boomer (Herb Jefferson Jr.) and nefarious Count Baltar (John Colicos), the traitorous human leader of the Cylons. Since it was essentially a "chase" series, there was plenty of battle action featuring spectacular explosions, panoramic shots of the Galactica's fighter fleet using laser cannons to destroy their Cylon counterparts, and tight close-ups of Apollo and Starbuck, capes flying, in hand-to-hand (or laser-to-laser) combat with their android enemies in exotic alien worlds.

Notable Quotable

"Earth? You can't be serious! That's nothing but a fable!"

—Count Baltar

If all this sounds as though it should've been called Battlestar Ripoff, that's the same impression Twentieth Century Fox cited when the film studio launched multiple lawsuits over the uncanny parallels between the television series and George Lucas's blockbuster movie *Star Wars*, which the studio had released a year earlier. It wasn't much of a stretch. For Apollo and Starbuck, substitute Han Solo and Luke Skywalker. For Count Baltar ("Imperious Leader"), fill in Darth Vader. Instead of Cylons, think Imperial Stormtroops. The producers of *Galactica* even hired special-effects wizard John Dykstra, who'd choreographed the distinctive look of the *Star Wars* battle scenes. Although a legal settlement was eventually reached, *Galactica* creator Glen Larson maintained his script was in development long before *Star Wars* was released and that his inspiration had come from the Biblical story of Moses (Adama) leading the lost tribes of Israel (humans) to the Promised Land (Earth) while being pursued by the Egyptians (Cylons).

Wherever the inspiration for *Battlestar Galactica* came from, the series never made a dent in the ratings and was cancelled with little fanfare after just one season. A little over a year later a streamlined version returned to ABC under the title *Galactica 1980*. Adama was the only original character brought back, and since the time frame had been advanced 30 years, the battlestar had reached Earth—with the Cylons close behind. The main story line revolved around the efforts of Capt. Troy (Kent McCord) and Lt. Dillon (Barry Van Dyke) to prepare Earth for the Cylon onslaught, but viewers were no more interested the second time around and *Galactica 1980* was euthanized after 10 episodes.

TeleTrivia

On *Galactica 1980*, little Boxey from the original series had grown to adulthood and was now Lt. Troy (Kent McCord).

The Least You Need to Know

➤ In the absolute worst episode of *Lost In Space*, the Robinsons were captured by giant English-speaking carrots who threatened to turn them into plants.

➤ The first inter-racial kiss in U.S. network history was between Capt. Kirk and Lt. Uhura in the *Star Trek* episode Plato's Stepchildren.

➤ The aliens on *The Invaders* were identical to humans, except they had no heartbeat and couldn't bend their baby fingers.

➤ The creator and producers of *Battlestar Galactica* were sued by Twentieth Century Fox over alleged parallels to the blockbuster motion picture *Star Wars*.

Chapter 19

We Gotta Get Outta This Place

In This Chapter

➤ Depths of despair: *Voyage To The Bottom of the Sea*

➤ Through the past, darkly: *The Time Tunnel*

➤ Unbreakable spirit: *The Prisoner*

➤ Large problems: *Land of the Giants*

➤ Monkey business: *Planet of the Apes*

Escape—like the sex act and the need to instantly change stations when a Barry Manilow song comes on the radio—is a primal urge. Fight or flight, and all that. When we're trapped, our first instinct is to run. When we're restrained, we try to get away (except the folks who like to advertise in those "personal" columns). That's just the way we're programmed; nothing more, nothing less.

The notion of being trapped in a hopeless situation or having to elude an all-powerful adversary is a device that's been employed in some of the world's most riveting literature, from the *Epic of Gilgamesh* in ancient Sumeria to H.G. Wells' *The Time Machine* and Franz Kafka's *The Trial*. It's no coincidence each of those works has frequently been cited as an inspiration by pioneers of TV science fiction, and no surprise that the shows claiming such noble lineage have generally stood the test of time. That's not to say they were all that good, as this chapter will show. Three of the five series discussed here were created and produced by Irwin Allen, so right there you know that the special effects budget was about $1.98 per episode. Still, Allen's work remains high on the list of

Boomer favourites for the same reasons many of us fondly recall our first dates: very cheap, very cheesy...and very memorable. The other two shows in this chapter have become cult classics despite having only a handful of episodes each—and the import from Britain is my No. 1 pick as the most thought-provoking series to appear on television in *any* era.

Voyage To The Bottom of the Sea

Series debut: Sept. 14, 1964 (ABC). Final telecast: Sept. 15, 1968 (ABC). 110 episodes.

When it came to recognizing the benefits of recycling, Irwin Allen was a good 20 years ahead of the rest of the planet. The ubiquitous writer/producer/director was left with miles of underwater film footage and a warehouse full of sets and props after making the hit motion picture *Voyage To The Bottom of the Sea* in 1961, but rather than let the stuff gather dust he simply retooled the script and pitched ABC the idea of a weekly series based on the movie. With visions of tiny production budgets dancing in their heads the network executives jumped at it, and in so doing launched the first of Allen's quartet of '60s sci-fi shows.

The series was set 13 years in the future, and the "star" was the 600-foot Seaview, a glass-nosed atomic submarine designed and developed by retired admiral Harriman Nelson (Richard Basehart), head of the top-secret Santa Barbara–based Nelson Institute for Marine Research. The sub was commissioned by the U.S. government for scientific research and placed under the command of Cmdr. Lee Crane (David Hedison), who was promoted to captain in the second season. Lt.-Cmdr. Chip Morton (Robert Dowdell) was the executive officer charged with the vessel's day-to-day operations, and the other

Admiral Harriman Nelson (Richard Basehart) and Capt. Lee Crane (David Hedison) battled everything from space aliens to fire-breathing dragons on Voyage To The Bottom of the Sea.

regulars included Chief Petty Officer Curly Jones (Henry Kulky), Chief Sharkey (Terry Pecker), Crewman Kowalsky (Del Monroe) and, from 1965 to 1967, young Stu Riley (Allen Hunt), an itinerant surfer who was "adopted" by the Seaview crew and served as a kind of on-shore emissary.

Though ostensibly designed for research, the Seaview was bristling with lasers, torpedoes and nuclear-tipped missiles, as well as a couple of high-tech "auxiliary command options"—a mini-sub called the Flying Fish that could rocket into the atmosphere at supersonic speed, and the self-propelled Sea Crab, which could leave the main ship and carry a small crew farther into the gloomy depths than even the great sub dared venture. With toys like that and a mandate to roam the seven seas, it was pretty difficult to avoid trouble—and the good ship Seaview found plenty of it.

In the first couple of seasons the villains were pretty run-of-the-mill: unrepentant Nazis (The Last Battle), giant whales (The Ghost of Moby Dick), mad scientists (The Sky's On Fire) and double agents (The Traitor). No problem there. But beginning in season three it seemed like every couple of weeks the gallant crew was threatened by some bizarre race of man-things. Worse, the episode titles in *TV Guide* always gave it away. There was The Mechanical Men (life-sized robots who use the Seaview to take control of the world); The Plant Men (humanoid seaweed beasts); The Fossil Men (the Seaview is invaded by hostile rocks); The Wax Men (evil wax replicas of the crew) and my personal favourite, The Lobster Men (Allen should have made this one a tasty two-parter by introducing The Steak Men the following week).

If all those "men" weren't bad enough, there was also an annoying reliance on pseudo-magic. In the episode Werewolf, Nelson and the senior officers were transformed into wolfmen. The writers thought it was such a neat trick that they scripted another

Notable Quotable

Admiral Nelson, responding to a report that the Van Allen radiation belt had caught fire, threatening life on a global scale: "I say we can stop the fire by detonating a giant nuclear device 3,000 miles up in the air. This will blow the burning gases clear of the Earth's magnetic field."

Scientist: "That sounds like a very dangerous plan!"

Sharkey: "Well, we'll never know until we find out."

Admiral Nelson: "I think we better go down to my cabin and discuss this."

outbreak of the "lycanthropy virus" in The Brand of the Beast a couple of months later. In The Deadly Dolls, Vincent Price guest-starred as Professor Multiple, a travelling puppeteer whose marionettes came to life, and The Mummy featured what looked like a life-sized 3,000-year-old roll of toilet paper casting a spell on Crane in order to seize the ship.

See where this is going? By season four the producers probably could have renamed the series Voyage To The Bottom of the Brain and we wouldn't have known the difference.

The Time Tunnel

Series debut: Sept. 9, 1966 (ABC). Final telecast: Sept. 1, 1967 (ABC). 30 episodes.

This was Irwin Allen's third series, after *Voyage To The Bottom of the Sea* and *Lost In Space*, and most Boomers justifiably regard it as his best.

In the premiere episode Drs. Tony Newman (James Darren) and Doug Phillips (Robert Colbert) are scientists working on Operation Tic-Toc, a top-secret government project located in an underground complex miles beneath the Arizona desert. The goal of Tic-Toc was development of a laser-actuated device to create a portal through the space-time continuum, but after a penny-pinching senator reveals government funding for the project is about to be cancelled, Newman prematurely tests the device by running through the portal—and promptly winds up on the deck of the *Titanic* hours before its fateful meeting with the iceberg. Fortunately, the crew back in Arizona has a fix on Tony's molecular structure that allows them to "tune in" and watch as he participates in the history being replayed on their screens, but they can't pull him back. The only solution is to send Phillips through the portal. He is likewise trapped, but his reunion with Newman creates a link that enables the Tic-Toc techs to blink the duo out of their current time and send them on another journey. Keeping tabs back at the control room were Lt.-Gen. Heywood Kirk (Whit Bissell), Dr. Ann MacGregor (Lee Meriwether) and Dr. Raymond Swain (John Zaremba).

Notable Quotable

"Don't gamble unless you have to, but if you have to, go for broke."

—Doug Phillips

All in all, *The Time Tunnel* was a pretty cool concept, and I always wondered why Newman and Phillips would even want to return to Arizona if they could keep travelling through time. Of course, they quickly discovered they couldn't change the past, which made it particularly painful for Tony when they landed in Pearl Harbor on Dec. 6, 1941, and he met both his father and himself as a child (The Day The Sky Fell In). His father would die in the Japanese sneak attack the next day, but there was nothing Tony could do to save him. The duo's other adventures included barely escaping being shot as spies by a British officer (Carroll O'Connor) on the eve of the final battle of the War of 1812 (The Last Patrol), and pursuing a mad bomber named Nimon (Robert Duvall) one million years into the future (Chase Through Time). In between, they landed in Sherwood Forest to help the Merry Men (The Revenge Of Robin Hood) and found themselves on opposite sides of the Civil War during the Battle of Gettysburg (The Death Merchant).

The Prisoner

Series debut: Sept. 29, 1967 (ITC in Britain); June 1, 1968 (CBS).
Final telecast: Feb. 2, 1968 (ATV); Sept. 11, 1969 (CBS). 17 episodes.

After five years of portraying John Drake on *Danger Man* and *Secret Agent* (see Chapter 16), Patrick McGoohan began pondering an intriguing question: What happens to spies when they quit? His equally intriguing answer turned out to be this darkly allegorical psychodrama, produced by McGoohan's Everyman Films in Britain and picked up by CBS as a summer replacement for *The Smothers Brothers*.

The series is a disturbing Kafkaesque combination of fantasy and science fiction, which tells the story of a fiercely independent man who resigns from the British intelligence service only to be knocked out by gas pumped into his London apartment as he's preparing to leave on vacation. When he wakes up he's in an exact duplicate of his home, but instead of being in London, it's in a mysterious community called The Village. He has no idea where the place is, nor can he be sure of the allegiance of his captors. Only two things are apparent: the people running The Village are after the sensitive secrets locked in his brain, and the prisoner—known simply as Number Six—will never escape alive.

Notable Quotable

- "I'm not making any deals with you. I will not be pushed, filed, indexed, stamped, briefed, debriefed or numbered. My life is my own."
  —Number Six

- "The butcher with the sharpest knife has the warmest heart."
  —A sign in The Village

- "I am not a number, I am a free man!"
  —Number Six

In each eerie episode Number Six and the other residents of The Village (all of whom once worked for the government) are under 24-hour surveillance by hidden cameras and microphones. They're subjected to brutal brainwashing techniques by Number Two, the nominal head of the place who presumably answers only to Number One. There was a new Number Two for every episode, but Number One's identity wasn't revealed until the finale (and no I won't...that would be telling). The only other regular character was The Butler (Angelo Muscat), who never spoke a word through the entire 17 episodes.

The Village itself looked pleasant enough—brightly painted buildings, a concert hall, lovely fountains. It had its own shops and cafés, an old folks home, a taxi service...even a newspaper called The Tally-Ho. But the telephone operator would accept only local calls, and the taxis would never venture off the main roads. The Village was located in the middle of a small wind-swept island ringed by miles of sandy white beaches, but anyone who attempted to swim or sail away was immediately attacked by one of the "Rovers"—giant white balloons that seemed to materialize out of thin air with a menacing roar. If Number Two was in a particularly snarly mood, the Rovers could also be programmed to kill.

So what did it all mean?

"I believe passionately in the freedom of the individual, and the show is basically about dehumanization and the loss of individuality that is so prevalent in our society today," McGoohan told *TV Guide* in 1968. "In one way or another, we are all prisoners in the society we have created for ourselves. With *The Prisoner*, each person can look at it and, I hope, have a different interpretation of what it's supposed to be about. That's the intention...to be left hanging somewhat. As long as people look at it, think about it and argue about it, I think I've done my job."

During its initial run critics either totally ignored *The Prisoner* or dismissed it as a sort of Disneyland gone insane, a disjointed show that meandered along with no rhyme or reason, with a protagonist who was consistently guilty of a TV hero's worst crime: failure. Yet right from the start it was a series that inserted viewers directly into the story, forcing us to make choices and live with the consequences. The fact everybody who watched it came away with a different interpretation only made it more fascinating. That unique aspect was best exemplified in the episode Living In Harmony, in which Number Six is transported out of The Village to a generic town reminiscent of the Old West. He's tricked into becoming sheriff, but steadfastly refuses to pick up a gun or do any killing. In a last-ditch effort to break his resolve and bend him to their will, Number Six's captors inject him with hallucinogenic drugs. Considering the symbolism, and the fact this particular episode was scheduled to air during the peak of the anti–Vietnam War protests, it's not difficult to see why CBS censors, on recommendation from the government, yanked it off the air. More disturbing is that the same Big Brother mentality prevented Living In Harmony from airing on any American network until 1988.

That's as good an indication as any as to why *The Prisoner* remains entertaining, enigmatic and infuriating all at once. It's one of the handful of series from the 1960s that will never go out of style as long as television exists because my interpretation of what it all means is no more or no less valid than yours. Be seeing you....

Land of the Giants

Series debut: Sept. 22, 1968 (ABC). Final telecast: Sept. 6, 1970 (ABC). 51 episodes.

The final instalment in Irwin Allen's sci-fi quartet was this bizarre hybrid of *Gilligan's Island, Lost In Space* and *Gulliver's Travels*. Seven passengers and crew aboard the sub-orbital ship Spindrift were on a routine flight from Los Angeles to London in 1983 when the ship was sucked into a mysterious vortex. When it emerged from the white mist several minutes later none of the flight controls were operating and it crash-landed on a world that was an exact duplicate of our own—except everything was 12 times normal size! The trials and tribulations faced by the castaways in trying to survive and repair the ship while being menaced by giant children, monstrous insects and a general population bent on exterminating all "little people" furnished the simplistic plots for the rest of the run, but as trite as those story lines became, it was still fun to tune in to see the giant-sized props.

The leader of the stranded Earthlings was Capt. Steve Burton (Gary Conway), who along with co-pilot Dan Erikson (Don Marshall) and flight attendant Betty Hamilton (Heather Young) made up the crew of the Spindrift. The passengers were engineer-tycoon Mark Wilson (Don Matheson), heiress Valerie Scott (Deanna Lund), 12-year-old Barry Lockridge (Stefan Arngrim), his dog Chipper and a secretive blowhard named Col. Fitzhugh (Kurt Kasznar). In the first episode (The Crash), Chipper dug up a chest containing a tape-recorded message from previous crash-survivors from Earth. As if being imprisoned in doll houses, thrown into giant wastepaper baskets and being tormented by marauding cats wasn't bad enough, the recording warned of a security agency called S.I.B. that was responsible for hunting down "invaders" from Earth. Halfway through the first season the group had their first encounter with sadistic S.I.D. Inspector Kobick (Kevin Hagen), who subsequently became a semi-regular on the series.

Land of the Giants isn't as fondly remembered as Allen's other three shows, but it probably should

Freeze Frame

A pair of famous prizefighters appeared in different episodes of *Land of the Giants*. Former world welterweight and middleweight champion Sugar Ray Robinson starred as a kind-hearted singer in *Giants And All That Jazz*, while heavyweight contender Jerry Quarry, ranked No. 2 in the world at the time, portrayed a menacing thug in *A Place Called Earth*.

be—if only for the kitschy look and the form-fitting outfits worn by Heather Young and Deanna Lund. The props (slices of bread fashioned from four-foot slabs of foam rubber, 10-foot papier-mâché pencils) had to be made "giant-sized" in order to maintain the physical perspective of the actors, and that was a main reason for the huge production cost—around $250,000 per episode. The sets were colourful and expansive, and there was a certain robust abandon to the overall look that helped make the stories seem just a little more believable. Hey, at least the Spindrift survivors never battled a giant carrot....

Planet of the Apes

Series debut: Sept. 13, 1974 (CBS). Final telecast: Dec. 27, 1974 (CBS). 14 episodes.

Astronauts Alan Virdon (Ron Harper) and Pete Burke (James Naughton) were transported 1,000 years into the future when their space capsule passed through a time warp while re-entering Earth's atmosphere. When they emerged from their craft after a crash-landing, it was into a pre-industrial world ruled by apes who regarded humans as unwanted reminders of a dark, blood-drenched past.

Based more on Pierre Boulle's original allegorical novel than the hugely successful string of Apes movies, this unappreciated series made some salient observations about morality, fear and prejudice as Virdon and Burke roamed the planet in search of the "forgotten technology" that might return them to their own time. Aiding their quest was the sympathetic chimpanzee Galen (Roddy McDowall, reprising his movie role), while the dreaded General Urko (Mark Lenard) and his gorilla storm troopers beat the bushes searching for them. The other regular cast member was Zaius (Booth Colman),

Roddy McDowall reprised his movie role as the renegade chimp Galen on Planet of the Apes.

leader of the orangutan ruling council, who grudgingly accepted the "secret and terrible knowledge" that man had once ruled the planet and Burke and Virdon were indeed from the past.

When CBS pulled the plug on *Planet of the Apes* after just 14 episodes (24 had been ordered), most of the developing story lines were far from resolved. As a compromise, the network later re-inserted unused footage into some of the completed episodes and spliced them with others to make 90-minute movies, which still show up periodically on late night marathons. If you ever get the chance, check 'em out. For my money this show was one of the real gems of the 1970s, and I'm keeping my fingers crossed it'll one day be released on home video or DVD.

TeleTrivia

Beneath that four-hour simian make-up job, Mark Lenard (General Urko) would be instantly recognized by Boomers as Sarek, Mr. Spock's father in the *Star Trek* episode Journey To Babel.

The Least You Need to Know

➤ *Voyage To The Bottom of the Sea* was the first of Irwin Allen's four sci-fi shows in the 1960s.

➤ Robert Duvall portrayed a mad bomber who fled one million years into the future on *The Time Tunnel*.

➤ Other than Number Six, the only character to appear in every episode of *The Prisoner* was The Butler (Angelo Muscat)—but he never uttered a single word.

➤ The production cost of *Land of the Giants* was $250,000 per episode.

➤ Roddy McDowall reprised his big-screen role of Galen in the short-lived TV version of *Planet of the Apes*.

Chapter 20

The Fright Stuff

In This Chapter

➤ Unlocking the door: *The Twilight Zone*

➤ Awe and mystery: *The Outer Limits*

➤ Bound by blood: *Dark Shadows*

➤ Artful terror: *Night Gallery*

➤ Intrepid interloper: *Kolchak: The Night Stalker*

For those of us who like our TV menu spiced up with a side order of terror, the 1960s and '70s were wonderful times. To put things in context, suffice it to say that the contrived creepiness on the *The X-Files* and the phony fright on *Buffy The Vampire Slayer*—to name a couple of celebrated present-day equivalents—can't remotely compare to the pulse-pounding excellence of Rod Serling's black-and-white nightmares or the spine-tingling plights of a rumpled reporter working the Chicago night beat. Why? It's a matter of degree. Instead of numbing us with scenes expressly intended to register shock value, Boomer classics like *The Twilight Zone* and *Kolchak: The Night Stalker* creeped us out by taking the subtle approach, methodically raising the suspense through brilliant writing and wonderful characterizations before throwing an unexpected curve that hit like a jackhammer.

In my humble opinion the five series outlined in this chapter remain, to this day, the scariest shows ever to air on network television—if you don't count *Jerry Springer* and all those *Barbara Walters Specials*.

The Twilight Zone

Series debut: Oct. 2, 1959 (CBS). Final (original) telecast: Sept. 10, 1965 (CBS). 156 episodes (138 half-hour episodes; 18 one-hour episodes).

With this ground-breaking series writer/creator Rod Serling proved that intelligent, literate anthology drama wasn't the exclusive domain of movies and live theatre. A playwright himself, Serling intuitively understood that science fiction could be a vehicle for presenting stories that were in essence little morality plays. At the same time, he was able to hook into the sort of primal fears capsulized in universal concepts like death, solitude and paranoia. The result was a show that was altogether captivating. Every episode offered up stories that were so unusual, so off-beat that the viewer was often left emotionally drained by the time the show ended. The fright factor was always important to Serling, but not as important as leaving a strong impression or establishing an empathic link with the main character(s).

That unique style was showcased in the very first episode of *The Twilight Zone*, which aired on Oct. 2, 1959. Titled Where Is Everybody?, it's the story of Mike Ferris (Earl Holliman), an amnesiac dressed in an airman's uniform who wakes up to find himself completely alone in a large town. He explores a coffee shop and the police station, a movie theatre and a drug store, all the while with a growing uneasiness that he's being watched. Finally, nearly hysterical with fear, he collapses against a crosswalk sign, pushing the "walk" button over and over again. As the scene shifts, it becomes apparent Ferris is in fact an astronaut-trainee, sealed in an isolation booth to simulate a flight to the moon. After nearly 500 hours alone he has cracked under the pressure, repeatedly pressing the panic button to alert those monitoring him. In another classic, Time Enough At Last, Burgess Meredith portrays a bank teller who can never find enough time to read. On his lunch break one afternoon he slips into the vault for some peaceful reading time, only to have the door slam shut as a great roar shakes the building. When the time lock on the vault door opens he walks out into a dead city; everybody has been killed in a nuclear attack. Overwrought with grief, he considers suicide...but then realizes he now has "all the time I want...all the time I need," to pursue his favourite activity. As he's happily stacking books at the public library, trying to decide where to start, he slips and shatters his glasses. Without them he is totally blind.

Notable Quotable

"There's a saying: 'Every man is put on Earth condemned to die; time and method of execution unknown.' Perhaps this is how it should be."

—Rod Serling

Over the course of five years and 156 episodes—the vast majority of which were written by Serling—the series explored themes ranging from magic to horror and genres from fantasy to straight humour. The one constant was that the characters remained the focus of the stories; there was never a reliance on gimmicky props or fancy effects to carry the plot. Guest stars like William Shatner, Charles Bronson, Lee Marvin, Frtiz Weaver, Telly Savalas, Elizabeth

Montgomery and Robert Redford all landed memorable roles, but in the end it was simply the quality of the writing that made the series so great. Earl Hamner, who wrote a handful of *Twilight Zone* scripts years before creating and developing *The Waltons*, called Serling's work "the embodiment of great storytelling. It harkens back to a time when we all sat around fires and had animal skins for clothing....There were great stories told around campfires, and those same principles are at work in *The Twilight Zone*. It doesn't surprise me at all that it's achieved such a universal appeal. They're simply great stories, well told."

The Outer Limits

Series debut: Sept. 16, 1963 (ABC). Final telecast: Jan. 16, 1965 (ABC). 49 episodes.

"There is nothing wrong with your television set...."

Except for that ominous opening line, I don't remember much about the debut of *The Outer Limits*. I just remember watching in the darkened living room of my childhood home on the West Coast, alone and just a little bit afraid. Was this one of those Emergency Broadcast System tests? Were the godless Commies finally swarming over the North Pole? As oscilloscope sine waves pulsated across the screen, the faceless Control Voice droned on: "Do not attempt to adjust the picture. We are controlling transmission....We will control the horizontal. We will control the vertical....For the next hour, sit quietly and we will control all that you see and hear. We repeat: There is nothing wrong with your television set. You are about to participate in a great adventure. You are about to experience the awe and mystery which reaches from the inner mind to...The Outer Limits."

You never knew what kind of bizarre adventure was in store each week on The Outer Limits—*only that it would be scary.*

TeleTrivia

Stefano's original series title of Please Stand By was rejected by ABC as "too frightening," considering that just a year earlier millions of viewers had been glued to their televisions during the Cuban missile crisis. The 1964 *Outer Limits* episode The Invisible Enemy, starring Adam West as an astronaut on Mars battling killer sand sharks, aired the same year as West's cult sci-fi movie *Robinson Crusoe on Mars*.

Well, at least it wasn't the Red Army. To this day the Control Voice has one of the highest recognition factors of any catch phrase in television history. We never knew if the voice was human, alien or mechanical...only that it served as a sort of pre-Ted Koppel TV tranquilizer, preparing us for the weekly dose of monsters and mayhem guaranteed to follow.

Created by Leslie Stevens and Joseph Stefano (who wrote the screenplay for the movie *Psycho*), *The Outer Limits* is generally considered the best fantasy/horror series of all time—and deservedly so. Stefano, who agreed to change the original title of Please Stand By, insisted from the outset that the series would explore both ends of the emotional spectrum. The high road invariably involved an optimistic portrayal of humanity, and each episode had to be consistent with scientific knowledge and man's quest for answers. But Stefano also insisted on the low road. In an interview with *TV Guide* he summed up his philosophy by stating: "Our viewers must know the delicious and consciously desired element of pure terror." In other words, every show had to have a monster.

The premiere episode, entitled The Galaxy Being, starred Cliff Robertson as a radio engineer who makes contact with an alien from another galaxy with the aid of a crude 3D television set. Robertson was paid the unheard of sum of $10,000 for the role and became the first of many name stars to appear in the series. Over the next 48 shows, Robert Duvall, Martin Sheen, William Shatner, Martin Landau and Robert Culp were just a few of the others. The second season kicked off with Soldier, an episode starring Michael Ansara as a killing machine from the future. Written by Harlan Ellison, it won a Hugo Award as the best sci-fi presentation of the year and remains a cult favourite of Boomer sci-fi aficionados.

Dark Shadows

Series debut: June 26, 1966 (ABC). Final telecast: April 2, 1971 (ABC). 1,245 episodes.

A little over a year after poor ratings permanently silenced the Control Voice on *The Outer Limits*, ABC jumped back on the fright TV bandwagon with the debut of *Dark Shadows*, television's first Gothic soap opera.

Created and produced by Dan Curtis, the daytime serial at first revolved around the exploits of Victoria Winters (Alexandra Moltke), who had been hired as governess for a 10-year-old boy in the remote fishing village of Collinsport, Maine. She was employed by the wealthy Collins family at their huge seaside estate ("Collinwood") and veteran screen actress Joan Bennett was featured in the role of Elizabeth Stoddard, the estate mistress. After several months on the air, however, the series wasn't attracting a large enough audience with its conventional Gothic suspense formula, so Curtis did the unthinkable: he introduced a vampire.

In April 1967, Canadian-born Shakespearean actor Jonathan Frid joined the cast as Barnabas Collins, a 175-year-old blood sucker. Frid's stunning portrayal was an instant success, and within a couple of months he was receiving upwards of 3,000 fan letters per week from female fans. Although he could have been a menacing creature in the tradition of Dracula, Frid portrayed Barnabas as a sympathetic man, guilt-ridden by his insatiable appetite for human blood. He added humanity to his characterization by playing the vampire as a tragic figure, and the audience ate it up. As the ratings continued to soar, more supernatural aspects were added to *Dark Shadows*. Ghosts, witches and werewolves appeared as the show cleverly alternated the story line between the present-day Collins family and their ancestors. David Selby, who would go on to fame and fortune in *Falcon Crest*, made his TV debut as vampire Quentin Collins in an

Venerable Canadian stage actor Jonathan Frid starred as tragic vampire Barnabas Collins on Dark Shadows.

elaborate flashback to 1897, and future *Charlie's Angel* star Kate Jackson also had a recurring role.

In 1970 MGM released the theatrical film *House of Dark Shadows* with the original series cast reprising their roles and surrounded by more elements of blood 'n' guts than could be shown on daytime TV, and it was successful enough to spawn a sequel entitled *Night of Dark Shadows*. The series was still No. 1 in its time-slot when it was cancelled in 1971, and it continues to be wildly popular in syndication and on home video.

Night Gallery

Series debut: Dec. 16, 1970 (NBC). Final telecast: Aug. 12, 1973 (NBC). 43 episodes.

Rod Serling's last major TV work before he died of cancer at age 51 was this horror anthology, which opened with him in a darkened art gallery, describing the grotesque paintings that foreshadowed the three vignettes in the episode to follow. It was a neat gimmick, even though the stories were invariably dark and depressing—and unusually bloody for Serling. The best segments ended up being those that looked like they came from *The Twilight Zone*, including one with old Serling favourite Burgess Meredith as a discredited doctor living on skid row who finds a medical bag containing cures from the future. Vincent Price guested in another memorable story as a teacher from the future who came back to give present-day students a lesson in hate.

Two of Serling's scripts from *Night Gallery* were nominated for Emmy Awards: They're Tearing Down Tim Riley's Bar, about a lonely widower who sees the destruction of his favourite drinking spot as a metaphor for his life, and The Messiah of Mott Street, starring Edward G. Robinson (in one of his last TV appearances) as a terminally ill Jew who wants to see the coming of the Messiah before he dies.

As he did on *The Twilight Zone*, Serling attempted to keep the stories character-focused, but since he had no creative control (he was contracted only to serve as host) many of the scripts he submitted were completely rewritten. It was a totally unnecessary and humiliating put-down of the man who was arguably the greatest writing talent in the history of the medium.

Kolchak: The Night Stalker

Series debut: Sept. 13, 1974 (ABC). Final telecast: Aug. 30, 1975 (ABC). 20 episodes.

Darren McGavin introduced the character of rumpled reporter Carl Kolchak in two enormously successful made-for-TV movies in 1973–1974: *The Night Stalker*, in which he chased a modern-day vampire around Las Vegas, and *The Night Strangler*, which saw him pursue a 150-year-old killer in Seattle. Loud-mouthed, pushy and decked out in a poorly fitted white suit and straw hat with an impossibly large camera perpetually slung over his shoulder, Kolchak was a walking stereotype of bad newsroom clichés—but for a few months viewers couldn't get enough of him.

In the series, Kolchak worked out of the small office of Chicago-based Independent News Service. His boss was editor Tony Vincenzo (Simon Oakland), while Ron Updyke (Jack Grinnge) wrote musical reviews and Emily Cowles (Ruth McDevitt) handled the lonely hearts column. The news desk was a magnet for the kind of stories Kolchak loved to tackle: unusual murders, unexplained disappearances, psychic phenomena—and there was no shortage of them. Over the 20 episodes he had run-ins with the "real" Jack the Ripper, Aztec sun-worshippers who ate human hearts, a werewolf, a headless biker who went around slashing up members of rival gangs, and a 12th-century knight who somehow ended up in Chicago to settle a medieval score.

Even though the stories were well crafted and genuinely scary, the endless parade of monsters and maniacs finally got to be a bit much even for McGavin, who was obviously having fun playing Kolchak as a kind of hybrid of Barney Fife and Maxwell Smart. Naturally, his stories rarely saw the light of day in the newspaper, and Vincenzo spent most of the series screaming: "For once, Kolchak, just once, I'd like a nice, normal little story to appear on my desk. Just once, Kolchak...."

What I couldn't figure out was how a guy who never got anything published still always managed to get his boss to sign those expense vouchers.

The Least You Need to Know

➤ Earl Holliman portrayed a hallucinating trainee astronaut in the premiere episode of *The Twilight Zone*.

➤ Cliff Robertson was paid $10,000 to guest star in the debut of *The Outer Limits*.

➤ Veteran Canadian stage actor Jonathan Frid portrayed a 175-year-old vampire on *Dark Shadows*.

➤ Rod Serling was nominated for two Emmy Awards for stories he wrote for *Night Gallery*.

➤ *Kolchak: The Night Stalker* was a spinoff from two highly rated TV movies that aired during the 1973–1974 season.

RIPPP!

Chapter 21

One of a Kind

In This Chapter

➤ Up, up and away!: *The Adventures of Superman*

➤ New and improved: *The Six Million Dollar Man* and *The Bionic Woman*

➤ Gills and guile: *Man From Atlantis*

➤ Femme fatale: *Wonder Woman*

➤ The beast within: *The Incredible Hulk*

Years ago, in cleverly explaining why she was dumping me, an old girlfriend fixed me with a withering stare and tersely opined that the only thing we had in common was "we're both carbon-based." To this day I can't recall why she figured that would bother me, but I believe it had something to do with our divergent views on the relative worth of uniqueness. I did (and still do) put a high premium on it. She, on the other hand, wanted a more symbiotic relationship. I mention this here because uniqueness—or lack of it—has long been a recurring theme in sci-fi television, but it wasn't until the cusp of the Boomer era that several "freakazoid" characters (one of Jack McGee's pet names for the Incredible Hulk) crowded the network landscape and were treated with dignity and respect.

All the shows discussed in this chapter revolved around a character who wasn't like you and me, and their "freakazoid" nature gave the writers ample opportunity to place them in situations that shed new light on old themes like loyalty, loneliness and prejudice. For the most part, they did it quite well.

The Adventures of Superman

**Series debut: Oct. 1952 (syndicated). Final telecast: Nov. 1957.
104 episodes.**

One of the great mysteries of Boomer TV—right up there with why the Howells took a trunk of clothes to Gilligan's Island and how the Incredible Hulk repaired his pants—is why Superman almost always ducked when the bad guys threw stuff at him. It didn't matter what it was—empty pistols, chairs, rocks. I mean, the guy could smile while letting bullets bounce off that big red S in the middle of his chest, but then he'd duck like a scared rabbit to get out of the way of a flung baseball bat. Go figure.

Non sequiturs aside, *The Adventures of Superman* was a thoroughly entertaining series that seamlessly meshed with the temper of the times. The production budget averaged just $15,000 per week, but most of the effects were surprisingly good. For example, when Superman (George Reeves) used his X-ray vision, there was a pretty cool-looking beam of light emanating from his eyes. His flying sequences were equally well done, even though Reeves was often suspended on wires in front of a moving backdrop. Other effects weren't quite as successful. In the series-opening episode the bad guys were two midgets with what looked like Holiday Inn shower caps on their heads, and their "super-weapon" was a not-so-cleverly-disguised Electrolux vacuum cleaner (probably from the same Holiday Inn). When he wasn't "on the job," Superman appeared as his alter-ego, mild-mannered reporter Clark Kent of The Daily Planet. Of course, no one could tell they were the same guy because Clark wore horn-rimmed glasses and a fedora...but Lois Lane (Noel Neill) had her suspicions. Rounding out the regular cast were cub reporter Jimmy Olsen (Jack Larsen), crusty Daily Planet editor-in-chief Perry White (John Hamilton) and Inspector Bill Henderson (Robert Shane), a plodding Metropolis police officer who somehow managed to get assigned to every case involving Superman.

Notable Quotable

Lois (mooning over Superman): "Clark, does spring mean anything special to you?"

Clark: "Baseball."

Lois (embarrassed): "Do you think spring means anything special to Superman?"

Clark (sternly): "He doesn't have time for baseball!"

Another plus for *The Adventures of Superman* was that it was a faithful adaptation of the comic book mythos familiar to millions of North American kids in the '50s. An alien from the planet Krypton, Superman's real name was Kal-El. He was sent to Earth in a rocket by his parents, Jor-el and Lara, just before their planet was destroyed, and when the rocket crash-landed outside the town of Smallville in the heartland of America, the baby was rescued by Martha and Jonathan Kent, who named him Clark and raised him as their son. At age 25 Clark moved to Metropolis to join The Daily Planet, and Superman quickly established himself as the nation's greatest defender of "truth, justice and the American way!"

After the series went out of production, Reeves continued to be typecast as the Man of Steel— including in a hilarious 1958 episode of *I Love Lucy*

TeleTrivia

John Hamilton, who portrayed Perry ("Don't call me Chief!") White, wasn't particularly good at memorizing his lines. As a solution, his scenes were invariably shot while he was sitting behind a desk covered with papers, one of which contained his lines!

in which the zany redhead, disguised as the hero, met Superman face to face. For two years after leaving the role Reeves found very little work in front of the camera, but he remained heavily involved in film production. All of that ended on June 16, 1959, when he was found dead of a gunshot wound to the head. The police ruled it a suicide, but many colleagues of the actor believed there was a more sinister motive behind his death—a mystery that is still hotly debated to this day.

The Six Million Dollar Man

Series debut: Jan. 18, 1974 (ABC). Final telecast: March 6, 1978 (ABC).

The Bionic Woman

Series debut: Jan. 14, 1976 (ABC). Final telecast: Sept. 2, 1978 (NBC).

These two series will always be linked for several reasons, the most obvious being that *The Bionic Woman* was a direct spinoff. But there was more. Col. Steve Austin (Lee Majors) and tennis pro Jamie Sommers (Lindsay Wagner) were engaged before Austin became an astronaut, but over the years they'd drifted apart. After Steve was almost killed during the test-flight crash of an experimental moon lander in the Arizona desert, he lost track of Jamie completely—not a big surprise, considering that Dr. Rudy Wells (Martin Brooks) had to perform radical experimental surgery in order to save his life. When all the cutting was done, Austin was a full-fledged "cyborg"—half man, half machine—with new legs that allowed him to run at more than 60 miles per hour, a bionic right arm that could lift a truck and a computerized left eye that gave him incredibly accurate vision, even at great distances. Obviously now far too valuable to be a run-of-the-mill astronaut, he was transferred to the Office of Scientific Information (OSI) under the auspices of Oscar Goldman (Richard Anderson), who dispatched him on covert missions all over the planet. Usually the bad guys were foreign operatives, but occasionally Steve also battled mad scientists and, in one memorable two-parter, Bigfoot!

After a slow start, *The Six Million Dollar Man* gradually gained a loyal following, and in January 1975 Jamie Sommers was introduced on the show as "the girl who got away." Unfortunately, she too was now grievously injured (the result of a skydiving accident), but when Rudy attempted the same cyborg cut-and-paste job that had saved Austin, her body rejected the bionic hardware...and she died. At least we all thought so.

When *The Bionic Woman* debuted in January 1976, it was revealed that Jamie had only been in a coma, and was now fully recovered and working as a schoolteacher on an army base near her home town of Ojai, California. Her "special goods" included bionic legs, a bionic right arm and a bionic right ear. Grateful to the OSI for having rebuilt her, she naturally agreed to work for Goldman while maintaining her cover as a teacher.

For a short time after *The Bionic Woman* was up and running (pun intended), there were occasional crossovers between the two shows when Jamie and Steve were both assigned to the same mission, but the injury had wiped out some of Jamie's memory—including her romantic feelings for Steve. For the remainder of her series (one more season on ABC before moving to NBC), Jamie and Steve worked independently, although Oscar and Rudy appeared on both shows to maintain the sense of the OSI "family."

Taken together, *The Six Million Dollar Man* and *The Bionic Woman* were an interesting experiment in parallel programming, and on the whole, the two shows pulled it off pretty neatly. The idea that either hero could appear on the other's show next week— perhaps to rekindle that old flame—was an intriguing hook for viewers that never really

Lindsay Wagner was absolutely adorable as tennis pro turned cyborg Jamie Sommers on The Bionic Woman.

wavered until Lindsay Wagner moved to NBC. Both shows also made an effort to introduce intelligent science fiction to their story lines, above and beyond the bionics. Austin and Sommers eventually both had run-ins with extraterrestrials, but the writers wisely chose not to return to that theme too often. One of the best pure sci-fi plots on *The Six Million Dollar Man* was the episode Burning Bright, which featured William Shatner as an astronaut pal of Steve's who returns from space with the ability to communicate with dolphins. Another was The Pioneers, with Mike Farrell as one of a pair of cryogenically frozen astronauts who gains super-human strength after being "thawed." On *The Bionic Woman*, Jamie's best adventures included a battle against a band of sexy mechanical "FemBots" in Las Vegas, and a "mission" with daredevil Evel Knievel that took place deep behind the Iron Curtain.

TeleTrivia

Lee Majors and Lindsay Wagner reprised their series roles in *The Return of The Six Million Dollar Man & The Bionic Woman* (1992), and two years later finally tied the knot in another made-for-TV movie, *Bionic Breakdown*, in 1994.

In the third and final season of *The Bionic Woman* Jamie got a bionic dog (Maxamillion), and in the very last episode of the series (On The Run), the writers spoofed Patrick McGoohan's *The Prisoner* (see Chapter 19) by sending her to a special camp for ex-agents after she resigned from the OSI.

Man From Atlantis

Series debut: Sept. 22, 1977 (NBC). Final episode: July 25, 1978 (NBC). 13 episodes.

After watching Steve Austin and Jamie Sommers make bionic leaps into the top 15 of the ratings, NBC eagerly bought this series about the last survivor of Atlantis, hoping to cash in on the "freak-hero" trend.

The premise definitely had some potential: an underwater disturbance uncovers the last "Atlantean," a handsome, exceedingly polite "gill man," (Patrick Duffy). Washed ashore unconscious, he's found by Dr. Elizabeth Merrill (Belinda Montgomery), who just happens to work at the Foundation for Oceanic Research. Though he appears human, the Atlantean has webbed hands and feet...and no lungs. He also has super-human strength and senses, swims faster than a porpoise and has the ability to make tenuous telepathic connections with certain sea creatures. In a nutshell, he's the perfect secret weapon. After being nursed back to health by Dr. Merrill (she kept him in a big aquarium), he reveals he can only survive on land for 12 hours before it's necessary to return to the sea to "breathe," but grateful for having been rescued, he agrees to return and join Merrill and her team in a project to learn more about undersea life.

Given the cover name "Mark Harris," the Atlantean intially had a tough time adjusting to his new dual world (often with humourous results), but once he got used to riding around in the Cetacean (the Insttute's submersible vehicle) and got the hang of hangin' with those wild and crazy "landlubbers," some real possibilities for good sci-fi opened up—especially when evil Mr. Schubert (Victor Buono) appeared on the scene, hoping to kidnap Mark. Unfortunately the series ended before any of those possibilities could be explored, and Mark presumably returned to the briny deep for a few years before swimming up the shower pipe at Bobby Ewing's place.

Wonder Woman

Series debut: Sept. 18, 1977 (ABC). Final telecast: Sept. 11, 1979 (CBS). 57 episodes.

Charles Moulon's comic book superheroine of the 1940s finally made the break to the small screen when Cathy Lee Crosby starred in the 1974 made-for-TV movie, but it wasn't until former Miss World–USA Lynda Carter donned the magic bracelets and the star-spangled hot pants that we really noticed.

Carter's original series was set in the 1940s, when Amazon princess Diana Prince left her idyllic home on Paradise Island to help a dashing fighter pilot, Maj. Steve Trevor (Lyle Waggoner) kick some Nazi butt. Diana had a personal score to settle as well. The Nazis were in control of Paradise Island and had even created a Third Reich ripoff of Wonder Woman named Fausta, so you had to figure there'd be some decent cat fights down the road. When the series moved from ABC to CBS the following season it was retitled *The New Adventures of Wonder Woman* and the time frame was updated to the present. Diana hadn't aged, of course, and Steve Trevor Jr. (Waggoner again) was the head of an undercover organization called the International Agency Defence Command (IADC). On his father's recommendation, he recruited Diana to join the fight against the sworn enemies of democracy and free enterprise: a mad toy-maker (Frank Gorshin), a psychic vampire (Wolfman Jack), a greedy mad scientist transported back from the 22nd century (Joan Van Ark). The stories were lively, there was enough action to sustain the comic book feel, and the steady parade of colourful villains (Roddy McDowall and Henry Gibson were two of the best) gave the show a campy, light-hearted look in the tradition of *Batman*. Carter was at her sexiest best delivering a stylish kick to the stomach or batting those baby blues...but as Wonder Woman's alter-ego, Diana Prince could be almost as smoldering.

Even when the time frame was advanced 30 years, the producers made a point of maintaining the original Wonder Woman legend, which told of the renegade band of Amazons who fled ancient Greece and Rome to escape male domination. On Paradise Island they found the magic substance Feminum, which when shaped into a golden belt gave them super-human strength. Formed into wrist bands, it could deflect bullets.

The Incredible Hulk

Series debut: March 10, 1978 (CBS). Final telecast: June 2, 1982 (CBS). 80 episodes.

In terms of longevity, this series about the big, green guy created by Marvel Comic artist Stan Lee ranks second only to *The Adventures of Superman* among TV shows inspired by comic book superheroes. But in terms of quality, it's No. 1. Beginning with the feature-length pilot episode, in which research scientist Dr. David Banner (Bill Bixby) accidentally exposed himself to a massive dose of gamma radiation, the series was expertly written and superbly acted, and consistently featured plots that were both intelligent and poignant.

Dr. Banner began experiments to discover a way to tap into the human body's reserve of super strength after watching his wife burn to death in a car accident. Exposure to the gamma rays caused a molecular mutation that triggered his Jekyll-and-Hyde transformation into the Hulk every time anger, pain or frustration overcame his normally placid emotions. Watching the diminutive doctor "Hulk-out" into the snarling seven-foot beast was a highlight of every episode. His shirt was always ripped to shreds and his shoes mysteriously disappeared, but somehow his pants always stayed on (after all, this was a family show)—albeit with some token rips and a distinct pedal-pusher look. The Hulk (former Mr. World and Mr. Universe Lou Ferrigno) didn't speak, just snarled and growled a lot. In the fight scenes he wasn't shy about picking up the bad guys and hurling them against walls or over cars, but he never killed anyone (at least not on purpose). When the situation was resolved and he'd calmed down, the Hulk would transform back into mild Dr. Banner. The transformations were filmed in progressive quick cuts and were really well done.

Another neat thing about the show was that there was a quasi *Fugitive* feel about it. Banner was constantly on the move, taking odd jobs while maintaining fleeting contact with trusted colleagues in the scientific community who might be able to help him find an antidote. Hot on his trail was Jack McGee (Jack Colvin), a crass headline-hunting tabloid reporter who suspected Banner and the Hulk were one and the same and wanted to break the story. Their cat-and-mouse chase heightened the urgency of Banner's plight, and because Colvin's quarry (like Dr. Kimble) had a propensity for placing himself at risk to help others, it provided some intriguing secondary story lines.

TeleTrivia

Between being crowned Mr. Universe and his first acting job—opposite Arnold Schwarzenneger in *Pumping Iron*—6-foot-5-inch, 280-pound Lou Ferrigno had a brief tenure with the Toronto Argonauts in the Canadian Football League. A sensitive man, he was so distraught after breaking a teammate's legs during a scrimmage (Lou was blocking), he quit the game for good.

Six years after *The Incredible Hulk* was cancelled, the big green guy was resurrected in *The Incredible Hulk Returns* (1988), a feature-length television movie that scored huge ratings and led to two more: *Trial of The Incredible Hulk* (1989) and (sniff!) *The Death of The Incredible Hulk* (1991).

TeleTrivia

Bill Bixby never forgot his TV roots while wandering the country as Dr. David Banner. In the fifth episode of *The Incredible Hulk*, Bixby was reunited with young Brandon Cruz, who portrayed his son on *The Courtship of Eddie's Father* (see Chapter 2). In an episode from the third season called My Favorite Magician, the guest star was Ray Walston, who co-starred with Bixby in *My Favorite Martian* (see Chapter 6). Bixby, who died of cancer in 1993, also appeared in *The Joey Bishop Show* (1962), *The Magician* (1973–1974), *Masquerade Party* (panellist, 1974–1975), *The Book of Lists* (host, 1982) and *Goodnight, Beantown* (1983–1984).

The Least You Need to Know

➤ Disconsolate over being typecast as television's Superman, George Reeves died under suspicious circumstances in 1959. His death was officially ruled a suicide, but to this day many people who knew Reeves believe he was murdered.

➤ Before *The Bionic Woman* became a series, Jamie Sommers (Lindsay Wagner) apparently "died" on an episode of *The Six Million Dollar Man*.

➤ *Man From Atlantis* star Patrick Duffy went on to play Bobby Ewing in *Dallas*.

➤ *Wonder Woman* star Lynda Carter was crowned Miss World in 1973.

➤ Lou Ferrigno, who portrayed the green monster in *The Incredible Hulk*, was once a member of the Toronto Argonauts of the Canadian Football League.

WEST FARGO PUBLIC LIBRARY

Murray Greig's Top 20 Boomer TV Ratings

All the following shows are profiled in more detail elsewhere in this book; please refer to the Contents. Boomer westerns, variety shows and cartoons are rated in Appendix 2. For the Boomer TV Hall of Shame, see Appendix 5.

Sitcoms

1. *All In The Family*
2. *The Honeymooners*
3. *The Bob Newhart Show*
4. *Fawlty Towers*
5. *The Odd Couple*
6. *The Andy Griffith Show*
7. *Leave It To Beaver*
8. *Get Smart*
9. *The Phil Silvers Show*
10. *Green Acres*
11. *I Love Lucy*
12. *Hogan's Heroes*
13. *The Mary Tyler Moore Show*
14. *The Adventures of Ozzie and Harriet*
15. *The Dick Van Dyke Show*
16. *Monty Python's Flying Circus*
17. *When Things Were Rotten*
18. *Gomer Pyle, U.S.M.C.*
19. *That Girl*
20. *M*A*S*H*

Guilty Pleasures (C'mon, ya know ya love 'em!)

1. *Gilligan's Island*
2. *The Brady Bunch*
3. *I Dream of Jeannie*
4. *Batman*
5. *The Beverly Hillbillies*
6. *The Addams Family*
7. *Happy Days*
8. *Father Knows Best*
9. *The Munsters*
10. *Family Affair*
11. *Petticoat Junction*
12. *The Partridge Family*
13. *Car 54, Where Are You?*
14. *My Favorite Martian*
15. *The Flying Nun*
16. *My Three Sons*
17. *The Real McCoys*
18. *Mork and Mindy*
19. *My Mother The Car*
20. *Welcome Back, Kotter*

Dramas

1. *The Fugitive*
2. *Combat!*
3. *Mission: Impossible*
4. *Hawaii Five-O*
5. *The Waltons*
6. *The Untouchables*
7. *Perry Mason*
8. *Twelve O'Clock High*
9. *The White Shadow*
10. *The Rockford Files*
11. *The Life and Times of Grizzly Adams*
12. *S.W.A.T.*
13. *Ben Casey*
14. *Sea Hunt*
15. *The Streets of San Francisco*
16. *Lassie*
17. *The Rat Patrol*
18. *Starsky and Hutch*
19. *Man With A Camera*
20. *Flipper*

Sci-fi and Spies (for some memorable openings, see Appendix 3)

1. *Star Trek*
2. *The Prisoner*
3. *The Outer Limits*
4. *The Twilight Zone*
5. *The Invaders*
6. *Planet of the Apes*
7. *Kolchak: The Night Stalker*
8. *The Adventures of Superman*
9. *The Avengers*
10. *The Time Tunnel*
11. *The Incredible Hulk*
12. *The Man From U.N.C.L.E.*
13. *Land of the Giants*
14. *Night Gallery*
15. *Danger Man/Secret Agent*
16. *The Six Million Dollar Man*
17. *Voyage To The Bottom of the Sea*
18. *The Saint*
19. *The Bionic Woman*
20. *I Spy*

Top Boomer TV Westerns, Variety Shows and Cartoon Shows

Westerns

1. Rawhide (1959–1966)

Wrangler Rowdy Yates (Clint Eastwood) and trail boss Gil Favor (Eric Fleming) led TV's longest cattle drive. And who can forget Shep Wooley in the role of Pete Nolan? Wooley recorded the novelty hit "Purple People Eater," while the "Rawhide" theme, sung by Frankie Lane, also made the charts.

Was there a cooler Boomer western hero than Paladin (Richard Boone)? Not!

2. Have Gun, Will Travel (1957–1963)

Nobody, but nobody was cooler than Richard Boone as the black-clad Paladin. For years I thought his first name was "Wire" because that's how it was written on those great chess-head calling cards of his: "Wire Paladin, San Francisco."

3. Gunsmoke (1955–1975)

In terms of longevity, this one's the king. Marshall Matt Dillon (James Arness) maintained law and order in Dodge City for 20 years after John Wayne turned down the starring role (but he agreed to introduce the premiere episode).

4. The Lone Ranger (1949–1957)

"The daring and resourceful masked rider of the plains" (Clayton Moore) and his faithful Indian companion Tonto (Jay Silverheels) were inseparable—except for the period 1954 to 1956, when John Hart was the man behind the mask.

5. The Gray Ghost (1957)

The only western ever made that showed the Confederates as good guys. Tod Andrews starred as Maj. John Singleton Moseby in this all-but-forgotten classic, which was forced to air exclusively in syndication after CBS sponsors kept pulling out over concerns it would rekindle Civil War hostilities.

6. Kung Fu (1972–1975)

Yes, grasshopper, this Eastern western rates as one of the all-time greats, combining powerful, well-written stories with David Carradine's terrific performance as loner Kwai Chang Caine.

7. Wagon Train (1957–1975)

Maj. Seth Adams (Ward Bond) started the wagons rollin' westward from St. Joseph, Missouri, in the series debut and stayed on the trail for four years. When Bond died prior to the 1961–1962 season, the role of wagon-master was turned over to John McIntire.

8. The Life and Legend of Wyatt Earp (1955–1961)

Wyatt (Hugh O'Brian) and his custom-made "Buntline Special" .45 were next to invincible in defending the town of Tombstone, Arizona, from the scourge of the plains.

Ward Bond was tough-but-fair wagon-master Maj. Seth Adams on Wagon Train.

Hugh O'Brian cut a powerful figure as the immortal Wyatt Earp.

9. The Rifleman (1958–1963)

Widowed rancher Lucas McCain (Chuck Connors) was not a man to be trifled with—especially when he pulled on those leather gloves and took aim with that snazzy repeating rifle. But no matter how busy he got while bailing hapless marshal Micah

Torrance (Paul Fix) out of trouble, he always seemed to find time to whip up a decent meal for his son Mark (Johnny Crawford).

10. Bonanza (1959–1973)

For 14 years "Ponderosa power" was a cornerstone of NBC's weekend dominance. By the time the series ended, Adam and Hoss had left (Roberts in 1965; Blocker died just prior to the start of the 1972–1973 season), and Candy (David Canary) had come on board to help Pa and Little Joe around the ranch. But Hop Sing (Victor Sen Yung) kept those corn biscuits comin'.

The Cartwrights: Adam (Pernell Roberts), Little Joe (Michael Landon), papa Ben (Lorne Greene) and Hoss (Dan Blocker). Dedicated Bonanza *freaks will recall that Hoss' real first name was Eric.*

11. The Big Valley (1965–1969)

This was a thinly disguised copy of *Bonanza*, with Barbara Stanwyck as head of the Barkley clan in California's San Joaquin Valley. Her sons Jarrod (Richard Long) and Nick (Peter Breck) got most of the good lines, but daughter Audra (Linda Evans) and stepson Heath (Lee Majors) were the ones to watch.

12. The Rebel (1959–1961)

Johnny Yuma (squinty-eyed Nick Adams) was an ex-Confederate who drifted from town to town, battling injustice and making long, rambling entries in his journal. There was pretty good gun play, considering he hated violence, and the theme song by Johnny Cash was terrific.

13. The Wild, Wild, West (1965–1970)

This western version of *The Man From U.N.C.L.E.* featured James West (Robert Conrad) and Artemus Gordon (Ross Martin) as undercover operatives for President Ulysses Grant's new Secret Service. They lived on a very cool train, had tons of neat little gadgets (my favourites were the switch blades in the toes of West's boots and the smoke bombs in the hollow heels), and in the end they always got the girls.

14. Tombstone Territory (1957–1959)

Sheriff Clay Hollister (Pat Conway) was the man in charge in "the town too tough to die," but when he needed help he turned to Harris Claibourne (Richard Eastham), heroic editor of the Tombstone Epitaph. Eastham also narrated the series, which featured a very catchy theme song.

15. Wanted: Dead or Alive (1958–1961)

This show made Steve McQueen a star as bounty hunter Josh Randall. A man of few words, he usually let his trusty "mare's leg" sawed off carbine do the talking.

16. Maverick (1957–1961)

In most Boomer oaters the heroes spent their time chasing bad guys, fighting Indians or rounding up stray cattle. Not the "Maverick" boys. Bret (James Garner), Bart (Jack Kelly), Brent (Robert Colbert) and cousin Beauregard (future James Bond Roger Moore) were craven cowards who liked nothing better than to win a crooked game of poker before slinking out of town before the fighting started. It was a lot of fun, even after Garner quit over a contract dispute prior to the 1960–1961 season.

17. Bat Masterson (1958–1961)

The real-life Masterson was a rough-around-the-edges rogue from Canada who made a name for himself in the Old West largely because of his friendship with Wyatt Earp. On TV, Gene Barry portrayed him as a derby-wearing, cane-toting "dude" who preferred to talk his way out of dicey situations.

18. Sgt. Preston of the Yukon (1955–1958)

"On, King! On, you huskies!" With that forceful command, Sgt. Preston (Richard Simmons) of the Royal Canadian Mounted Police whipped his dog team into action to apprehend the scourge of the far north. Yukon King was the lead dog and often performed such Lassie-like stunts as chewing pistols out of the hands of bushwackers with really bad French-Canadian accents. The series was filmed in the Sierra Nevada region of northern California.

19. Alias Smith and Jones (1971–1973)

Hannibal Heyes (Peter Deuel, then Roger Davis) and Jed "Kid" Curry (Ben Murphy) were amiable ex-outlaws trying to go straight. After being promised a pardon by the governor if they stayed out of trouble for a year, they assumed the identities of "respectable gentlemen" Joshua Smith and Thaddeus Jones, but chaos just seemed to follow them. Davis replaced Deuel after the latter was found dead of an apparent suicide in his Hollywood apartment on New Year's Eve 1971.

20. The Guns of Will Sonnett (1967–1969)

Grizzled old Will Sonnett (Walter Brennan), a former scout for the U.S. Cavalry, spent two seasons roaming around with his grandson Jeff (Dack Rambo) in search of the boy's father, James. They never found him, but in the very last episode they crossed paths with a man who claimed to have killed James in self-defence two years earlier. Hey, thanks for the tip.

Variety Shows

1. The Ed Sullivan Show (1948–1971)

Everybody who was anybody eventually wound up on this Sunday night showcase, which was usually the only time the whole family got together to watch TV. Elvis, The Beatles and The Rolling Stones all dropped in, but Ed's all-time favourite act was the Canadian comedy duo of Wayne and Shuster. Geez, even that little Italian mouse, Toppo Gigio, was funnier than those guys.

2. The Smothers Brothers Comedy Hour (1967–1969)

Tom and Dick Smothers were threatened with cancellation almost every week because their material was so topical, but the real draw on this show was stone-faced Pat Paulsen, who performed a weekly "editorial" and ran a low-key campaign to get himself elected president of the United States.

3. The Sonny and Cher Comedy Hour (1971–1974)

Cher's "vamp" sketches and the "Sonny's Pizza" bit were always worth tuning in for and there was a steady parade of big-name musical guests, but the theme song of "I've Got

You Babe" didn't hold up after the couple was divorced in May of 1974. After both bombed with solo efforts, they reunited (professionally) for *The Sonny and Cher Show* (1976–1977), but it just wasn't the same.

4. SCTV (1977–1981)

The original version of this wickedly funny parody of network television was produced in Canada where it became a monster hit before starting a two-year run on NBC in 1981. Starring John Candy, Joe Flaherty, Harold Ramis, Dave Thomas, Rick Moranis, Andrea Martin, Eugene Levy and Catherine O'Hara, it was a non-stop assault on everything from *Leave It To Beaver* to *Hockey Night In Canada*. The spoofs were interspersed with commercials for "sponsors" like The Evelyn Wolf School of Speed Eating, and during programming breaks wheelchair-bound station owner Guy Caballero (Flaherty) and manager Edith Prickly (Martin) concocted bizarre plans to wring more revenue out of their lame-duck advertisers. One of the most popular segments was Canadian Corner, short ad-libbed sketches featuring Thomas and Moranis as Bob and Doug McKenzie, a pair of bacon-frying, beer-guzzling "hose heads" who became an overnight sensation.

5. Saturday Night Live (1975–present)

This landmark series debuted on Oct. 11, 1975, with comedian George Carlin as the first guest host, and over the years the ensemble cast has included some of the biggest names in Hollywood: Dan Aykroyd, John Belushi, Albert Brooks, Chevy Chase, Billy Crystal, Jon Lovitz, Julia Louis-Dreyfus, Dennis Miller, Eddie Murphy, Randy Quaid, Martin Short and Mike Meyers. Featuring the preposterous Weekend Update news segment along with The Not Ready For Primetime Players repertory company, big-name musical guests and over-the-top skits featuring such unforgettable characters as The Coneheads ("We're from France!"), Gilda Radner as brassy newscaster Rosanne Rosanna-Dana and Eddie Murphy as Gumby, SNL was and still is 90 minutes of outrageously topical lunacy—and 21st-century TV's last great link to the '70s.

6. Rowan & Martin's Laugh-In (1968–1973)

This zany mix of comedy, music and mayhem was the hottest show on the tube for about 18 months after debuting in January 1968. Along with hosts Dan Rowan and Dick Martin, the huge cast featured Goldie Hawn, Ruth Buzzi, Lily Tomlin, Judy Carne, Art Carne ("Verrrrry interesting!"), Henry Gibson and more than two dozen other semi-regulars. The show's goofy catch phrases quickly crept into everyday use ("Sock it to me!" "Here come de judge." "You bet your sweet bippy!"), but my favourite line from *Laugh-In* is still Tomlin's signature sign-off as the telephone operator: "We don't care. We don't have to. We're the phone company."

239

7. The Original Amateur Hour (1948–1960)

Hosted by Ted Mack (who always looked like he needed a couple of shots of Geritol, one of the show's sponsors), this intriguing program was a showcase for up-and-coming kazoo-players, knife-throwers, mimics and other amateur performers looking for their big break. With unfailing geniality Ted made 'em all feel like stars, and when the acts were finished, the studio audience helped pick a winner.

Cartoons

1. Rocky and His Friends (1959–1961)

Rocket J. Squirrel and Bullwinkle J. Moose were sensational all by themselves, but throw in Boris Badenov, Natasha Fataly, Mr. Peabody and his boy Sherman (get it, a dog and his boy!) and intrepid Mountie Dudley Do-Right and this show had "timeless classic" written all over it right from the start.

2. Jonny Quest (1964–1966)

The first prime-time "serious" cartoon was the story of a 12-year-old boy who travelled the globe with his renowned scientist father Dr. Benton Quest and their bodyguard, Roger "Race" Bannon. Jonny's best pal, an adopted Indian kid named Hadji, and their dog Bandit rounded out the team. What was so cool about this toon was that the kids learned how to use Dr. Quest's ultra-sophisticated equipment, which usually turned out to be quite an advantage when they were battling space invaders, mutated jungle beasts and all the other interesting creatures they met along the way.

3. Tennessee Tuxedo & His Tales (1963–1966)

Don Adams (*Get Smart*) provided the voice for Tennessee, a wisecracking penguin who was always looking for a way to escape the Megopolis Zoo. With his trusty (but dimwitted) pal, a walrus named Chumley, Tennessee finally succeeded in busting out, and they promptly made friends with Phineas J. Whoopee, a kindly old professor who used a three-dimensional blackboard (the famous "3D-BB") to impart the wisdom Tennessee and Chumley needed to survive "outside." They soon decided to return to the zoo, but Mr. Whoopee remained a close friend and never failed to put his magic blackboard to use in helping solve their problems.

4. The Road Runner Show (1966–1968)

The question has haunted Boomers for decades: If Wile E. Coyote had enough money to buy all those rockets, slingshots and hand grenades from the Acme Co., why didn't he just order out for pizza instead of trying to eat the Road Runner? No matter. The thrill of the chase is what made this show so great—along with those shots of the Coyote running off the cliff and falling way, way, way down into the canyon....

5. Underdog (1964–1966)

"Have no fear...Underdog is here!" That was the rallying cry of a humble little "shoeshine pup" when he transformed himself into the caped defender of truth and righteousness. Wally Cox provided the voice for Underdog, while Norma McMillan was the voice for his true love, Sweet Polly Purebread.

Honourable mentions: *Atom Ant; The Heckle and Jeckle Show; Magilla Gorilla; George of the Jungle; Top Cat; The Jetsons; Josie and The Pussycats; The Archies; The Beany and Cecil Show; Sinbad the Sailor.*

Openings for Some of Boomer TV's Classic Sci-fi Shows

The Adventures of Superman (1952–1957)

"Look! In the sky!"

"It's a bird!"

"It's a plane!"

"It's Superman!"

"Yes, it's Superman, strange visitor from another planet, who came to Earth with powers and abilities far beyond those of mortal men. Superman, who can change the course of mighty rivers, bend steel with his bare hands; and who, disguised as Clark Kent, mild-mannered reporter for a great metropolitan newspaper, fights a never-ending battle for truth...justice...and the American way!"

Battlestar Galactica (1978–1979)

Prologue: "There are those who believe that life here began out there...far across the universe, with tribes of humans who may have been the forefathers of the Egyptians or the Toltecs or the Mayans. Some believe there may yet be brothers of Man who even now fight to survive, somewhere beyond the heavens."

Epilogue: "Fleeing from the Cylon tyranny, the last battlestar, Galactica, leads a rag-tag fugitive fleet on a lonely quest for a shining planet known as—Earth."

Captain Video and His Video Rangers (1949–1956)

"Captain Video! Master of space! Hero of science! Captain of the Video Rangers! Operating from his secret mountain headquarters on the planet Earth, Captain Video rallies men of goodwill everywhere. As he rockets from planet to planet, let us follow the champion of justice, truth and freedom throughout the universe!"

Rod Brown of the Rocket Rangers (1955–1956)

"CBS Television presents: Rod Brown of the Rocket Rangers! Surging with the power of the atom, gleaming like great silver bullets, the mighty Rocket Rangers' spaceships stand by for blastoff! Up, up, rockets blazing with white-hot fury, the manmade meteors rise through the atmosphere, breaking the gravity barrier, pushing up and out, faster and faster and then...outer space and high adventure for...the Rocket Rangers!"

The Invaders (1967–1968)

(Pilot episode): "How does a nightmare begin? For David Vincent, architect returning home from a business trip, it began a few minutes past four on a lost Tuesday morning, looking for a shortcut that he never found. It began with a welcoming sign that gave hope of black coffee. It began with a closed, deserted diner, and a man too long without sleep to continue his journey. In the weeks to come, David Vincent would go back to how it all began many times...."

Note: In subsequent episodes William Conrad's introduction included a reference to the landing of the aliens and concluded with: "Now David Vincent must try to convince a disbelieving world that the nightmare has already begun!"

The Outer Limits (1963–1965)

"There is nothing wrong with your television set. Do not attempt to adjust the picture. We are controlling transmission. If we wish to make it louder, we will bring up the volume. If we wish to make it softer, we will tune it to a whisper. We will control the horizontal. We will control the vertical. We can roll the image, make it flutter. We can change the focus to a soft blur, or sharpen it to crystal clarity. For the next hour, sit quietly and we will control all that you see and hear. We repeat: There is nothing wrong with your television set. You are about to participate in a great adventure. You are about to experience the awe and mystery which reaches from the inner mind to...The Outer Limits."

The Prisoner (1968–1969)

"Where am I?"

"In The Village."

"What do you want?"

"Information."

"Whose side are you on?"

"That would be telling. We want information."

"You won't get it!"

"By hook or by crook, we will."

"Who are you?"

"The new Number Two."

"Who is Number One?"

"You are Number Six!"

"I am not a number, I am a free man!"

(Laughter from Number Two)

Note: Some televisionaries believe the answer to the long-standing riddle of Number One's identity is revealed simply by inserting a comma after the word "are" in the second-to-last line in the opening to *The Prisoner*. Does the series finale bear that out? That would be telling....

Space Patrol (1950–1956)

"High adventure in the wild, vast regions of space! Missions of daring in the name of inter-planetary justice! Travel into the future with Buzz Corey, commander in chief of...the Space Patrol!"

Star Trek (1966–1969)

"Space...the final frontier. These are the voyages of the starship Enterprise. I's five-year mission: to explore strange new worlds, to seek out new life and new civilizations...to boldly go where no man has gone before!"

The Time Tunnel (1966–1967)

"Two American scientists are lost in the swirling maze of past and future ages during the first experiments on America's greatest and most secret project: The Time Tunnel. Tony Newman and Doug Phillips now tumble helplessly toward a new fantastic adventure, somewhere along the infinite corridors of time!"

Tom Corbett, Space Cadet (1950–1956)

"Space Academy, USA, in the world beyond tomorrow. Here the Space Cadets train for duty on distant planets. In roaring rockets, they blast through the millions of miles from Earth to far-flung stars and brave the dangers of cosmic frontiers, protecting the liberties of the planets and safeguarding the cause of universal peace in the age of the conquest of space!"

The Twilight Zone (1959–1965)

Version 1: "There is a fifth dimension beyond that which is known to man. It is a dimension as vast as space and timeless as infinity. It is the middle ground between light and shadow, between science and superstition, and it lies between the pit of man's fears and the summit of his knowledge. This is the dimension of imagination. It is an area which we call the Twilight Zone."

Version 2: "You're travelling through another dimension, a dimension not only of sight and sound, but of mind; a journey into a wondrous land whose boundaries are that of imagination. That's the signpost up ahead—your next stop, the Twilight Zone!"

Version 3: "You're travelling through another dimension, a dimension not only of sight and sound, but of mind; a journey into a wondrous land whose boundaries are that of imagination—next stop, the Twilight Zone!"

Boomer TV's All-time Greatest Signature Phrases

Comedies

1. "Stifle yourself!"
   "Get away from me...all of yuse."— Archie Bunker, *All In The Family*

2. "Sorry about that, Chief."
   "Would you believe..."
   "Missed it by *that* much!"—Maxwell Smart, *Get Smart*

3. "Oh, you're a riot, Alice!"
   "Bang! Zoom! To the moon!"—Ralph Kramden, *The Honeymooners*

4. "I know nussing...NUSSING!"— Sgt. Hans Schultz, *Hogan's Heroes*

5. "Ooooh doggies!"—Jed Clampett, *The Beverly Hillbillies*

6. "Holy [fill in the blank]!"—Robin the Boy Wonder, *Batman*

7. "He's from Barcelona."—Basil Fawlty, *Fawlty Towers*

8. "God will get you for that, Walter."—Maude Findlay, *Maude*

9. "Oh, Willlllburrrrrr."—Mr. Ed, *Mr. Ed*

10. "Nip it! Just nip it!"—Barney Fife, *The Andy Griffith Show*

Dramas and Westerns

1. "Book 'em, Danno."—Steve McGarrett, *Hawaii Five-O*

2. "Goodnight, John-Boy."—Any of the other 10 Waltons, *The Waltons*

3. "Two hundred a day, plus expenses."—Jim Rockford, *The Rockford Files*

4. "It's the ginchiest."—Kookie, *77 Sunset Strip*

5. "Time to saddle up..."—Sgt. Saunders, *Combat!*

6. "Hey, who was there—you or me?"—Sgt. Same Troy, *The Rat Patrol*

7. "Solid!"—Linc Hayes, *The Mod Squad*

8. "I never draw my gun unless I intend to use it."—Paladin, *Have Gun, Will Travel*

9. "I don't hang anyone—the law does."—Marshal Matt Dillon, *Gunsmoke*

10. "Eeeeeeeeeeeee."—Flipper, *Flipper*

Sci-fi and Spies

1. "I am not a number, I am a free man!"—Number Six, *The Prisoner*

2. "He's dead, Jim."—Dr. McCoy, *Star Trek*

3. "There is nothing wrong with your television set..."—The Control Voice, *The Outer Limits*

4. "Open Channel D!"—Napoleon Solo, *The Man From U.N.C.L.E.*

5. "Mrs. Peel, we're wanted."—John Steed, *The Avengers*

6. "Forget it, pal."—Oscar Goldman, *The Six Million Dollar Man*

7. "To the Batcave!"—Batman, *Batman*

8. "Oh the pain of it all!"—Dr. Zachary Smith, *Lost In Space*

9. "Faster, Kato!"—The Green Hornet, *The Green Hornet*

10. "Arrrrrrrrrraggggghhhh!"—The Incredible Hulk, *The Incredible Hulk*

The Boomer TV Hall of Shame

The Five Absolute Worst

1. The Starlost (1973)

This Canadian sci-fi series starred Keir Dullea as Devon, Gay Rowan as Rachel and future game-show host Robin Ward as Garth, three travellers aboard the massive Earthship Ark, which was launched from Earth in 2285 in the hope of finding another world for humans to colonize. Dullea, who starred in the big-screen epic *2001: A Space Odyssey*, should have known better. The incredibly cheap visual effects included filming the entire show on videotape in front of a solid blue background, which made the human figures look like they'd been cut out and pasted onto a giant felt board. The stories were equally idiotic, including one in which the trio confronted the Tube People—a society of angry teenagers. Inexplicably, *Star Trek*'s Walter Koenig (Chekov) appeared in 2 of the 16 episodes as an alien named Oro.

2. Turn-On (Feb. 5, 1969)

Hyped as ABC's answer to *Rowan & Martin's Laugh-In*, this was the only series in television history to be cancelled during its premiere episode! Tim Conway was the featured guest on that historic telecast, but he had nothing to do with how terrible it was. Producer Digby Wolfe sold the network on the idea of "a visual, comedic, sensory assault involving animation, videotape, stop-action film, electronic distortion and computer graphics"—all generated by the show's "star," a giant mock-up computer. The large supporting cast, which included Teresa Graves (star of the short-lived cop drama *Get Christie Love*), was reduced to screaming out sexual double entendres and brainless observations between the mind-numbing "psychedelic" visuals and sound effects.

Dozens of ABC affiliates pulled the plug after the first few minutes, and when the network switchboard lit up with angry calls from the major sponsor, the decision was made to dump the show after that one ignominious telecast.

3. Saturday Night Live With Howard Cosell (1975–1976)

This short-lived variety program proved that success in one branch of television entertainment doesn't necessarily mean it's transferable to another. Cosell was the No. 1 talking head on the phenomenally popular *ABC Monday Night Football* when somebody came up with the idea of putting The Mouth That Roared in front of a live audience to host a splashy *Ed Sullivan*–type showcase. The debut effort certainly looked promising: John Wayne, Frank Sinatra, John Denver and Evel Knievel checked in as guests, along with a live-via-satellite musical performance by the red-hot Bay City Rollers. But it was all downhill after the first one, and by show number four Howard was reduced to trying to warble a song (coached by Andy Williams) between guest appearances by embarrassed-looking stars from other ABC programs. The series was mercifully cancelled after half a season.

4. Hotel de Paree (1959–1960)

Let me preface this by saying I'm a big fan of Earl Holliman. He was great as Cookie in the cult movie *Forbidden Planet*, he was terrific as the star of the very first episode of *The Twilight Zone* (see Chapter 20), and he put in four sterling years as Lt. Bill Crowley, Angie Dickinson's boss on *Police Woman*. So what was he thinking when he made this asinine excuse for a western? Here's the premise: Sundance (Holliman) returns to the quiet town of Georgetown, Colorado, after spending 17 years in prison for accidentally killing a local resident. The owners of the Hotel de Paree, relatives of the man he killed, turn around and give him a job as their "strong-arm." Although he's quick on the draw, Sundance is still haunted by guilt over killing the wrong guy, so rather than rely on his prowess with the pistol in his new duties, he goes out and gets himself a fancy new hat, custom-made with shiny silver discs all around the band. Why? So that when he's trying to diffuse a troublesome situation he can just tilt his head a little and let the reflection of sunlight off those spiffy silver discs blind the bad guy! Neat trick, huh?

5. The Gong Show (1976–1980)

The bottom-feeder "reality" game shows of recent years (*Survivor, Big Brother, Temptation Island*) owe at least a passing nod to this effort dreamed up by Chuck Barris, who originally envisioned it as nothing more than a parody of amateur talent competitions. Instead, inside of a few weeks, Barris had a monster hit on his hands—not to mention a steady parade of freaks and weirdos anxious to get their 15 minutes of fame by winning the top weekly prize of $712.05. All they had to do was step out in front of the celebrity judges and perform an "act" without getting gonged. Judging was done on a scale of 1 to 10, and the highest rated performance won the dough. There was a 300-pound woman who belched to the tune of "The Star Spangled Banner." There was a guy who played the trumpet with his navel. There was a girl who whistled "Dixie" through her nose. And to keep things lively between acts, there was The Unknown Comic (he appeared with a brown paper sack over his head) and Gene-Gene the Dancing Machine, a big stagehand who would run onto the floor and frantically gyrate while the judges threw garbage at him. Yup, this was funny, funny stuff.

Index

About the Author

MURRAY GREIG is a real person based on a composite of fictional television characters. A former TV critic for *The Edmonton Sun*, he's described by his very tolerant wife Judy as "a combination of Archie Bunker, Oscar Madison, and that cartoon penguin, Tennessee Tuxedo."

WEST FARGO PUBLIC LIBRARY